POSTCARDS
from the ledge

Greg Child

POSTCARDS

*from
the
ledge*

Collected
Mountaineering
Writings of
Greg Child

THE
MOUNTAINEERS

Published by
The Mountaineers
1001 SW Klickitat Way, Suite 201
Seattle, WA 98134

Ckoth edition: first printing 1998.
Paper edition: first printing 2000, second printing 2003

Published simultaneously in Great Britain by Cordee, 3a DeMontfort Street, Leicester, England, LE1 7HD

Manufactured in the United States of America

Edited by Linda Gunnarson
All photographs by Greg Child except those on pages 32 (Randall Leavitt), 43 (Simon Carter), and 170 (Leo Dickinson).
Cover design by Helen Cherullo
Book design by Alice C. Merrill

Cover photograph of Greg Child: Michael Kennedy
Frontispiece: Woodcut © Randy Rackliff

Library of Congress Cataloging-in-Publication Data
Child, Greg.
    Postcards from the ledge : collected mountaineering writings of
Greg Child. — 1st ed.
        p.   cm.
    Many of the writings were previously published in Climbing
magazine.
    Cloth: ISBN 0-89886-584-0
    Paper: ISBN 0-89886-753-3
    1. Mountaineering. 2. Child, Greg. 3. Mountaineers—Biography.
I. Climbing (Aspen, Colo.) II. Title.
GV199.83.C45   1998
796.53'2—dc21   98-21175
                                                        CIP

To the memories of
Georges Bettembourg, Alison
Hargreaves, Steve Masceoli,
Geoff Radford, Steve Risse,
and Rob Slater

Contents

Foreword

I once believed that you could only write a mountaineering book if you were one of the leading climbers of your time. But on further reflection it seemed clear to me that this premise was utterly illogical. Top-notch, hard-core, main-lined mountain madmen spend far too much of their time, and imagination, hanging by their sensitive bits in alarming situations to possibly have a chance of writing a halfway coherent sentence.

Unfortunately after years of being comforted by this latter theory Greg Child comes along and proves me wrong. An exceptional world-class climber who must be regarded as one of the leading Himalayan climbers of his generation, he has climbed at the highest and most demanding standards on pure sports routes, high-altitude big walls, scary mountains like Gasherbrum IV and K2, heart-stopping ice cascades in North America—everything it seems that he can get his hands on. Yet he still claims to be unsure as to whether he is a climber who writes or a writer who climbs. He suspects somewhat ruefully that he might have done a fair bit more climbing if he hadn't wasted so much time writing. Maybe it's a good thing he has his writing. I wonder whether it hasn't kept him alive over the years, not simply because it has reduced his time spent in dangerous places but perhaps more pertinently because it has made him a climber who thinks deeply about what he is doing.

More than any other pursuit writing makes one think about life. Thinking about life enables a perspective to form about what is important and what is not, about the bigger issues, the corny life and death questions, which in reality are the coinage with which the climber gambles. There are those who so gamble unwittingly, others who do so naively and learn the hard way, yet more who place their bets in search of questionable goals employing dubious ethics, and there are the hard-core egotists who climb in vainglorious desire of image and profile and adulation.

Foreword

Greg Child is none of these and he is a very good writer to boot. At once unassuming and self-deprecating, although without false modesty, he also possesses the authority of experience to speak forcefully about the sport he loves. Climbing is about good judgment, and good judgment comes from experience. Sadly, however, experience tends to come from bad judgment. An absurd Catch-22 that Greg Child seems delighted to acknowledge. He seems happy to admit to his failings and point laughingly at the absurdity of his errors, yet he refrains from praising his successes, and they are many. He has done his apprenticeship well, and it is clear that he has nothing to prove to anyone other than himself.

His writing reflects this and throughout there is always a sardonic Aussie humor, a delightful ability to puncture pomposity in others and egotism in himself; a wonderful tool for defusing harsh words and understating the incredible. He uses it well. It is a skill and an attitude much appreciated by British climbers, for whom taciturn black humor is a way of life that frequently baffles other nations.

I first heard of Greg Child when I read an elegiac piece he had written after the death of his friend Pete Thexton on Broad Peak in 1983. It was a stunningly emotive and beautiful evocation of loss and friendship, of joy and tragedy in the mountains. Any climber who has lost a friend in the hills would empathize with that poignant helplessness and the mute sense of despair experienced by Greg as he turns away from Broad Peak, down to follow the Braldu River, leaving his friend alone, buried high in a frozen eyrie. I knew many of the characters involved in that trip and when *Thin Air,* Greg's 1988 book, was published my neat theory about top climbers not being able to write was promptly exploded.

Mixed Emotions, a moving and sometimes hilarious collection of his mountaineering writing, further emphasized what a talented writer Child had become. This second volume of collected writings is in much the same vein, full of humor and drama and mixed with a bittersweet memory of a lifetime blessed with both adventurous fortune and a tinge of sadness.

The profiles of famous players are as incisive and intriguing as his meetings with Doug Scott and Voytek Kurtyka in *Mixed Emotions.* Child displays the unbiased, balanced voice of a journalist in his dispassionate but cutting analysis of Lydia Bradey and Tomo Česen. Fair-minded, but not one to shirk from sharp criticism when he deems it deserved, his voice is one of authority and concern for a sport that has defined and enhanced his life.

He is refreshingly scathing about the gathering of a yearly circus on Everest. "Just because it is the biggest shitpile on Earth doesn't mean it is the best shitpile on Earth," he announces, and then includes himself in his scorn when he describes assisting an amputee friend up that "tit of a hill" in "How I (Almost) Didn't Climb Everest." In "Death and Faxes" he turns a perceptively withering eye on the ballyhoo surrounding Alison Hargreaves' tragic death on K2 in 1995 and the consequent furor in the British media.

Never far below the surface is Child's sardonic and self-deprecating wit as "The Disgusting Mountains," "The Invention of the Chin Hook," the traveler's nightmare recounted in "Green Card," and "Lost in Lhasa" hilariously reveal. I think what is best about the collection is its ability to constantly surprise, intrigue, and amuse, to catch readers out and make them want to keep reading.

For me the shock of "Souls on Ice," an account of finding a teenage girl in the process of dying deep within the icy guts of a crevasse in the French Alps, is Greg Child at his best. He can make you cry as easily as he makes you laugh and that is a very special talent.

—Joe Simpson

"There is no rose without thorns."
Antonio Pigafetta
1485–1535

Introduction

Several years ago Michael Kennedy, editor and then-owner of *Climbing* magazine, suggested I write a regular-as-I-could-manage column for his publication. The brief for what this column would be about was undefined. "Wide-ranging, humorous, poignant, controversial," were words the editors at *Climbing* used to describe its intent; "I got to write any nonsense I liked," is the way I describe it.

The column, called *Postcards from the Edge* (with apologies to Hollywood's Carrie Fisher, who wrote a memoir of the same title), provided an excuse to dredge up numerous little climbing foibles that could never have made it as article-length pieces. The stories—about sport climbing, big walling, alpinism, travel, and "mountain thought"—revolved around my personal experiences and encounters with the climbers I have known. Sometimes the tales delved into ethics or history. Almost always they were laced with snide humor, a legacy of my Australian upbringing. At times, for effect, I resorted to the realm of the absurd, exaggerating circumstances to fantastical proportions to get a laugh out of anyone polite enough to read my column. So, don't take everything between the covers of this book too literally.

But not all I wrote for *Climbing* was tomfoolery. The editors also let me flex my brain as an investigative reporter, and I examined some troubling controversies in alpinism. You'll find those more somber pieces in the section "Scandals at Altitude." They are the product of dozens of hours of research. Also included in this collection are some personal accounts of expeditions and climbs—to Trango Tower, Mount Combatant, and the overcrowded flanks of Everest—published in *Climbing* and in *Outside*.

Thanks are due to the editors who helped polish these stories. At *Climbing*, Michael Kennedy, Alison Osius, Michael Benge, and Duanne Raleigh all battened down the hatches on my ravings. More than editing me, these folks

Introduction

allowed me to have a load of fun with my story telling. Brad Wetzler, formerly at *Outside*, was also a supportive ear. At The Mountaineers Books, publishers of my previous collection, *Mixed Emotions*, I am grateful to Margaret Foster, who encouraged *Postcards from the Ledge* into being, and to Linda Gunnarson, whose final round of editing gave coherence to a rather incoherent stew of climb-speak. I also want to thank my climbing companions from over the years who have let me tattle on them in my tale telling and who have done very little complaining about it. At least, they have never hit me.

The individuals to whom this book is dedicated—Georges Bettembourg, Alison Hargreaves, Steve Masceoli, Geoff Radford, Steve Risse, and Rob Slater—have all appeared in one or another of my books and stories over the years. Friends and colleagues with whom I spent my Himalayan days, all six lost their lives in mountain accidents and all are sorely missed.

—Greg Child

Manners
and Mothers

Michael Kennedy getting grotty on day 8 on The Wall of Shadows on Mount Hunter, Alaska.

The Disgusting Mountains

The years I have spent in the great ranges, cooped up in base camps, bivouacs, and snow caves, have taught me one abiding truth: mountains turn mountaineers into Neanderthals.

Table manners do not exist on expeditions. Talk is a patois of crude grunts, deranged utterances, and schoolboyish sexual innuendo. Restraint, dignity, and decorum, as they apply to bodily functions, are as absent from the alpine realm as a hot bath and a bar of soap, two things that might not grace an expeditioner's body for a month or more. The religiously inclined have said, albeit wistfully, that people scale mountains to get closer to God. If so, and if the old adage "Cleanliness is next to Godliness" is also fact, then the Great One would turn all mountaineers back from the summit ridge to Heaven's Gate and command they have a good wash before getting any closer.

Yes, we climbers are a grotty lot, but we love it. Now let me recount the ways my partners have most memorably disgusted me, and I them. If you have a weak constitution, read no further.

THE SPILLED PEE BOTTLE

The annals of alpinism brim over with tales of the fumbled piss vessel. This device—a simple water bottle, sensibly marked with skull and crossbones to prevent confusion between it and a drinking vessel—is used for emptying the bladder in the warmth of a tent. Yet despite its obvious virtues, the pee bottle is a hazardous thing in careless hands.

I once had a whizz in one of these things in a tent at 25,000 feet on

Makalu. The night was bitterly cold, and the jug was a welcome hot-water bottle inside my sleeping bag. But a meniscus of ice on the threads of the vessel's lid caused a faulty seal. As a torrent poured through my sleeping bag and tent, I sat bolt upright and let out an awful wail.

"What's wrong?" asked my tentmate, a Brit named Andy Parkin. Judging by my expression and my actions, he probably thought I had heard the thunder of an avalanche descending toward us.

"I've wet the bed!" I said instead.

The spillage instantly froze into a miniature skating rink, gluing our sleeping bags to the floor of the tent. By any standard this was disgusting, but, even worse, the tent and the sleeping bags did not belong to us, and the owner—a gruff, muscular Pole on another expedition—was that very morning cramponing up the slope toward us. We had invaded his tent because a violent wind had wrecked our own; under the circumstances our act of piracy was reasonable, but this mishap was not. Worried that he'd throttle us, we scurried about in the cold cleaning up the mess.

For once, cold was our ally. With spoons and cups we scraped frozen wee from the floor of the tent and shook freeze-dried yellow snow from the sleeping bags. After two hours of work, cold had sublimated all traces of my accident and the campsite was spotless. We headed down the mountain, just as the Pole appeared, a few hundred feet away.

"How are you today?" he asked as we passed him.

"Pissed off," replied Andy.

ORDEAL BY NOSE

To endure your tentmate snoring every night for the weeks it takes to climb a peak is a mind-numbing torture. The nocturnal snorts that emanate from a base camp—a range of notes somewhere between a buzz saw felling a forest and a piggery at feeding time—can, by sunrise, leave you ready to commit violence on your tentmate.

I once bivied on K2 with a man whose snoring was so bad that the members of our expedition drew straws to decide who would tent with him. While we were in the process of acclimatizing, the snorer and I reached the site of Camp 2 at dusk and then spent hours chopping a tent platform out of ice. Exhausted, cold, and with my head throbbing from 22,000 feet of newly attained altitude, I tried to sleep, but a relentless high-decibel nasal cacophony drove me mad. I kicked my partner and tickled and poked objects up his nose. I pleaded with him and shouted abuse at him. The noise went on. He slept like the dead; I slept not a wink.

As we descended the mountain the next morning, I felt drawn and sickly. My head hummed from sleep deprivation. Meanwhile, my friend bounded down like a gazelle.

"Have you ever considered getting a nose job?" I asked him.

"No, why?" he replied and trotted through the snow while I staggered in his footsteps, hoping that in the fabric of karma there will be payback for snorers.

TOURING THE ALIMENTARY CANAL

Everyone gets sick at one time or another in the Third World, and I've been mired in my own effluvium often enough, but nothing was more merciless than the night food poisoning hit me in a hardscrabble Tibetan village called Nyalam, a stopover on the highway to Lhasa. Mine was just a garden-variety gastrointestinal upheaval, but a couple of factors made this a stratospherically disgusting episode.

As I stood retching in an alleyway littered with Chinese beer bottles, a pack of dogs surrounded me. Tibetan curs are notoriously mean, infamous for ripping into travelers with pit-bull ferociousness. While my body convulsed in a violent fit of puking, I watched the leader of the pack advance and sit at my feet. I eyed him and he eyed me. Then he parted his chops to bare his awful yellow canines, snarled, and gobbled the now-externalized contents of my stomach.

With the last lick he flashed a black eye up at me and growled for more. Fear and revulsion brought up another belly-load. My barf never touched the frozen ground; he snapped it up in midflight. Quickly, his mange-ridden cohorts closed in around me, sealing off my escape, growling to be fed. Not wanting to be torn apart, I obliged, heaving like a human soda fountain, ad nauseum (if you'll excuse the pun), until my guts were empty. The dogs finally fled at the laughter of my companions, Jim Wickwire and John Roskelley, who had watched the whole show from the balcony of our hotel.

THE REDUCTION OF LANGUAGE

Deep in the mountains, the conventions of society are far away. Decorum disappears and climbers revert to primitivism. Language is the first casualty in the slide toward savagery. Mumbling and muttering, inane laughter, cussing and swearing, monosyllabic grunting, talking to yourself, and forgetting the art of conversation altogether, are signs you've been too long in the hills. When you start using reading material for toilet paper, you have hit rock bottom.

I once met an expedition of Brits who, after ten weeks, had learned to punctuate every sentence with at least four uses of the F word. For example,

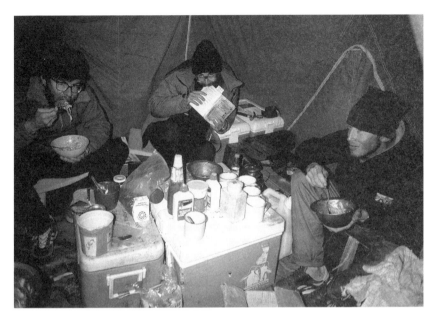

Base camp degeneracy in the Karakoram, below Gasherbrum IV, 1986. From left to right: Steve Risse takes in swill, Phil Balston takes in knowledge, and Tim Macartney-Snape takes in nothing at all.

when one showed me his broken ice ax, he described it like this: "This fucking fucker is fucking fucked." Gutter talk is strangely habitual, but it can be embarrassing when you reenter society and speak in this manner while presenting a slide show about your adventures to the local Rotary Club. But at least you'll never be invited back to give another lecture.

DRESS CODE AND CLEANLINESS

Lightweight alpinism dictates that one should carry the minimum of stuff on a climb, but living in the same clothes for two months at base camp is stretching this ethic to an unsavory limit. I once took ill on seeing my companion slobbing around base camp in nothing but unspeakably stained Y-fronts and a turban made from an old sock. But it was the well-aged blob of sunscreen on his nose, like an encrustation of sour cream, that really turned my stomach. Like a Venus's-flytrap, dozens of small insects were stuck to the blob. Right under my friend's nose, they fluttered, died, and sank in the zinc-oxide paste. He never noticed them, just as he never noticed his aroma, which was like the scent of a rutting tomcat.

I smelled no sweeter. We'd been rubbing sardine oil into our hands for weeks, building up a thick layer of body oil, grease, and grime to protect us from frostbite in the cold climate above base camp. The method worked—we came back with all our digits—but on the way home, when the head man from the first mountain village that we passed through begged us to wash and to please wear some trousers, we realized we had sunk a bit low.

BUGS AND PARASITES

The human body, with its multitude of creases and orifices, is a veritable motel for small creatures, a taxi service from village to base camp for lice, fleas, leeches, and parasites. What could be a bigger turn-off than sitting in a Kathmandu restaurant chatting to a pretty Swiss trekker and watching a six-inch-long tropical worm emerge from one of her nostrils and do a U-turn up the other? And how do you explain the ashen look on your face when she asks you back to her hotel room?

Still, mountaineering buggage is trivial compared to the zoo encountered by jungle thrashers or tropical river runners. I have been told, for example, of a small, spiny fish called the candiru that swims the Amazon, and of its strange affinity for the nether regions of people who swim in that river. Why it likes to swim up into one's most private passages is unclear, but once lodged there, the pain is, I'm told, "spectacular." Only surgery, or amputation, can remove the fish.

TENTBOUND

Becoming stormbound in tents and snow caves for days on end leads to regrettable behavior. Boredom is the culprit. My friend with the snoring problem taught me a game to pass time during storms. The rules are simple: each player hacks up a thick wad of mucous egesta from his or her trachea and spits it onto the roof of the tent. Bets are made as to whether your "magic nose goblin" will freeze to the fabric or drool down onto the sleeping bags. Like sport climbing, this game has limited audience appeal, as most visitors are immediately repelled when they enter a tent festooned with icicles of frozen snot.

EATING HABITS

Even before digestion converts food to the comedy of waste products, there is room at the expedition dining table to become disgusted. Hiring a Balti or Sherpa cook who spits on the cook-tent floor is a good start. Opening cans of local food—such as Asian tinned chicken, which consists entirely of chicken claws and rooster heads—can also prompt an abdominal spasm or two. Just trying to figure out what you're being served to eat in those dirt-floored wayside diners can provide hours of amusement; even five years after traveling through western China, I'm still at a loss as to the identity of a certain dish that had the appearance, texture, and flavor of shredded dog's nostrils, though I'll never forget the way it made me gag when I tried to eat it.

Studying your partners' table manners can be revolting. It may be better to turn away and not watch, or to eat in separate tents, as they slap, slurp, burp, and fart while they ladle their food into their maws with the rotary action of a steam shovel.

For me, the grand doozy of dinnertime gross-outs occurred in the mess tent of a Japanese expedition at the foot of K2 in 1987. Invited to a sumptuous multicourse meal by our Japanese neighbors, my friends and I reclined on a thick mattress of foam pads, scarfing down Japanese delicacies, quaffing round after round of sake, and joking and laughing with our hosts. It was the good life. Until, from a small tent pitched within the big tent, came a river of pee. A slumbering Japanese climber had overturned a brimming gallon-size pee bottle. It takes days to fill a vessel that size, and the stench was indescribable.

Nevertheless, the incident served as a test to separate the men from the boys, in terms of their ability to weather the disgusting.

As the wave scoured the dining area most people fled, with the Americans "goddamming" in indignation and the Japanese apologizing effusively, bowing, and wiping off our trousers with dishtowels. But, I'm proud to say, my friend the snorer, Steve Swenson, and I remained steadfast, squatting on our haunches, munching morsels with our chopsticks, unperturbed by the jaundice-colored sea lapping around our feet. Sitting like that, I remember the way we looked into each other's eyes, grinning and full-jowled. We knew then that we'd come a long way together in our mountaineering careers, and we felt safe in the knowledge that, come hell or high water, we could always count on each other up there where the air is thin and the going gross.

Matriarchs of the clan. Gloria at right, my grandmother at left.

Mother Knows Best

You cannot fool your mother. She may let you think you are fooling her for a while, but in the end, she will reveal that she has seen through your game all along.

I'd been climbing for a quarter of a century, but Mum had never witnessed me in the act of it, though she had read my magazine stories and my books, and had dutifully attended a climbing slide show I'd given. The slide show had been about the day my friends and I summited K2. It was a full house, which was gratifying, and which pandered to my sense of self-importance, but as the light from the slides bounced off the screen and illuminated the audience, I could see only Mum, planted in the front row, gazing at me. Her blue-rinse perm glowed in the reflected light like a 40-watt light bulb.

My mum is a meek woman, a happy woman, as accepting of the differences between people as the Dalai Lama. Possessed of a boundless ability to care for her brood, there is not a daunting or overbearing bone in her body. So I cannot explain why, up on the stage, my voice crackled with a sudden case of nerves, or why I felt compelled to address the rest of my narration directly to her, as if the paying crowd did not exist. But that is how it went.

I had reverted to the twelve-year-old boy scout of my past. Dressed in that ridiculous uniform—shorts with knee-high socks, lemon-squeezer hat, and sleeves weighed down by more merit badges than a Soviet general has medals—I stood at the podium of the local scout hall to receive an award for public service and make a mealy-mouthed speech. I was being honored for collecting more bottles for recycling than any other local scout. Truth was, my troop and I had fashioned Molotov cocktails out of hundreds more bottles and had created an inferno in a disused parking lot, rousing the fire brigade. As I said my bit, I looked into my mother's eyes. There was no fooling her. She knew about the fire bombs, the broken glass everywhere, the fire engine screaming to the bonfire. My award was a fraud, and no words need be spoken between us to define that fact.

My reflection on scouthood crimes came at the worst of times, at the point in the slide show where we were racing against dusk and storm to reach the summit of K2. This was gripping stuff, and I had to keep these people on the edges of their seats. But Mum alternated her gaze between the scenes of alpine desperation flashing on the screen and my face. I feared she might step onto the stage to adjust my collar, or lick her palm and wipe away some speck on my cheek—like a mother cat licking a kitten—as she used to do to me when I was a baby. I suspected she was scrutinizing my story for bullshit, wondering whether the Molotov cocktail maker had grown into a man, or not. It was then that I decided to simply tell it how it really was, up there on K2, minus the hype. Suddenly, Mum settled back in her seat and relaxed. She gave me that look that said, "Isn't it better to tell the truth?" and I got to the summit and off the stage with suitable applause.

"BUT IT'S SO DANGEROUS. How can it possibly be any fun?"

That was Mum, goddess of rhetoric and universal truth, responding to my phone call to tell her I was about to head off on another expedition. She knows there is no rational response to this question.

"Because it just is. I promise I'll be careful."

That was me, coming up with the best reason I could for why I had to go off again to climb some lofty pile of rubble. I suspect that Reinhold Messner, Sir Edmund Hillary, Doug Scott, and all the rest of them have had to contend with a protective mother.

The fact is, all the climbing literature in the world cannot persuade a mother that there is a good reason to risk your life for the sake of climbing. Mothers create life; mountains threaten to take life away. You might convince a spouse or a friend that there is spiritual merit within the hazardous framework of climbing, or that mountaineering is a treacherous pilgrimage to some inner fulfillment, but mothers know the truth: climbing is dangerous, and we climbers are very silly boys and girls and should get ourselves back home, right now!

As I was saying, Mum had never seen me climb, so I decided to take her to a local cliff to show her how it is done. My wife, Salley, would belay me

K2, object of a mother's angst.

and follow the pitch; then we'd come back to the ground, safe and sound, proving to my mother once and for all that climbing is a picnic.

I selected a crag with a ten-minute approach from the car. Mum is a good sport, and though she winced and pussyfooted around on the rocky walking trail in her powder-blue flats with the silk-ribbon bows, she reached the bottom of the crag only slightly out of breath.

"Now, this is the rope," I said as I uncoiled a ten-millimeter dynamic lead line, "and we tie it into our harnesses."

"Is it strong?"

"Yes, Mum, the rope is strong. You could hang a car from it."

"Well, I hope so. How will you get the rope up there?"

I sighed, wearily. I anticipate this sort of question from tourists, but I expected better from my mother after all the pictures of climbing she has seen. Salley muttered, "Be nice, she's only concerned for your safety," so I explained that I was going to forge a path up the cliff. Hearing this, Mum looked over the wall from end to end and cast me a perplexed glance.

"How will you know where to go?"

"I follow holds for my fingers and feet."

"I don't see any holds. It's smooth as a baby's bum up there. What if you get lost?"

"I won't."

"What if you fall?"

"I won't. Just watch and you'll see how safe it is."

The pitch I had chosen was rated 5.11 in difficulty, with an easy, but run-out start. I had it wired, having done it before; but a recent rainfall had dampened the initial holds, so I edged up carefully. Mum moved closer to the wall. She seemed to be examining my footwork. "Nice shoes; I like the color. They'd match my couch."

I smiled politely. My feet were a body length off the ground, and I stemmed onto a large foothold to place the first piece of protection. Unaccountably, the next second I was airborne. I heard Mum shriek, then heard a splash. Splash? I was on the ground, sprawled in a mud puddle.

Mum shuffled toward me, cooing nervously, kneading her handbag like a piece of dough. As Salley helped me to my feet, Mum produced a Kleenex from the handbag and began wiping my muddy knees, asking again and again if I was hurt. I assured her I was fine, but she had to touch each bone in my body to be certain. Underneath my new coating of mud, my face was red. I was unhurt, but fuming. Of all the days to grease off a foothold . . .

We decided to cut our losses and retire for tea and scones. Heading back up the trail Mum placed her arm in mine, as if I was one of the walking wounded, and escorted me up the steps at a fast trot. She mewled platitudes at me: "Never mind" and "It's okay." I was again her little boy, and I'd just had a big fright. I said nothing. I was beaten. But I took it like a man.

So now, when we discuss climbing in my family, there is no fooling my mother. She has seen the absolute truth, and the truth is that climbing is very dangerous. She resides in Sydney, Australia, where she lives in hope her son will find another hobby when he grows up.

Matters
of Technique

The author preparing to make a chin hook placement while bouldering in Sydney, 1975.

The Invention of the Chin Hook

The how-to books and magazine columns I see today about climbing all have this in common: they present the techniques for moving over rock as new discoveries and presuppose that climbers of the pre-sport era were bumblies incapable of figuring out a "back step" or a "dead point." This revisionist arrogance raises my ire, especially when I see the total omission of a move I invented, the chin hook.

I was just thirteen when I pioneered "jawing," and I still remember the Monday following the weekend of its invention, when, in the school yard, I was forced by my classmates to explain the sudden appearance of a prominent and unflattering rash on my chin, a scabby eruption that some kids taunted was the result of groveling to my teachers. Challenged to deny the charge of toadying, I set about accounting for the blemish and, in the process, revealed the circumstances surrounding the chin hook's premiere.

I should first point out, however, that climbing techniques don't just happen; they are devised or invented out of necessity. For example, until a nameless, unsung climber of some Neolithic era was chased by a saber-toothed tiger to the foot of a cliff, it was generally held that cracks were unclimbable. Spurred on by the will to live, he shoved his hand into a crack, flexed it, and found he had a solid wedge on which to pull his body upward, away from the hungry beast's claws. We now call this the hand jam, and, like the wheel, take it for granted. Less so with the chin hook, which made its debut at an Australian crag called Mount Piddington in 1970, on a route named Avago (a pun on the phrase "have a go").

The Invention of the Chin Hook

Though modestly rated at 14 (5.6 in U.S. ratings) and now ignored by modern climbers, who deride it as a chosspile of yesteryear, Avago—an overhanging sandstone crack and groove capped by a bulge—is harder than some climbs twice the grade, although I didn't know that at the time.

Belayed by a fellow apprentice climber, Chris Peisker, I must have looked a sight as I left the ground to do battle with Avago. I wore borrowed PA rock boots so big I had to wear two pairs of socks and stuff a wad of toilet paper into the heel to push my toes forward, baggy ex-army shorts, and an orange-colored fruit-bowl–shaped helmet strapped to my head. Our rack consisted of lengths of hexagonal aluminum rod threaded with shocking pink webbing. The nuts we knocked up with a hacksaw and drill press during metalwork class. In those days, a schoolboy allowance couldn't afford the imported American hexentrics by Chouinard Equipment that were just appearing in the Sydney climbing stores. A pity, because our homemade nuts didn't stick in the cracks properly and had to be bashed in with a few whacks of our hammers, which we carried in holsters on our waists.

Within fifteen feet of leaving the ground, I felt Avago begin exacting its toll on my body. The first symptom was a comprehensive skinning of my knuckles and hands. Seepage from these wounds stained the rock with patches of O+, which overlapped the bloody spots of past thrashers.

At twenty feet I was struck by an attack of leg shake so vicious it threatened to rattle me out of my boots. Sweat dripped from beneath the brim of my helmet, stinging my eyes. Like the tentacles of a spastic octopus, my knees and elbows wobbled all over the place, spurting blood from fresh gashes. March flies buzzed around my head, landing on my neck to stab me with their proboscises. When I pulled a hand from the crack to swat one away, I swung out like a barn door in a hurricane, nearly fell, and then lurched back onto the rock and clung on. I was out of control, hyperventilating. "Wow! This is *really* climbing," I thought to myself.

I continued to the groove and slid into it like a suppository. Then I hit the bulge. There, keeping my body as close to the rock as possible, I attempted to slither over it. This technique failed, so I down-climbed to a row of large, flat holds, clung to them with my scrawny arms while splaying my feet onto a lower hold, and rested before returning to the fight. My next tactic was to unleash a full-on tantrum of postpubescent strength at the obstacle. Yet even this frenzy of blood, sweat, and acne let me down. After another rest I tried the old standby of manteling onto my knee (another underused technique; few cruxes cannot be mastered by centering one's weight over a knee planted onto a hold and then "kneeing up," with one's foot jutting out behind, waving at the crowds below). My knee job resulted in

Peter Mayfield chin-hooking around a roof during the first ascent of Aurora on El Capitan, 1981.

more blood loss, but still the bulge remained inviolable. I had tried every trick I knew. Baffled, I slunk back onto the row of holds below the bulge.

I then detected the first signs of global pumpage. It began with a weakening of the will to hold on, progressed to a throb in the forearms, and then reached a critical stage with an agonizing meltdown from shoulder to wrist. Mind told body: you are going to fall. I had never fallen before, and I didn't like the idea of it. In fact, I panicked, especially when I looked down to see my protection—one of those homemade nuts that didn't work properly— teetering half out of the crack. Though it was at ankle level, it seemed a million miles away.

In reverse, I repeated my repertoire of moves—slithering, tantruming, knee-firsting—yet lacking serviceable arms, I was incapable of descent. I watched as the fingers of one hand peeled back, like three little piggies going to market. One engine down. My eyes skated to my other hand; those fingers cut loose, too. I closed my eyes and braced for the jolt of a fall, or the smack of the ground when the homemade nut ripped out.

That was when I had my great idea. A moment before falling backward, I thrust my chin at the large, flat hold my fingers had melted from, draped my jaw over the rock, and hung like a fish on a hook. The plan was to dangle like that until I de-pumped.

Salvation from falling was short-lived, however, as the maneuverability of a chin hook is limited. Anyway, my arms were so wasted I couldn't lift them to head level. In addition, it is difficult to speak while jawing stone, and Peisker, seeing my hands lank beside me, was led to shout prematurely, "Hey, a no-hands rest! You're cruising it, man!" His praise came too soon. My inadequately developed neck muscles caused my back to fold inward like a soggy pretzel, and sweat drooling from my nose, lubricating my chin, set me sliding backward, millimeter by millimeter. The march flies saw the chance to sting me repeatedly. Bug-eyed myself, I focused down the barrel of my nose at the rock in front of me and had my first Zen experience while meditating involuntarily on the starry configuration of sandstone crystals and on the small, crawly things that roam rock. To Peisker, I appeared to be suffering an epileptic fit. Then I peeled backward and flopped onto the homemade nut that didn't work properly. It held.

The welt on my chin and the scabs on my elbows and knees lasted a month, during which time it was fashionable for my classmates to refer to me as the crawler. I have never used a chin hook since, though it is a valuable trick to know for emergency rests—provided you have the neck for it. So, if you see some French sport-climbing star climb to a World Cup victory after draping a chin over a plastic bucket, you'll know where the move came from first.

Mark Witford (at right) and Rob Slater hunkering down in a bivy before a storm on Trango Tower, 1992.

Dialectical Bivouacism

I was corrupted as a youngster by reading the alpine memoirs of European climbers like Walter Bonatti, Kurt Diemberger, Heinrich Harrer, and Gaston Rébuffat (who we called Ghastly Rabbitfoot because we couldn't pronounce his name). These guys roamed the Alps in the Golden Age of mountaineering, from the 1930s to the 1950s, and they experienced many a hideous bivouac.

I envisioned their pinched and wan faces looking out from soggy, sleet-covered sleeping bags, from cramped snow caves, from butt-size ice ledges, and from hammocks dangling from cliffsides. Their teeth chatter like an orchestra of castanets. They are the Ghosts of Bivouacs Past.

I remember Rabbitfoot's tale, in the book *Starlight and Storm,* of a night he suffered on a peak somewhere above Chamonix. Zapped by repeated lightning strikes, he and his boys were slowly browned like slices of bread in a toaster. And there was Harrer in *The White Spider*, describing the Eiger's notorious Death Bivouac, a ledge where young Nordwand aspirants froze to death with grim Germanic regularity. The Death Bivouac was a romantic place to me. I fantasized sending a last postcard from there to a girl-friend: "My dearest, we have reached the Death Bivouac. Storm clouds fill the sky. With luck, we will meet again . . . "

The bivouac ordeals of Rébuffat et al. epitomized to my youthful mind the noble struggle of human flesh against the callous indifference of mountains. I wanted to master the art of bivouacking and be like "Fritz, the bivouac king," an Austrian lad in Diemberger's book *Summits and Secrets.* This tow-headed youth was as impervious to mountaineering discomforts as a barnacle on a sea cliff is to crashing waves. He could sleep anywhere, through rain, snow, hunger, and cold, even on the most cramped ledges. I didn't sleep through bivouacs, though. Instead, I lay awake, staring at the sky, haunted by the Ghosts of Bivouacs Past, and asking myself the eternal question of alpinism: what the hell am I doing here?

There are two types of bivouacs in this world. Good bivouacs are well planned and comfortable. Bad bivouacs, on the other hand, are not. You know what I mean: no tent, no sleeping bag, and caught by darkness, snow, or rain. Perversely, bad bivouacs have always been my long suit.

My first unplanned night on a mountainside taught me that a bivouac is a tunnel of discomfort that one enters in the hope of getting through to the other end. It took me longer to learn the deeper truth, that the bivouac is a pilgrimage. Just as Hindus hoof their way to the sources of the Ganges to have a cold bath and expiate their sins, or Moslems flog themselves into enlightenment, or tele-Christians send their money to tele-evangelists, climbers atone for their sins and find redemption by camping on uncomfortable ledges during storms.

Back in the autumn of 1993, I formulated a ten-point dialectic of bivouacking. At the time I hadn't bivouacked for months. Central heating and a roof over my head had made me soft. Life had become a routine of three square meals a day, then a measured climb up the staircase to a soft mattress and a down quilt. I itched to sleep under a blanket of clouds and moonglow, to wake up with my legs hung over a narrow ledge, with the sight of forests or winding glaciers far below.

Salvation came with a phone call from Perry Beckham, a Canadian friend, who suggested a climb on Slesse Mountain in British Columbia. He had a new route up his sleeve on Slesse's gothic eastern wall. It would require bivouac paraphernalia and bloodhound-sniffing to locate ledges for the night.

The first bivouac on Slesse was a disappointment. The ledge was so flat and wide there was no need to tie in. The weather was clear and warm. No rocks poked me in the back. I even slept. Nothing could be learned from such a bivouac. I could have been at home watching Ren and Stimpy on TV.

The next night held promise. As evening neared and Perry was in the lead, he began hunting for a ledge. Claiming he'd found a spot, he anchored the rope and belayed me up to him. It was a cramped triangular niche the size of a closet, with water trickling onto it. I looked up the cliff, into the fading daylight. The illusion of a ledge eighty feet higher sent me scampering up the wall. I was, I knew, responding to the first law of bivouacking—there is always a better ledge above.

One bivouac too many. The author signaling retreat from a 1986 attempt on Trango.

The ledge was a mirage. In its place I found a sloping ramp tilted about 30 degrees. A brush with an ancient glacier had polished it glass smooth. Bivouacking here would be like trying to sleep on the hood of a Volkswagen Bug. This proved the second law of bivouacking—there is never a better ledge above.

In darkness, I rigged an anchor and brought Perry up to me. "I think the other ledge was better," he said pointedly, as he shuffled about to get comfortable, while telling me about a recent bivouac he'd endured that made this one look like cake. It involved a rain-sodden night of the sort only the Canadian Coast Range can produce. This is the third law of bivouacking— one bad bivouac inspires talk about a worse one.

Making the best of our situation, we clipped our harnesses to pitons and hung on the slab. We pulled bivouac sacks over us and stuffed our feet into our rucksacks, which were also clipped to pitons. In this position, we half-stood, half-lay, suspended by a web of ropes and knots. I had heard of people paying good money in houses of ill repute for the strictures of such rope-bound confinement, but on Slesse we were getting it for free.

My initiation into bad bivouacking, years back, was on a "day climb" on Middle Cathedral Rock in Yosemite, with a chap named Marshall Rose. Unfortunately, the day passed faster than we could climb. On top, we found ourselves in darkness and inadequately dressed (the fourth law of bivouacking decrees that one neglects to bring extra clothing) on a windy, cold night. The only shelter was a three-foot-tall manzanita bush. When the sun rose it found us inside the bush, wrapped around its gnarled limbs like rattlesnakes, scratched from head to toe, wearing our day packs on our heads. If your feet are cold, bivouac experts say, wear a hat.

I carried what I learned in Yosemite (namely, being ill-equipped) to the Himalaya. On Gasherbrum IV, in Pakistan, my partners and I got benighted again, so we hunkered down in a tiny snow hole at 26,000 feet, without sleeping bags, bivy sacks, or even foam pads. As we massaged each other's feet to stave off frostbite, Tim Macartney-Snape asked me, through clacking teeth, "What's the worst bivouac you've ever had?" Did I really need to answer?

I outdid that debacle, though, on Trango Tower, when Mark Wilford and I got stuck in a two-man porta-ledge during a multiday blizzard. After one heavy snowfall I woke with my head pinioned by a snowdrift that had wedged between the wall and the porta-ledge. Mark, who was lying head-to-toe beside me, had to kick me about the noggin to break up the snow before I suffocated. During the day a football-size ice chunk clouted Mark's helmeted head. He hardly noticed it, though the impact sounded like someone clubbing a bucket. Our brains were addled, you see. We'd run low on food, gotten hypothermic, and were in another dimension with the cocktail of painkillers, circulatory stimulants, and sleeping pills we'd been driven to swallowing. We sobered up but the storm didn't, so we escaped the wall on the thirteenth day. Which brings me to the fifth law of bivouacking—whoever runs away lives to bivouac another day.

Back to Slesse.

As the night wore on, my harness, though of excellent and modern design, began to emasculate me, so I straightened my legs and stood up in the rucksack to take the weight off my waist. But this position cramped my legs into a vicious charley horse. As I leaned forward to massage my calf muscles, I lost my balance and fell sideways, sliding across the slab in my slick bivouac cocoon to collide with Perry. His only reaction was to grunt, so I lay like that for a while, my head cuddled on his lap, hoping he would not misinterpret my advances.

Lying in this position, I couldn't help noticing that Perry's bit of slab was 2 degrees less steep than mine. Somehow he had one-upped me in the sixth law of bivouacking—one should always finagle a better spot than one's partner. Nevertheless, I rested happily, knowing that by snuggling on Perry's lap I had achieved the upper hand in the seventh law. This establishes dominant and passive roles between bivouackers by the resolution of a simple question—who becomes the pillow?

A full moon beat down on Slesse, and full moons inspire the activity of nocturnal beasties. Around 2:00 A.M. a thousand half-inch-long, gray lobster-things decided to migrate from the crack on my left to the crack on my right. My face happened to be in their path, but that didn't stop them. Perry snored while I swatted them off.

At 3:00 A.M. the scurrying of rock rats gnawing at our food sack roused me from a snatch of sleep. This was serious. Rats love to chew climbing ropes and line their nests with the fuzzy nylon. I fought them off. Perry snored through that, too.

Morning came, and we greeted each other cordially, because—and this is the eighth rule of bivouacking—etiquette is essential, whether the bivouac is bad or otherwise. It's essential if only because the breaches of etiquette make the best tales. For example, some years ago on a granite plinth called the Watchtower in the Sierra, we were lying in hammocks, preparing dinner after a hard day of big-wall climbing. When I opened a can of sardines a foul stench met my nostrils. The fish had turned green, so I hurled the contents off the wall. This was unfortunate for my partner, a hard-partying, long-haired Bohemian named Roy Galvin, who hung in his hammock below me.

The botulism-chocked payload landed smack on his chest. I apologized for my oversight, but Roy's bivouac-savvy reply stole the day: "That's okay," he said. "I've spent too many nights sleeping in my own puke to worry about a few rotten sardines."

By the way, sitting on cold ledges gives you hemorrhoids. It is not widely known, but many climbers have failed to reach summits due to this undignified condition—not, as they claimed in their accounts, due to technical difficulties or storms. Bivouac-roids can be avoided by adhering to the ninth law of bivouacking—always carry a foam pad to sleep on.

As we emerged from our bivouac sacks they crackled with coatings of frost. The night had been chilly, but in the sacks we'd stayed passably warm. I always carry a bivy sack on alpine routes—the tenth and final law of bivouacking. I learned this the hard way, after too many nights spent saying, "If I had a bivouac sack over this sleeping bag, I'd be dry and warm, if I had a sleeping bag."

Anyway, Slesse's east pillar was a good route. We enjoyed the hospitality of the sun by day and the moon by night. We gazed over the vanishing forests of British Columbia (fiber farms and forest products, they are called up there), navigated a path through a sea of black gneiss, and enjoyed the camaraderie of cramped bivouacs. Five hundred feet above our second bivy, we encountered a Cadillac ledge, padded with moss as bright and green as a parrot's plumage. It would have been nice to lie on our backs on that ledge, but it would have been a shame, also, to dent that age-old colony of epiphytes with our bodies. So, we moved on to a more suitable site.

Be sure to carry this bivouac primer on your next overnight climb. You can burn it to stay warm.

A contestant runs the gantlet at Snowbird, 1988.

The Sporting Life

Vanity got the better of me on a visit to my native Australia and led me to compete in the 1993 Australian National Sportclimbing Championships, held at Mount Victoria, near Sydney. I used the ploy that I was entering for purely academic reasons, to see how I reacted under the pressure of rules and a competitive climbing atmosphere. It was a scientific experiment. I wasn't serious about trying to win, and to prove I was in it for a lark, I joked that in the qualifying round I'd climb dressed in lederhosen and bright red knee socks, like some old-fart alpinist of yesteryear.

But I didn't.

Back in the isolation room, I got serious. I couldn't help it. The mood there was funereal. Competitors sat silently in the autumn sun like dour young lizards, stretching, meditating, plugged into Walkmen, or pacing like death-row inmates counting the minutes before the noose was fitted to their necks. Swept up in the nervy mood, like everyone else waiting those three hours for their ten-minute session on the wall, I made endless visits to the portable john. My bowels hadn't been so efficient since I had dysentery in Pakistan in 1985.

Out in the arena where the forty-five-foot wall stood, we heard the audience screaming for blood as competitors in the division before us climbed up and then lobbed off. Our sweat took on the acrid odor of tension. I tried making conversation with my companions. Chat, I knew from stormbound mountain bivouacs and other scary alpine times, helps quell nervous jitters. But talk in the isolation tank consisted of lambasting the course setter and the moguls running the competition, and downgrading other climbers' routes, though I did strike up a conversation with a young skateboarder, who, with puffed pride, described his recent expulsion from high school for drug abuse.

Guards were posted everywhere, armed with boomerangs and muskets, to prevent us from sneaking around the back and peeking at the course. Nobody trusted us. Finally, our keeper got a message on the walkie-talkie to escort us to the wall for a three-minute preview of the route. We were paraded up to the wall past the suddenly silent crowd. It seemed a religious moment, as if the bulging plywood structure were a pagan edifice, the crowd a worshipful horde of pilgrims, and we the sacrificial lambs.

Our three minutes of route study began. Mark Baker, winner of most of the competitions Down Under, produced a pair of binoculars, no less, and began scanning the wall, inspecting holds and scribbling notes on a sheet of paper.

"Do the rules allow that?" I asked.

"Sure, they do it in France," he said. Then I noticed that other competition veterans were charting the wall with sextants, night-vision goggles, and X-ray specs and then speed-writing hieroglyphics and equations on notepads. Left to rely on my memory alone, which had been vaporized long ago from too many jaunts toward 8,000 meters, I realized I had no chance. All I saw were random blobs of plastic on a sea of plywood.

Herded back into isolation, the initial qualifying round of the comp began, and we were led to the wall one by one. The longer one waited, I found, the greater the volume of nervous byproducts one produced. It seemed that no sooner did I pee than my bladder would fill again. Where did it all come from? By afternoon the latrine was overflowing, and a nervous line of climbers blocked entry to it. Clearly, setting off on the wall carrying a dram of excess fluid would be disadvantageous. If an enema were available, we would have fought over it.

"Hey, Mister," I heard a young voice squeak from the sidelines, "are you one of the climbers?" Two kids on tricycles had evaded the guards and stood before me.

"Yes," I told them.

"What are you doing?" they asked.

"I'm peeing."

"Why?"

"Because I'm nervous."

"Do you think you'll fall?"

"Yes."

"Then what's the point?"

A climber pumping through The Pulse, a hard sport climb in Canada.

"Go away."

My turn to climb came. I got on the wall. My mind went blank for four minutes; then I found myself at the end of the route. Ohmigod, I thought, now I've got to go through this again for the finals.

Back in isolation, I sat with eleven contenders for the big finale. For this round I had contemplated pulling a can of beer from my chalk bag, popping it with a flourish of spraying foam, guzzling it down, and then chowing into a Dagwood-size burger before stepping onto the wall. Just to show I wasn't serious.

But I wouldn't.

Four hours passed before I got my turn to climb. I spent the time sitting silently, visualizing the layout of the plastic barnacles I'd soon be set adrift on. Thoughts of the route made my hands sweat furiously. Automatically, I began dipping into my chalk bag, even though I was sitting still. Before I knew it, the bag was half empty, and my hands were gummed with a white slime as viscous as a slug belly. I wiped it off and, in the process, noticed that my fingernails needed trimming. Fretting that my digits would have a micron less crimping area, I became neurotically body-conscious and detected another burgeoning reservoir in my bladder. But before I could rectify any of that, a guard connected me to a rope and pushed me onto the stage.

At the first Snowbird World Cup, in 1988, I had watched the French-man Patrick Edlinger stun the crowd and his peers when he sauntered to the top of a wall that had beaten the best that the world had to offer. Where others slapped for holds or quivered as they held on with gutbusting power, Edlinger danced catlike, weightless, and elegant with his blond shock of hair swaying in the breeze. Those who saw him climb that day learned the meaning of the term "poetry in motion," and they went away moist-eyed, convinced that climbing was, after all, art. In a climbing life, there are a few precious moments when everything comes together on a climb. It coincides with a heady electric tingle that you feel in every molecule of your body. Edlinger had it running through his veins that day, and whether your game was mountains or crags, big-wall routes or bolted sport climbs, 5.14 or 5.7, the Frenchman's fingers and feet tapped out a message that was the same for all: be there, be focused, be your best.

That was Edlinger, though, and this was me. Confronted by the wall and a cheering or jeering crowd—I couldn't tell which—my testicles retracted as if I were surrounded by a gang of skinheads armed with two-by-fours. A huge digital clock began counting out the first seconds of my climb. Keira, the four-year-old daughter of a friend, waved to me from the crowd. I took it as encouragement; she was too young to hold a grudge against me, and I'd read to her from her storybook that very week. Then I faced the plywood, latched onto a hold, and stepped into the fray.

Negotiating a route through judges, photographers, and TV camera-men dangling on ropes and from scaffolding, I climbed ten feet up and crouched beneath a four-foot roof. Clipping a quickdraw, I then began feeling out the first crux. Streaks of chalk and bloody bits of fingernail embedded in the plywood indicated my predecessors' high points and told me the move was burly. Gripping a troublesome pocket with one hand and a buttock-shaped plastic blob with the other, I eyed the hold I needed to crank to and began high-stepping toward it, concentrating for all I was worth.

The noise from the crowd intensified as the gap between my fingers and the hold shrank. It was a rousing sound, a positive note, and it coaxed my fingers a millimeter closer to their destination. Above this noise I heard the cheers of Keira: "Come on, Greg! Come on, Greg!" she yelled. Her voice caused images from the children's storybook that I'd read to her to cloud my thoughts. Instead of focusing on a precise crank, my mind's eye tracked the progress of a purple hippo in a tutu bouncing across the frontal lobe of my brain.

"Shut up, Keira. Shut up, Keira," I thought. Then I saw my reflection mirrored in a TV camera lens pointed toward me. "Shit," I thought,

"I don't look like Patrick Edlinger at all. I look like the picture on my driver's license."

The blood rushed out of my hands, leaving them cadaverous and cold, and flowed into my forearms, which swelled like sausages. My legs wobbled, and my feet sketched about the wall. I felt suddenly very heavy, as if a brick had been slipped into my pants. It was do or die, so I flapped at the hold.

My fingers missed their rendezvous. I clutched a handful of air, then dropped onto the rope. A sad noise rose from the crowd, and then they applauded. It all happened in two-and-a-half minutes.

Soon after, Mark Baker took the title, the crowd went to the pub, and workers began dismantling the wall. I didn't place last, but I was a long way from the front of the pack. My experiment had been a success. For one thing, I learned that earplugs are essential equipment to block out the sound of noisy fans. Next time I'll bring a telescope, too. And to prove I'm not serious at my next comp, I'll embark up the wall with ice axes and crampons. I'm certain there's nothing in the UIAA rules forbidding that.

Pills, crystals, amulets. Essentials for the sport climber.

Among the Believers

The Insult of Injury

"All you guys ever do is talk about your injuries." That comment from a bored eavesdropper at a party.

True, we are standing around complaining again about the inexplicable, incurable aches that assail our wrists, elbows, shoulders, ankles, knees, and backs, our muscles, tendons, nerves, ligaments, cartilage, and bones. As it did for our grumpy, gouty, rheumatic, and bunion-plagued grandfathers, the onset of winter weather has multiplied the colonies of gremlins that infest our limbs and joints.

Yet we are not granddads, but in our thirties, not sedentary, but active. We run, cycle, pump iron, ski, stretch, eat well—all to train for climbing. Yeah, we like to climb a lot, climb anything: plastic, rock, mountains. But one day we awoke a day older, pulled on a hold a bit too hard, ran a mile too far, and from that moment on our aches became legion. We are the ibuprofen generation. This is the season of our discontent.

Standing in this circle of the walking wounded, it comes my turn to whine. I display my elbow, which sports a fresh scar from the surgeon's scalpel—the latest chapter in my battle with tendinitis. My problems began two-and-a-half years ago while I was lapping a juggy, overhanging traverse in a climbing gym. I crouched into undercling mode on two big buckets, and then, when I weighted my arms, I heard the faint rip of tearing fabric. The next instant it felt like someone was using my elbow to stub out the hot ember of a Camel. So this is tendinitis, I thought.

What had happened was this: my flexor muscles—developed to un-natural proportions by two decades of climbing—had played tug-of-war with the tendons connecting them to the bony nubs of the inner elbow, the medial epicondyl. The result: a colossal whupping of the zone where meaty muscle turns to Kevlar-strong tendon. So I rested my elbow, iced it, warmed it with hot towels, and wore a brace.

Elbow got worse.

"Rest won't cure tendinitis," someone advised. "You've got to train through it, pump blood into the injured area." This made some kind of sense, since tendons are poorly endowed with blood vessels, so I tried climbing again.

Elbow got worser.

Then some pill-head said in my third month of agony, "Take stronger anti-inflammatories." My guts already rattled with ibuprofen, but I upped the dose anyway, until I was warned, "Your kidneys will shrivel up if you take too much of that stuff." So I switched to aspirin, which, among other side effects, thins the blood. I took so many that I got paranoid I'd bleed to death if I cut myself shaving.

Elbow got worsest.

Next I tried a powerful prescription nonsteroidal anti-inflammatory. It caused depression and nausea.

Elbow cramped up and died.

Saw a doctor. Saw several doctors. "Describe the pain," said one. I wanted to scream, "Maggots with hacksaw mandibles gnawing rotted tendons, injecting them with acidic venom, laying eggs in my joints, the vile brood hatching, chewing tunnels through my muscles, spiraling in conga lines 'round my nerves, their thunderous footsteps charged with a thousand itchy volts."

Instead I told him I couldn't twist lids off jam jars, slice bread, change gears on my car, turn doorknobs, lift a suitcase. Pulling lint off my shirt hurt. Diagnosis: medial epicondylitis, commonly called golfer's elbow. "But I don't *play* golf," I whined.

Six months after the injury, I was injected with cortisone, a steroidal drug with legendary powers for reducing inflammation. That was the good news. The bad news was too much of the stuff corrodes the joint. But I was assured that one or two doses were harmless.

Did it work? Yo! That tendon shrank like an erection in an icy river. The pain faded as if I'd been hit with morphine. I started pulling at rock again. But eight months later, tendinitis crept back. This time, though, the

No wonder my elbows blew out. The author authoring a route in the Blue Mountains.

stiffness consumed both elbows, and like some antibiotic-resistant virus, a second cortisone job barely quelled the inflammation. Modern medicine had failed me.

The months that followed were bleak as I watched my bouldering shoes gather dust and the calluses peel from my fingertips. I was a coyote caught in a bear trap, gnawing its leg off. I snapped and barked and begged for help.

Vitamin therapy was recommended, so I gobbled antioxidants like vitamins E, C, and B6, minerals like magnesium and calcium. I munched amino acids. I even tried powdered bovine trachea, the logic being that cow gullets are made of substances similar to tendons and ligaments. This sounds like the cannibalistic custom of eating the heart of your enemy to gain his strength, but I swallowed the stuff anyway. "Expensive urine," said one doctor, laughing and citing studies that showed virtually no supplements are absorbed by injured cells.

An acupuncturist stuck needles into my ear, neck, and arm to stimulate the flow of *chi* energy in my body. A chiropractor wrenched my neck and elbow until the joints made alarming clicks. Physiotherapists performed cross-tissue and deep-tissue massage. Herbal poultices and hot ginger compresses were applied. Homeopathic potions imbibed. I decreased my intake of coffee, liquor, meat, gluten; when nothing came of this, I increased my intake of liquor, meat, coffee, gluten.

Along the way I learned that doctors scoff at alternative cures, and alternative practitioners diss conventional medicine. Yet, who could heal me?

A hippie who suggested I lie in a circle of crystals and place magnets on my elbows advised me to adjust my attitude. "You won't get better unless you believe in the healing method," he said. My memory dredged up a scene from my childhood, of the old Presbyterian minister at school who preached that we'd never get through the Pearly Gates if we didn't believe in God.

Belief, the power of the mind. It is the key to the executive bathroom. A witch doctor can point a magic bone at a man, and because the tribe believes the bone has the power to kill, the man dies. "Visualize healing," the hippie said. "I'm trying," I replied, straining so hard on a mental image of my tendons being crocheted together that I wet my pants.

It was suggested that I find a practitioner to realign the plates of my skull. And one to replace my dental fillings with nonmercuric compounds. One climber claimed that a mystical therapist cured her tendinitis by looking into her mouth and finding a root canal in need of repair. I told my dentist this. He looked at me to make sure I wasn't overdosing on his Novocaine, then characterized the notion as "crazy."

Someone else recommended an herbal enema to flush out my gripey bowels. Get hypnotized. "Your astrological chart predicts this injury," nodded a friend with a bent toward star gazing. Try electrotherapy to stimulate the muscles. Ultrasound to fibrillate the affected region. Visit a faith healer in the Philippines—yeah, right, watch him extract chicken gizzards from my elbow. Meditate. Yoga. Get worry beads. Apply leeches to the elbows to siphon off bad blood.

"See a shrink. Maybe your injury is the manifestation of some neurosis lurking in your psyche; maybe deep down you're trying to quit climbing, and your injury is a device of your subconscious," I was told. After hearing that, I walked around depressed for a week, convinced I was a hypochondriac.

I read about transferral technique, in which the patient writes an essay about his problem, then puts it in a box. That done, the ill is symbolically out of the body. I went further, I drove a hundred miles, dug a hole, buried the box containing the essay, then spat on the grave.

I also compared notes with others who had wrenched their bodies. Another climber solved his arm pain with an operation called a fasceotomy, in which a surgeon sliced open the Saran Wrap-like sheath surrounding his overly buff forearm muscles. The pent-up muscle oozed out, like the innards of an overcooked sausage on a barbecue. The relief, I understand, is like removing a too-tight climbing slipper from your foot on a hot day. Olympic runner Mary Decker had the job done on her ballooned-out calf muscles, and she still runs like a gazelle.

Another guy had nodules of cartilaginous grit that wandered around his elbow joints like mice, turning up in a different place every time he had an x-ray. Others had flexed so hard that a tendon had ripped off a sliver of bone— an avulsion fracture. Still others had a tendon snap like rubber and twang back up a limb, necessitating a surgical fishing expedition to find and reattach the tendon.

I met many victims of carpal tunnel syndrome, an exquisitely painful condition that occurs when a tendon located in a groove in the wrist inflames and rubs against bone. And there were dislocations; I once saw Henry Barber's shoulder slip out of place while he was climbing—the tendons strapping his arm into his shoulder socket got sloppy—and I watched him flip about on the ground like a trout plucked from a stream. Typists, keyboard operators, and women cradling babies were also among the ranks of the injured. They suffered from RSS, repetitive stress syndrome, caused by performing repetitive work tasks.

No one was safe from the tyranny of tendinitis.

Two-and-a-half years after the onset of my injury a surgeon cut open my elbow to see what could be done. He went in expecting to do a flex release, a serious procedure in which the tendons of the flexor muscle are cut and relocated to a less tightly strung position. Footballer Joe Montana had had it done, and he was throwing again; Jerry Moffat had it done too, long ago, and he cranks like the proverbial disease. In the end, my doc performed a cleanup job instead, slicing out a cubic centimeter of degenerated tendon and ripped-up fascia.

"Maybe it'll work for me, maybe not," I tell my fellow sufferers in the circle of injury, adopting a fatalistic tone that suggests I've tried it all.

Then Smith, a friend with a wretched hand ligament, corners me at the party and presents me with a small box. He'd recently had luck with a *milagro*, an amulet popular among Latino folk. Appropriately, Smith's amulet was shaped like a hand. I open the box. It contains a tiny metal charm fashioned into the likeness of an arm, elbow, and hand. Smith tells me he is contemplating having his *milagro* supercharged with the blessing of a Santeria priestess. Santeria is a mix of West African, Catholic, and West Indian faiths that incorporates ecstatic trances, magic, and animal sacrifice.

I cradle the tin charm in my palm, forming a mental picture of a big chanting Jamaican woman cutting the head off a chicken and spraying hot blood all over my elbow and amulet. A puzzled look crosses my face as I ponder the political correctness of this form of therapy.

"You've got to believe, Child," Smith says. My amulet sits on my bedside table. Lately my elbow has been feeling better. I think.

Travels

in La-La Lands

A dyno from the dawn of time: an aboriginal hand stencil.

Report from Quinkin Country

It was the finest cliff I had ever seen, a leaning sheet of sandstone, tungsten hard and glistening with a burnished patina of silica more orange than a sunset. Beyond it stretched a hundred other flaming walls—Buoux, Arapiles, and Smith Rock all crammed into one place. Ten lifetimes of climbing surrounded me. But there, in a remote place called Quinkin Country in an isolated part of the crocodile-infested tropics near the Cape York Peninsula in northeast Australia, there were no bolts, no climbs, no climbers.

I was not the first to eye these rocks with infatuation. At the base of every cliff, where rocky overhangs formed shelters, were "galleries" of ancient paintings left by the aboriginal people who dwelled here eons ago. Working with natural paints of ochre mixed with animal blood and fat they had decorated the rock with images of men and women, animals they had hunted, plants they had gathered, and the strangely misshapen spirits of their fears, the Quinkins, the poltergeist-like demons that the Ang Gnarra still believe inhabit the heart of the rock and slip out through cracks. They also left their signatures—hundreds of them—in every stony nook and cranny, in the form of simple stencils painted by blowing a mouthful of ochre over a hand placed palm-down against the rock.

I had seen such signatures before, but those—the chalky white hand smears of rock climbers—belonged to a more modern breed of cliff dweller, a tribe with different ceremonies. And though it is a stretch to say that the dark-skinned ancients of Quinkin Country could have had anything in common with the sons and daughters of the white invaders who shot their way through this stretch of land a century ago—and in so doing blew away our chance to understand the deeper meaning of these paintings—the figures and hand stencils daubed around me made me wonder if, in some remote sense of the spirit, those long-vanished people and we climbers were distant cousins.

That the ancients were lovers of the rock was obvious. They chose only the most architecturally spectacular outcrops and caves to decorate and to shelter themselves from the seasonal monsoon and blazing sun. But the way they incorporated the natural shapes, pockets, and flakes of the rock into their dreamtime murals suggested that they possessed a sensitivity to the tactile feel of the stone that comes only from handling it, from studying it, from climbing it. They didn't just paint rock, they interpreted it, as carefully as climbers feel out holds on a vertical path. Proof of this lay everywhere on the cliffs: beside an ochre emu, a row of deep, oval huecos, or potholes, had been utilized to represent the eggs of that huge, flightless bird. Farther on, a finger-size monopocket had become the eye of a kangaroo. Near that was a row of hand stencils. For those, the artist had made his clan members stretch high up a wall and, seemingly, cling to small edges while paint was sprayed over their hands. The hands appeared to be moving up the wall—perhaps depicting an ascent, a dyno from the dawn of time.

Just when these works were created is uncertain, but whoever decorated the thousands of cliff galleries of Quinkin Country had been doing it for millennia. The paintings overlapped one another, again and again, so that faded figures of great antiquity hovered like ghosts in the backgrounds of every gallery. Predating all of that lay the engravings of an even more ancient race, who chipped and pecked strange shapes into the rock. The descendants of these people, the aborigines of the Ang Gnarra clan, believe most of the paintings predate their arrival to this land. Anthropologists have dated relics in the shelters to 32,000 years ago, but other experts believe the engravings are 150,000 years old, making them the world's earliest known rock art.

Climber and sufferer of tunnel vision that I am, my eyes wandered from the paintings to the wall above, where the monopockets and crisp edges peppering the 150-foot cliff carried me on an imaginary journey. Tracing the paths of my dream, I pictured my fingers stabbing into abrupt puncture-wound pockets, my arms lunging through rocky waves, my feet toeing sharply hewn flakes and ripples. All that was needed was a power drill and a dozen bolts. But evil-looking spirit-figures at one end of the wall and a lively scene of hunters spearing kangaroos at the other stood like guardians, warning me against touching this splendid wall. There could be no climbing here. The place was too sacred.

Years before, in America, I had been strolling along the base of a sport-climbing cliff with a traditionalist friend who saw only ugliness in the bolts above. He was of the old school that believed a climb should begin at the bottom and follow a line using natural protection, so that after the climbers had left, there was no trace of their visit. I tried to persuade him that the bolts were okay, that the rock was the canvas where the next generation of climbers was pushing the art of climbing. He wasn't impressed. To him, the bolts had violated the cliff. "Some places just shouldn't be climbed on," he said.

Even so, as I pushed sweatily through thick scrub and walked from gallery to gallery and from one world-class crag to another, I found it impossible to imagine that these ancient people did not indulge in some form of climbing of their own. So, scrambling in an area outside the gallery, I looked for signs that the aborigines had made vertical detours on their walkabouts. I didn't have to search for long.

The first hint came at a deep cleft in a wall where cool air rushed out of a jam crack. Twenty feet of 5.9 climbing led to a narrow, peapod-shaped cave entry. With cracks all around me, it seemed unlikely that I'd find traces of aboriginal ascent so quickly, but immediately I saw that the rock was polished by many hands and feet. And sure enough, beside the cave entrance were two faded hand stencils. For whatever reason, people had found cause to climb this crack and enter the dark cave that disappeared into the cliff, probably for ceremonial reasons, maybe to communicate with Quinkins, whose mischievous shapes stood a few paces away.

The sun was low now, the cliffs amber, and dingo howls resounded through the valley. I walked at a brisk pace, wishing for more daylight, more clues. Farther along the scarp, below a long, easy chimney splitting a wall bedecked with the 5.12 face routes of my dreams, I bouldered onto a ledge and found a painting of a small man beside a hand stencil. The symbol looked like a sign for travelers, an ancient topo symbol saying "climb up here." So I did. Massive jugs blazed a 5.6 trail through the steepness. The holds were worn smooth. They had been here, too. Before I knew it, I was eighty feet off the ground, nearing the top.

As I climbed down I realized that for the agile ancients, even with spears in hand, this line would have been a highway to the hunting grounds atop the plateau, and a good escape route from the murdering whites of the British Empire who wiped out the last of these people in the 1870s. Ironically, it was around that time in Europe that the "first" climbers were venturing onto the crags of England and the European Alps. Those events are duly recorded in climbing histories. Unrecorded, of course, are the climbs of the peoples of

Rock art: a Quinkin stalking emus.

antiquity: the Andeans who left the treeline and climbed ice-clad volcanoes more than 20,000 feet high to make sacrifices to their gods, the Native American hunters who climbed Longs Peak and left a small wind shelter there, the barefoot boulderers of Quinkin Country. I see no reason not to believe that these people—lean and sinewy as the best sport climbers and raised in the shadows of cliffs that would make a modern climber drool—indulged in some form of recreational bouldering. To create such a body of art, they had time to play, and what more obvious thing to do in a field of boulders than to try and climb them?

Every civilization has its glory days, and every civilization declines into faded paintings or the rubble of fallen castles. In the distant future, long after climbing has ceased to be fashionable and the last crag rat's bones have been eaten by worms, the anthropologists of another race will visit Buoux in France, Arapiles in Australia, and Smith Rock in America, and they'll stroke their beards in puzzlement over the age-pitted pieces of steel protruding from the cliffs. Maybe they'll declare them the trappings of religious ceremonies. Certainly, they'll say, "Here was a race of eccentrics who worshipped the vertical." Chances are the boffins of a future millennium won't understand climbers any better than we, today, understand the rock dwellers of Quinkin Country.

The prow of our dragon boat cuts past a limestone tower.

Tights, Camera, Action

In Vietnam they don't eat just any dog; it has to be a certain fluffy type of puppy. I saw a two-ton truck loaded with wire cages full of them, all destined for the wok, on the ferry from Bai Cha to Ha Long City, where we were to board a boat to explore the sport-climbing potential of the 3,000 limestone towers that rise out of Ha Long Bay.

But more about the dog. It is served barbecued, head and all, with a sauce made from fermented shrimp heads. When I was passing through Hanoi's old quarter a few days earlier, I had noticed that the dog stalls do a lively trade, though not all Vietnamese indulge in such eating habits. I had stood there looking at a roasted pup head and carcass, wondering for some time if I could get it down my neck, since I try to dine native when I am in Asia. But my conscience couldn't handle it. Instead, lunching in a *pho*, or noodle shop, I ate a plate of fried silkworms. Yummy.

Vietnam isn't on the grand tour of rock climbing yet, but it may soon be, if you've got the patience to deal with the baroque bureaucracy running this delightful totalitarian country, because around Ha Long Bay's labyrinthine and warm emerald-watered passages there is more climbable limestone than a mono-puller could ever conquer. Admittedly, a fair bit of it is jungle-covered choss, and where the rock is black and slabby, or even vertical, it is so rope-shreddingly sharp that you need welder's gloves and a flak jacket to survive it unscathed. But, just as in Thailand, where the rock overhangs in tangerine waves, it is enamel hard and peppered with everything from one-finger pockets to man-eating huecos.

Vietnam's climbing history is brief. Todd Skinner and his entourage checked it out in 1991 and found that the sport was illegal. Nevertheless, Todd's team covertly bolted and climbed a couple of routes—one they called "Charlie Don't Crank"—above a rice paddy on the mainland. Todd said the routes are so obscure that no one will ever find them again; yet for this transgression the Skinner gang was briefly arrested and urged to write self-criticisms. The lifting of the U.S. trade embargo on Vietnam, and the fact that Nam is now a thriving tourist center, especially among the French and Aussies, has led Vietnam's Ministries of Information, Foreign Affairs, and the Interior to rethink their policies about quirky activities like climbing. The change in attitude can be attributed to the country's scramble for much-needed foreign currency, and its need to fill the many new hotels sprouting around the tourist hangouts. Even though this is still a country where the locals can go to jail for standing on a street corner and publicly criticizing the government, the new philosophy seems to be that free enterprise and money in your pocket are cooler things than the drab collectivism of communist ideology. So bring on the tourists.

It was 1996 and I was in the country to participate in a British TV film about climbing and travel to exotic locales. The film's director, Richard Else, of Triple Echo Productions, had faxed me a few months earlier, inviting me to be one of the two climbers who would "star" in the film. My partner would be Andy Parkin, an old British friend of mine who is a ferociously bold alpinist and a gifted artist. We had last climbed together in 1988, on Makalu in Nepal, when Andy was getting back into climbing after a cartwheel down the north face of the Matterhorn, in 1984, had rearranged his body for him. The fall had left him with a blocked hip that gave him a rakish, peg-legged gait and an elbow fused at the angle of a Napoleonic pocket-slot. But now he was climbing hard again, putting up wild mixed routes around his digs in Chamonix. Yet you'd never know he was the victim of horrendous injuries if you saw him dance a jig at the Hanoi Roxy, the vogue nightclub in Hanoi. That spot, and a club called Apocalypse Now, where the decor includes helicopter rotor blades for ceiling fans and bits of U.S. warplane wreckage, are the hot spots in local nightlife, where foreigners gather like moths to a candle.

Richard's idea for the film was to explore a place untouched by rock climbers. Fair enough, but casting two leading men better known for alpine masochism than for sport-climbing feats and having them sail off in search of the new promised land of stone seemed a bit off course to me. So I faxed Richard a warning to the effect that Andy and I had both spent the summer mountaineering in the Karakoram (he on K2, I on Shipton Spire) and were totally out of shape for cragging. Furthermore, I cautioned, we would never in a million years be able to prance over stone like a Jerry Moffat or a Ron Kauk, two gifted rock climbers who have starred in many climbing films. "That's one of the reasons I chose you," Richard answered, saying that guys like the aforementioned make climbing look too easy. They never sweat or gasp or thrash. At that point, I saw this director's modus operandi: Andy and I *would* thrash, gasp, and sweat, and TV viewers would see looks of bug-eyed fear in us as we inevitably fell off routes. Cunning director, he also planned to do a film in which sport climbers went mountaineering. I'm looking forward to watching that film.

Driving by bus for five hours from Hanoi to Ha Long Bay, we entered a traffic jam of vehicles, motor scooters, and bicycles. It was impressive to see what could be carried on two wheels. A woman pedaling a bike that had a three-piece lounge set roped onto it, with two lads running alongside like outriggers to keep the balance, was memorable, but the motor scooter that overtook us with two live pigs strapped to its rack, their snouts pointing skyward, was unsurpassably comic.

We spent a night in the coastal resort town of Bai Cha in one of those hotels full of faux marble and clocks set to Hong Kong, New York, and Paris time. Bulldozers working outside the window all night kept me awake. The next jet-lagged morning, around 6:00 A.M., I stood on the balcony watching a tropical sunrise sketch in the hazy forms of bulbous islands and rocky karst towers across the bay. I also saw that the nocturnal bulldozing was to construct a beach, first by paving a clay foundation over a mudflat, then by sprinkling golden sand on top. Same time next autumn, tourists would be lounging on deck chairs, sipping cocktails served with little umbrellas poking out of the glasses.

That day we moved onto a "dragon boat" for the three-hour journey to the islands. On board were Andy, me, the five members of the film and rigging team, Dag Goering, a Canadian sea kayaker who had explored the area extensively, and seven Vietnamese: a cook, a skipper, a tour guide, two deckhands, and a couple of card-playing, chain-smoking guys from the ministry-of-keep-an-eye-on-the-foreigners-to-make-sure-they-don't-secretly-film-a-documentary-about-MIAs, or something else they didn't like.

The boat sported a huge wooden dragon head on the bow, and it would be our home for the next week. At the dock, street hawkers peddled maps, phrase books, postcards, and bootleg copies of Graham Greene's moody Vietnam War-era novel, *The Quiet American*. Duncan McCallum, the cameraman, bought a postcard showing a tombstone-shaped cliff poking out of the sea. He showed it to the skipper and said, "Take us to that one." The skipper nodded and we cast off.

The best way to describe the landscape of the eighty-mile stretch of islands that streak along the coast north of Ha Long Bay is to compare it to a perfect garden in a Zen temple—like a miniature landscape of rocky turrets decorated with bonsai plants, surrounded by a placid sea of raked pebbles. Some formations are sea stacks as well defined as the stone heads of Easter Island, others are thumb-shaped islands that display their rock faces like portraits, framed by fringes of vines and jungle. Everywhere you sail, ten crags appear, ranging from fifty to three hundred feet tall. Caves abound, with drip-formed tufas thick as tree trunks dangling from their roofs. Some of the caves tunnel from one side of an island to the other, and at low tide can be kayaked through; at high tide, the caves can be submerged. The tide-level bouldering is unmappable in quantity.

Two things I expected to see in Vietnam that I did not: junks and bombed-out landscape from the "American War," as locals call it. Ha Long Bay cries out for the romance of a junk on the horizon silhouetted against the red ball of the sinking sun, but they were all scrapped a few years ago in favor of the ear-shattering two-strokes and Russian-made diesels that power the ramshackle fleet of these parts. To see junks in Ha Long Bay, either rent the video *Indochine*, about the French period in Vietnam, or pay out big bucks for an adventure travel trip on one of the boats that motor around the islands sporting an ersatz junk sail.

As for the war, there is no doubt plenty of moldering wreckage to be seen in the south, but aside from some wrecked bridge footings, a moss-covered concrete bunker, and frequent shrines to the war dead, I saw little sign of the conflict during my brief stay around Hanoi and the coast. Nevertheless, I gleaned from a bit of research that the port city of Hai Phong, across the water from Bai Cha, was flattened by B52's, and that strategic parts of Ha Long Bay had been mined back then to deter foreign tankers and supply ships from trading with the communist north. I had also learned, from reading a book called *Derailed in Uncle Ho's Victory Garden*, by a gutsy and colorful Vietnam War correspondent named Tim Page, that in a later war between Vietnam and China, in the very area where we were vacationing, "one of the most vicious battles in military history was fought with hardly any coverage by anybody." Wrote Page, "Almost total censorship was drawn across the border zone stretching from the Tonkin Gulf at Ha Long Bay, with its 3,000 dolomitic stack islands, all the way to Pa Tan, just about on the Lao border. During six weeks in the autumn of 1979, probably 70,000 soldiers and untold numbers of civilians perished as China made its displeasure felt over [Vietnam's invasion of] Cambodia."

We spent the first night on our boat surrounded by bathtub-size coracles, 　　55

*Andy Parkin leading the first pitch of our climb. A minute later he ripped off a
stalagmite and fell thirty feet, just missing the water.*

sampans, and net-festooned trawlers, all lashed together into little floating villages. The occupants of these fishing rigs slept in hammocks and, probably, seldom set foot on the shore. The morning that we planned to make the ascent of Duncan's postcard wall we were awakened by a large explosion. Across the cove from where we were anchored a fisherman was tossing dynamite into the water. The depth charges brought up a lot of fish, which he effortlessly netted, but the practice also wrecked the coral reef below and slaughtered everything from plankton to young fish.

The first big scene began with Andy and me diving heroically into the sea, swimming toward the cliff with our gear in a dry-bag, and bouldering up out of the water to a belay stance. While Duncan swam beside us filming with the camera in a watertight housing, two women wearing conical straw hats rowed past in a bamboo coracle. They gave us no more than a quick glance, evidently totally uninterested in our tomfoolery. The wall above us gave two pitches of 5.10, but by the time we had climbed it the tropical sun and 98 percent humidity had boiled our minds to the consistency of soggy noodles. After rappelling back to the oyster-encrusted shore, we cooled ourselves by diving into the briny sea. Back on the boat, we normalized our core temperatures by pouring Tiger beers into our bellies.

A couple of days later we were ready to film the next climb. On an earlier reconnaissance by speedboat we had sighted a prow of pocketed rock that overhung about forty feet in two hundred. When Richard saw how excited Andy and I got at the sight of this Buoux-like totem, he determined that we had to film an attempt on it, even though I was skeptical that we had the physical oomph to pull off what could easily be a 5.13 route. Not only was the climb probably beyond our stamina levels, but we had only three days left before the trip ended. That gave us one day to rappel it, bolt it, and rig ropes for the camera team, one day to climb it and film it, and one day to get back to Hanoi so that the ministry factotums could review the videotape to see that we hadn't filmed any state secrets. Trying to climb the prow was a huge risk, because if Andy and I failed pathetically on it, not only would we look like a pair of old has-beens (which we were rapidly becoming), but Richard's film would be scuttled. Regardless, we went for it.

Andy and I sketched out a topo of where on the cliff we wanted the bolts placed and handed it to the rigging team of Brian Hall, Mark "Digger" Diggins, and the climbing genius Dave "Cubby" Cuthbertson. They then proceeded to physically wreck themselves as they created the route and the rope line for Duncan's camera work. The previous night, while discussing the route, talk had turned to whether we should film a discussion about the ethics of using bolts for protection on these limestone towers, especially since we were using a battery-powered roto-hammer to place them. In Britain, bolts are quite uncommon due to a long tradition of using natural and removable forms of protection, as compared to Europe, where bolting is accepted without reservation. An Englishman would argue that there are too many bolts on the Continent. Due to their bolt-conservative backgrounds, the Brits felt guilty about having to bolt the climb, and they felt their viewers would want to hear the stars have an anguished confessional about the morality of all this. I defused the need to film this scene by asking, "How can we be worried about the environmental impact of a few bits of metal sticking out of these cliffs when you consider all the lead that was dropped on this country in the war?"

Meanwhile, Andy and I lounged about on a sandy beach near a Buddhist temple, contemplating the excellence of having finally become so famous that servants were bolting our routes for us. We even toyed with the notion of having the very fit Cubby stand in for us as our action double on the hard bits.

While we waited, the skipper was in the temple, engaged in a coin-tossing session with the spirits who watch over the waterways. Using a pair of well-worn tokens that resembled I Ching coins, he threw them repeatedly at the feet of a statue of a fearsome-looking deity.

"It's not going well; the outcomes of the tosses are unfavorable," said Dag, who explained that the sailors hereabouts take these ceremonies seriously. If he didn't get an auspicious coin toss, the skipper might insist that we head back to port.

The skipper threw a sixth time—a total of ten tosses are allowed. Again he shook his head. The boat's cook, a woman, lit another incense stick as appeasement. Dag made an offering of a cookie at the altar, and I donated a banana I was about to eat.

"Money is better," said the cook.

Dag upped the ante by a U.S. dollar bill. American aid produced a favorable outcome on the skipper's seventh toss, and we got the word that the climb could continue.

It was dark when the riggers rappelled the fixed rope down the overhanging wall straight onto the deck of the dragon boat.

"Do you think the route will go?" I asked Cubby as he unclipped from the line. "I woodna like ta say," he said dourly in perfect *Trainspotting* English.

The next day we found that the fixed ropes set in place for the camera team had been shortened fifty feet by some fishermen who'd come with knives under cover of darkness. Well, how could they resist that lovely, strong, ten-millimeter static cord? Nevertheless, it was tights, camera, action by 11:00 A.M. By 11:05 Andy had ripped off a melon-size tufa and fallen twenty feet, stopping a foot above the sea, and I was nursing an aching knee where the force of the fall had rammed me into the rock. Andy is genuinely fearless (the night before he'd told me about a stormy rappel down the Supercouloir on Fitzroy in Patagonia, where he'd punched through the surface of the ice gully and found himself inside a waterfall. Wet to the bone, he extricated himself and continued down, only to punch through again; this time though, the whole gully slid below him, in a massive avalanche. He continued down the rubble, sleeping under a boulder in his frozen clothes.), and he got back on and completed the pitch. It went at 5.11, on natural protection.

The next lead was mine. As I clipped the first bolt, an armada of sampans and coracles appeared in the channel below us. These little boats were all lashed to a larger mothership that putt-putted along, drifting and circling past our rocky port like a cluster of space junk orbiting an asteroid. Boat folk—mums, dads, grandparents, and kids—stared up at us with varying degrees of comprehension. I'm certain none knew what the hell we were doing on that cliff. They probably thought we were harvesting swallow nests, which in these parts are collected for sale to China, where they are made into a tonic. Ounce for ounce, the nests are as expensive as gold. But we were doing nothing so profitable; we were climbing.

Resting sweatily before the bulgy crux, I poked my leg into a deep hueco lined with bat shit. From the boat people came a cacophony of laughter. Rock eats white man's leg—a good joke. Then I heard a splash as their skipper dropped anchor. They had decided to stop and watch. While I huffed and puffed on my no-hands rest, I stared down at the emerald water and saw the boat folk chopsticking rice into their mouths. Our ascent had become lunchtime entertainment.

With Duncan hanging on a rope and nosing his massive video camera almost into my ear, I warned Andy to brace for a fall, as I was about to try the hard move. I crimped my fingertips over a matchbook-size flake, reset my feet, sucked in some air, and then threw my hand at another big hueco, a long way away. For reasons still unclear, I found myself hanging from the desired hold, legs swinging, and I swarmed into the next hueco. Above that, I clutched a few grips of black flint that resembled fossilized whale turds; then I nested inside a cave belay.

"How hard?" asked Brian, who dangled alongside me.

"5.11+."

Andy sailed off on the third pitch, clipping into runners of cord threaded through pockets and tufas. It was truly impressive to watch him battle up the wall. With one arm permanently bent at an inconvenient angle, he had limited reach on his left side, and his fused hip prevented him from executing high steps. No matter, he had developed a unique "twisting" style to get around this limitation, and he wasn't scared to fall while trying a pitch. I caught him on another fifteen-foot plummet; then he solved the move that had rebuffed him—solid 5.11—and climbed up a shallow corner paved with crystals to get to a foot ledge and an anchor.

Resting there, we watched the ropes swing below us in the afternoon breeze. Swallows chattered and flitted through the air. The boat people fired up their engines and headed off. The sea was a crazy shade of green, woven into changing patterns by the incoming tide. The water eddying around the towers reminded me of glaciers flowing around mountains. The boat below was our base camp. Above stood the jungle-covered summit. And in front of us was the final pitch, which from our stance looked to be a forearm-wrenching series of roofs and bulges on huge pockets and clamshells of limestone.

I was halfway up that fourth and final lead when I realized I was getting critically pumped. The weight of the battery pack of the remote microphone taped to my back, and the stoppers and cams dangling from a sling around my neck, weren't making it any easier. A hard heel hook and mantel to pull around a beergut of rock left me raining sweat. I tried to engineer a rest above this, but it only made me gasp. Craning my head around the final roof, I saw the razor-blade jugs of the summit, just twenty feet higher. I figured I had two minutes at most before I reached complete pumpage, so I got moving. The pockets were enormous, yet the bulge kept me on my arms, arms that had become so worthless I couldn't even clip the last bolt. Breathing like an emphysema patient, I exclaimed something that was censored from the film broadcast; then I told Andy to "take," and I dropped into space. I hate falling, but there was an opiate relief to letting go and accepting the cushion of the air a dozen feet below. Duncan, who had filmed the fall, grinned from ear to ear. "Great stuff," he said. I was happy that my skill at falling had been so appreciated.

After spinning on the rope for a while, my arms consented to lead me to the top. Andy followed. Then we rappelled off to the deck of the dragon boat, just as night engulfed Ha Long Bay and bats emerged from their lairs.

That route, on a blob of rock west of Dao Hang Trai Island, was among the best climbs I've ever done, but I doubt you will ever find it again. There's no need to, as a million other routes await your first ascents.

Everyone is curious: a street scene in Rawalpindi.

Green Card

"Travel is glamorous only in retrospect," wrote the globe-trotting storyteller Paul Theroux. His words also apply to that particular breed of lunacy—the Himalayan expedition—where getting to, or home from, a mountain can be harder than the climb.

Take, for example, the summer of 1992, when I got stranded in Islamabad, the capital of Pakistan. It was the end of a successful expedition to Trango Tower in the Karakoram Range, and, like all expeditioners after a sojourn in Asia, my cohorts, Mark Wilford and Rob Slater, and I were desperate to get home.

Expeditioning in the Third World frays the nerves. Two months earlier, we had arrived as polite as choirboys; but now the insufferable heat, bribe-sucking officials, tragic beggars, and the indignity of diarrhea had warped us into three petulant travelers, as diplomatic as Harvey Keitel on a bender. If one more taxi driver attempted to overcharge us, we would tear off his head and make a curry from it.

Which brings us to Islamabad International Airport, where we were trying to elbow our way onto a flight to New York. The scene around us was chaos. The plane was overbooked, and we were trying to fly standby. Scores of wanna-be passengers mobbed the counter, pleading, bullying, trying to pay their way on. It looked like the exodus at the fall of Saigon.

It was then, when checking my travel documents, that I discovered that my Green Card was missing. Carried with my Australian passport, this little laminated card identified me as a U.S. resident-alien and let me enter America freely. Because I owned the Green Card, a U.S. visa had never been stamped in my passport; without the card or a visa, I had nothing to prove that I lived in America, nor any hope of escaping Pakistan.

With only half an hour before departure, I went as crazy as a rat in a coffee can. Ripping into our duffel bags, I scattered pitons, ice axes, sleeping bags, and dirty underpants across the floor. But alas, no Green Card. Instead of flying home, I realized, I was stuck for who-knows-how-long in a city where the idea of nightlife is sipping a 7-Up while trimming one's fingernails and watching geckoes chase bugs across the ceiling.

Misery overcame me. I slumped onto our baggage. Mark and Rob looked on with pity. We had shared great torment to climb Trango Tower, and had we been in the mountains, my friends would have waded rivers or dared avalanches to save me; but I was nuts if I thought they were going to spend one more minute in Islamabad just to keep me company. They skedaddled home.

Back in town that night, I bivouacked on the office floor of my trekking agent. The British mountaineer Doug Scott lay beside me, shaking and moaning from an attack of malaria. In the morning, after Doug staggered feverish onto a flight home, I waved down a taxi.

"Please take me to the American Embassy," I told the driver.

"Yes, no problem," he said. A long ride to the outskirts of town brought us to a shack surrounded by oxen. Behind it, men with hatchets chopped at ox carcasses.

"No. This is a slaughterhouse. Take me to the American Embassy."

I can only imagine that the words "American Embassy" somehow mimicked the Urdu sounds for butcher shop. I repeated my desired destination; then on a piece of paper I sketched a building with Old Glory flying over it. "Ah, yes! American Embassy. No problem!" he exclaimed, and drove off, this time to the embassy, an imposing fortress surrounded by surveillance cameras, rebuilt to repel invaders after a Shiite mob had destroyed it during the Iran hostage crisis. But today the embassy was closed.

"Why closed?" I asked the driver.

"Today holiday. Birthday of Islamic prophet."

I closed my eyes and sighed, the first of many such surrenders I would make that week. That morning I had phoned my wife, Salley, in Seattle and instructed her to ask U.S. immigration authorities at home to reissue my Green Card. But it was Labor Day weekend, and everything was closed there, too.

The next day at the U.S. embassy, I pleaded my case to a two-inch-thick panel of bulletproof glass, behind which sat a secretary. I told her I had

A movie billboard in Islamabad reflects my mood at the time of this tale.

lost my Green Card and couldn't go home, and I asked her to do whatever necessary to get me home.

"But you cannot go to America. You don't have a Green Card," the secretary replied.

"I know. That's why I'm here. For help," I said. "Please get me your supervisor."

"He is busy. Come back tomorrow."

I went ballistic. "I'm a taxpayer!" I shouted. "I have a job to get home to, a wife and family to support." Furthermore, I told her, I was penniless and had frostbite from two months in the mountains. Half of this was a lie, but I felt compelled to maximize my pathetic situation to gain her sympathy.

A supervisor appeared. I repeated my story. He then called for his supervisor, and I told her as well. Then they told me they could not give me an official letter to enter the United States; the State Department forbids such letters being issued in Pakistan because they are often forged by terrorists.

63

Worse, I was told that there was no U.S. immigration office in Pakistan, and I would have to go to Delhi or Bangkok to find one.

"Can't you phone the office in Delhi and ask them to help me?" I asked.

"I can't act on your behalf because you are not an American citizen," one supervisor answered.

"Then I'd like to apply for a tourist visa to enter America. You can stamp it in my Australian passport, and I'll be out of here."

"I can't do that because you've told me you have a Green Card, and tourist visas can't be issued to Green Card holders."

Only Kafka could have scripted a Catch-22 as seamlessly confounding as this. I stared into the bulletproof glass my taxes paid for. It wasn't glass, I decided, but a special screen that filtered out logic and compassion—stealth glass, a CIA invention. I knew the person to whom I was talking was a decent human being, if only I could get through to her. Then something tweaked and I started raving about being treated like a second-class citizen and writing letters to congressmen. The surveillance camera zeroed in on me. I imagined marines in the next room pegging me as a security threat and itching to monster me. I got paranoid and left.

Back at my trekking agent's office I phoned U.S. immigration in Delhi. Public holiday. Office closed. So I sent them a fax, which they never answered. When I visited the Indian Embassy to get a visa for going to Delhi, it, too, was closed for the holiday.

Days passed. My cash dwindled. I was forced to move out of the cockroach-infested Flashman's Hotel into something cheaper. I stayed at Flashman's because it was one of the few hotels in this prohibition town where I could obtain a quota of beer, though only after filling out a declaration pledging I was not a Muslim. At night, bottle in front of me, I watched Pakistani TV till I felt as if I'd had a frontal lobotomy. Aside from Islamic soap operas, TV was mostly prayer, with sporadic CNN broadcasts that blacked out at the first hint of women in short skirts, couples dancing, or anything suggesting that men and women ever come within thirty feet of each other. My new hotel room didn't even have TV, let alone plumbing. When I called for washing water, a bellboy brought a bucket of suspicious-smelling brown liquid pumped out of a ditch beside the hotel.

While I rotted in Islamabad, back in Colorado Mark had recovered from the bottle of Pakistani rum he'd poured down his neck on the flight home and was poking around the gear we'd shoveled into duffel bags at Trango base camp. He found a life preserver he'd pilfered from the Pakistan International Airlines 747; then, amongst a pile of miscellany, he saw it: my

Green Card. When a fax rolled out of my trekking agent's machine announcing that my Green Card was jetting toward me, special delivery, everyone in the office rejoiced, happy that soon they'd be rid of me.

That is, if I could get on a plane. The flights were booked full for a month. At PIA headquarters I barged into a manager's office and implored him for help. He had heard the sob stories—stranded, broke, ailing mother—a thousand times before. He pretended to hear me out while listening to a cricket match on the radio and was about to give me the bum's rush when I said, "Yes, cricket is truly the finest game. As a matter of fact, I went to school with the son of Sir Donald Bradman (a cricket star of Michael Jordanesque status)." I lied. I hate cricket, and as for Bradman, if he ever had a son, I wouldn't know him if he jumped up out of my soup bowl.

Bullshitting changed everything. The manager handed me a cup of tea and promised to try and get me on a flight. After a lively discussion of cricket, which I faked very well, I rushed to the airport to get my Green Card from customs. Customs was closed, another national holiday.

Two days later I had my Green Card, but my prospects were dim for escaping Islamabad. My cricket-loving friend at PIA had cut off the flow of tea and now gave me the brush-off. But while walking back to my hotel, I passed a travel agent shopfront and entered it on an impulse. I told the ticket agent my problem.

"Would you pay $250 to fly tomorrow?" the woman, Anita, asked.

"Is the Pope Catholic?"

"What?"

"Never mind. It's a deal."

Next morning, Anita and a surly fellow hiding behind Raybans met me at my hotel, took my cash, passport, and airline ticket, and said, "We'll be back in a few minutes." Ten minutes later my friend from PIA phoned. "Good news. You are booked to fly tonight," he said. I put the phone down and marveled at my stupidity: I had just given everything I owned to two people I didn't know, while I got my reservation anyway.

Hours passed with no sign of Anita. I was panicked that I'd miss my flight and began to wonder if I'd been ripped off. Two British climbers had told me that day that they'd been held at gunpoint by policemen outside their hotel and had lost a small fortune. My paranoia redlining, I caught a taxi to Anita's office.

The only person at the office turned out to be the manager, a beefy Pakistani who told me he lived in Texas, where he operated a chain of laundromats in addition to this travel agency. When I explained why I was looking for Anita, he went berserk, screaming that I'd just proved what he

Greg Child

had long suspected—Anita was running a black-market ticket agency under his roof.

I began to feel mighty uncomfortable. "I don't want to get anyone in trouble. I thought it was business as usual," I said.

"You can't be blamed. You are just a poor dupe, desperate to get home."

"Right. Furthermore, I'm an idiot."

He thanked me for exposing Anita's nefarious trade and apologized for the corruption eating at his country. "Now you must tell my brother this story," he said, escorting me to a room where a dignified gentleman—obviously the don of this family operation—knelt on a prayer rug, facing a framed photo of Mecca, mouthing a verse from the Koran. I stuttered out my story. He hammered his fist on the floor. "Fire the bitch!" he roared.

Next I was hustled into a Mercedes with a security guard cradling a sleek, automatic machine pistol in the back seat. Suddenly I wondered if this whole charade wasn't an elaborate plot to take me hostage. Don't laugh. It happens. In 1986 a friend of mine, Michael Thexton, was on a flight taxiing down the runway at Islamabad when terrorists hijacked the plane. When the hijackers' demands weren't met, they grabbed Michael and held a .45 to his head: he was going to be the first to die. Luckily for Michael, Pakistani commandos burst in, and he dived out a door amid grenades and bullets. Afterward, Bryant Gumbel on the "Today Show" asked him why he didn't try to overpower his captor. "Because he had a gun pointed at my head," Michael said very slowly, just so Bryant didn't miss the point.

"Where are we going?" I asked as we screeched through the streets of Islamabad.

"We are gonna nail Anita," the driver says.

Wonderful, I thought, I was about to see a drive-by shooting. Frankly, I couldn't have cared less if Anita was running heroin. I just wanted to be on that flight in four hours, but things had spiraled out of control.

After checking the airport and several other sleazy hangouts, we found Anita waiting at my hotel. Her mouth dropped when she saw her boss. A massive argument followed. Onlookers gaped while our gunman passed the time combing his hair and inspecting his reflection in the car mirror. Everyone kept pointing at me and apologizing on behalf of Pakistan. I felt like an insect, and I shrugged my shoulders at Anita to say, "Sorry," then took my ticket, my documents, and a refund and made a beeline to the airport.

Going through Pakistani immigration, it occurred to me that Anita's gang might avenge themselves on my lousy rat-fink hide by spinning a story to the famously corrupt airport police that I was smuggling drugs. This thought made me break into a guilt-smelling sweat. While an official inspected my documents I tried to look casual, but the more casual I tried to be, the more nervous I appeared. A machine-gun-toting cop frisked me, while another one opened my camera and inspected it closely. He made me remove the batteries, "in case there is a bomb inside." Visions of the movie *Midnight Express* filled my head. I expected to be pulled aside for a full-body search; some gloating sadist would plant a brick of hashish in my pants and then drag me off to a prison and subject me to unspeakable abuses. I gulped with relief when my camera was returned.

As the immigration officer stamped my passport, he noticed that I had been to Pakistan six times.

"Oh, my God," he said, smiling. "You have visited us too many times."

"Yes," I replied. "Too many."

The Potala Palace in Lhasa.

Lost in Lhasa

Five minutes after driving into Lhasa I realized I'd gotten there ten years too late, and that the "golden era" that trekkers refer to—when the city was still unchanged and ancient—had ended. On my way to Everest, I had arrived in this city on the high plains of Tibet with an illusion of what I would find, an illusion built on books such as Heinrich Harrer's *Seven Years in Tibet*, a tale of two Western travelers stumbling into the Tibetan capital during the closing months of World War II. Harrer's book, and others of its era, with their photos and tales of monks, lamas, and wild-looking yak-men, described a Buddhist kingdom hidden behind Himalayan walls, a land locked in a medieval time warp, where life and customs were so different that a Westerner could imagine he had been transported to a distant planet.

But what I found—after landing at the turbulence-addled Lhasa airport, driving past the dust-caked cement factory, the walled Chinese compounds, the People's Liberation Army barracks, the fields littered with blue plastic shopping bags flapping in the wind, and the old yet freshly-painted-for-tourists Buddha etched into a cliff—was just another big, ugly Chinese city. Only the great white ziggurat of the Potala Palace distinguished the view around me from downtown Chengdu or Shanghai.

What stunned me about Lhasa was this: the old is being replaced by the new, at a frenzied pace. I encountered roads and traffic jams in a city that had scarcely seen a vehicle before 1950, when Red Army trucks rolled into town. When I went hunting through the back streets for the Lhasa of legend, I saw bulldozers, picks, and shovels eradicating antiquity, and workers erecting the tumble-down schlock of Chinese architectonics: concrete monuments, marble-faced banks and hotels, neon-lit shopfronts hawking cheaply made goods, and rows of ramshackle nightclubs, video parlors, karaoke bars, and brothels thumping out the disco twang of Asia-a-go-go.

What did I expect, a Buddhist Disneyland? Probably. After all, I *was* a tourist, fed a diet of books and slide shows in which a visit to Lhasa and a bit of Buddhist sightseeing was a rite of passage for a north-wall-bound Everest tripper. The reality of the Lhasa I was seeing was one of photographs carefully cropped to exclude the background of change wrought by Chinese occupation.

I went to the Potala in a Toyota Landcruiser. The driver escorted us climbers to a huge wooden gate that creaked on its hinges when a watchman opened it. While paying our admission fee we were mobbed by a dozen Tibetan women, all weighed down by beads and trinkets looped round their necks and arms. They grabbed and prodded us, elbowing each other out of the way, laughing, discounting one another's prices, and imploring us to buy their wares, until the watchman, a Tibetan, rushed into the fray, cracking a whip made from a hefty rubber fan belt nailed to a stick. Gently flogged yet smiling, the women dispersed, and we headed on.

Yes, the Potala was magnificent, a labyrinth of chambers painted with frescoes and jammed with countless statues of deities, all illuminated by the yellow glow of butter-burning lamps. Illuminated, too, were the video surveillance cameras and the plainclothes police, with their crackly sounding hand-held radios, who we encountered at every turn.

Photographing the Potala from outside was tricky. I found it hard to emulate the postcard image of the place because of the forest of new buildings, telephone lines, and towers that have sprung up around it in modern times; whatever lens I used, there was always a cable or a steel structure in my shot. The most intrusive of these steel hulks stands atop a pimple-shaped hill called Chagpori, adjacent to the Potala. The hilltop was formerly the site of the Tibetan medical school. It was blasted by Chinese artillery in 1959, renamed Victory Hill, and became the site for a television antenna.

Perhaps the Chinese were under the impression that if they surrounded the Potala with enough structures, the Potala might disappear. Whatever the case, the modern view was what we had, and it was a vision of realpolitik.

More potent in my memory than any temple in Lhasa was the MIG warplane monument in a park in front of the Potala. A tribute to what—peace? war? Chinese conquest? I was unsure, and I wondered if, for the sake of authenticity, the Chinese had selected a MIG that had actually strafed a monastery?

70   *Inside the temple in Barkhor Square, Lhasa.*

Lost in Lhasa

When I previously visited Tibet, in 1990, it had been illegal to possess pictures of the Dalai Lama. Tibetans owning such photos could be beaten or jailed, and foreign meddlers importing them could be fined or deported. This time, however, I saw many pictures of His Holiness, who lives in exile in India. People carried his photo in lockets and necklaces; temples and even some restaurants displayed his photograph. But this didn't mean the Chinese were loosening their grip over the Tibetans; it meant, more likely, that the Chinese know they have conquered Tibet, and quibbling over a photo of an exiled spiritual leader is no longer a concern to them.

After my first day in Lhasa I woke up to an interesting realization: I had seen very few Tibetans. The staff of our hotel were Han Chinese. So were all the shop owners on the street. And the vehicle drivers. And the policeman who stood on duty underneath the huge concrete statue of the Chinese conquerors of Everest in the square below my hotel window.

Where were the Tibetans? The next day, when I walked through the back streets to Barkhor Square and the Jokhang Temple—the remnants of old Lhasa—I found plenty of Tibetans, circling the temple, selling and buying crafts, all dressed in furs and ragged finery, the men with long knives tucked into their waistbelts. But they were outnumbered in their own city.

At the beginning of the 1950 "liberation," or Chinese takeover, Lhasa's population was 30,000 Tibetans, and the built-up area of the city was three square kilometers. Today, official figures peg the population at 180,000, though unofficial estimates (cited, in 1995, in the Asian magazine *Himal*) go as high as 400,000, with a city size approaching forty square kilometers. Officials say 87 percent of Lhasa's residents are Tibetans, but other studies say only 20 to 30 percent. From what I could see, Tibetans are the minority, and the Han Chinese and Hui-zhou Moslems from Sichuan (these migrants enter Tibet freely, while Tibetans find it hard to travel unhindered in, or leave, their country) run the businesses.

There is no love lost between Tibetans and Chinese, and this makes Lhasa a tense place. As recently as 1987, angry Tibetans, fed up with their lot under Chinese occupation, rioted and burned Chinese property, a move answered by Chinese troops with widespread beatings and arrests of monks and citizens. Highlights of truncheon-wielding soldiers thumping monks a la Rodney King were videotaped and played by Western news programs. A tinderbox of revolution is said to await a match in this city.

I'd seen Chinese soldiers putting the boot into Tibetans before, on other visits. But on this visit all was quiet. Perhaps that was due to the platoons of Chinese troops marching around town, the video surveillance cameras and rooftop guards on every street, the eight prisons and sixteen military bases surrounding the city.

On my last night in Lhasa we left the Lhasa Holiday Inn (we'd moved to this posh hotel because some of our group had complained that our downtown digs were inadequate, that the televisions, hot water, and toilets didn't work; my experience is that they never work in Tibet or China) and tramped off into the cold night to a restaurant where a banquet had been arranged for us.

At the intersection of a road called Dzuk Trun Lam and Beijing Street, we passed two enormous gold-painted, concrete yaks. These were unveiled in 1991 to celebrate the "peaceful liberation of Tibet." On the day of the unveiling, foreign journalists were banned, tourists confined to hotels, monks and nuns confined to monasteries and nunneries, roadblocks set up, and thousands of police and soldiers deployed. Locals jokingly call the yaks Tenzin and Raidi, two Beijing-installed Tibetan officials in the Communist Party of Tibet.

By the time we got to the restaurant it was dark and quite cold. Our destination lay in a street of nightclubs and Chinese eateries. We passed one swank neon-lit joint where bouncers were checking the IDs of the movers and shakers trying to get in—PLA officers and well-dressed business dudes, all with girls in fur coats and hot-pants hanging off their arms. No Tibetans were among them.

As we filed into the restaurant I saw a glossy poster on the wall of a bright red Ferrari with a blonde, bikini-clad girl sprawled provocatively across the hood. Behind me I heard a woody-sounding noise: clop, clop, clop. I turned and saw a teenage boy seemingly crawling along the street. Covered in grime and soot, he was dressed in a threadbare leather apron; on his hands were wooden clogs. The boy was making a circuit around the Potala. The young practitioner of this pilgrimage was alternately standing and then prostrating himself flat onto his belly, again and again, for mile after mile. With each movement the boy muttered a prayer. Cars and motor scooters zipped around him. The clogs protected his hands—clop, clop, clop—the apron protected his knees.

Our eyes connected. He stared at us, all well-dressed, modern-thinking, white-skinned, and free, and we stared at him, a medieval vision, his eyes shining out of his filthy face, bright with something wild and maybe wise. Both he and I were stunned by the encounter. He swayed on his feet, as if delirious. I wished for something to say, some gesture to make, but we were from other worlds and failed to make contact.

We paused like this a second; then he went on his way, a snort of steam streaming from his nose as he faced his path and prostrated himself again. I wonder what he makes of us, I asked myself as he disappeared into the night. He was probably wondering the same about us.

The mountain and the men who jumped off it, Nic Feteris (at left) and Glenn Singleman (at right).

Madmen Offering Themselves to the Brink of Disaster

Irena called her husband's plan to leap from the 5,500-foot cliff of the Great Trango Tower the *kasmat*, a Russian word meaning nightmare. She and Glenn Singleman had been married for less than a year. They met while he was climbing Mount Elbrus in Russia. Even then, the plan to climb to Great Trango's 20,500-foot summit ridge, step off the edge of the north face, and then free-fall through space before opening his parachute and landing on a glacier, was oiling his mental gears. She married him anyway.

It mattered little to Glenn that he had made only a handful of parachute jumps and that his highest BASE jump (BASE is an acronym for Building, Antenna, Span, or bridge, and Earth, or cliff) was from a 300-foot crane. But, I knew from the time I had spent around Glenn in our base camp at the foot of the Trango Towers during that summer of '92, he had a higher twitch level than the average bystander. The deficit of experience amplified the excitement. "I like the volume of life turned up to ten rather than four," he once said, to account for the part of him that could be labeled adrenaline junkie, risk taker, or explorer of mortality's boundary. An emergency room doctor by vocation, his "hobby" was creating film documentaries about life on the edge. His adventure resume included stunts such as being lowered inside a steel cage into a frothy frenzy of white pointer sharks, and crewing a yacht through storm-lashed southern oceans to Antarctica to ski up a glacier to climb an untrodden peak called Mount Minto. That was his first taste of alpinism. He ended up with frostbite from it. True, Glenn likes to tackle horror head on, but he is a meticulous and calculating planner.

Equal partner in Glenn's plan to BASE jump what they dubbed the biggest unjumped cliff on Earth was Nic Feteris. Like Glenn, Nic was Australian. Affable and modest, a public relations expert by profession, and a veteran of 500 BASE jumps, the boy-faced Nic is one of the coolest, most calculating jumpers ever to step into free fall. Nic doesn't have the same relationship with gravity that most of us suffer. He's on friendly terms with it, as was apparent when I saw a video of him stepping as easily off a cliff as one would dive into a swimming pool.

In their plan, Nic would swan dive from Great Trango a second after Glenn. Movie cameras strapped to their bodies and helmets, and cameras in the valley and on the mountain, would record them plummeting like rocks and then sprouting wings and flying like birds. Or, if the scheme went awry, it would document two young men rocketing to terminal velocity and then exploding against cold granite in venous blossoms of guts and parachute nylon.

I first met Glenn, Irena, and Nic in 1991, when they and the British filmmakers Leo and Mandy Dickinson visited me to pick my brain about the Trango Towers. It was a part of Pakistan I knew well from several expeditions. Over cups of tea we discussed the logistics of expeditioning in the Karakoram Range, and I told Glenn we would meet there, because I planned to climb Trango Tower, otherwise known as Nameless Tower. That was when Glenn dropped the punch line, telling me that their real objective was to parachute from Great Trango's awesome wall. They hoped I would endorse this as a great idea and tell them about a perfect natural diving board up there that I just happened to know about. Instead, I tried to talk them out of it.

I warned them about the bone-chilling concoction of sleet and snow that often shrouds the Trango Towers, about unpredictable winds that could snatch their chutes and send them careening into the wall, of the 100-foot ice cliffs that cap Great Trango and that regularly peel off, and of the mounds of jagged boulders they would have to land among—if they got that far. Even though they planned to reach their jump site by climbing up the comparatively easy southern snow slope, I cautioned them that deep snows had halted many climbers who had tried that route.

But what did I know about parachuting off cliffs? Zip, to be exact. So I told them to call Randy Leavitt, who had been with me on an attempt to climb Trango Tower, and who had BASE-jumped from El Capitan and other monoliths. "It's a low-percentage jump," Randy warned them.

Later, Glenn told me that after hearing my pessimism, he and Nic had driven home silent and moody, for the experts had pronounced their plan impossible. Even Nic admitted that the photos of the tower I had shown them revealed a jump fraught with dangers. Yet as they drove, watching the orbs of oncoming car headlights streak past their windscreen, they found themselves looking across the darkness between them, smiling at each other. No words were needed. They knew then that they would go to Pakistan to try their jump.

"I still don't think they'll do it," I whispered to Mark Wilford on Jump Day, six months later below Great Trango Tower. Mark and I sat on rocks on the Dunge Glacier, staring up at Glenn and Nic's take-off point, 5,500 feet above. Secretly, I half-hoped they wouldn't jump, because if they botched it and ended up hanging half-dead on the wall or spread out like a bloody yard sale across the huge couloir in front of us, the task of a rescue (or body recovery) would fall to Mark and me. The ascent of Trango's south face that Mark and I had just completed had provided us with plenty of drama, delivering rockfall, storms, and frigid bivouacs. Additional excitement would be gluttony.

Two days earlier, while we were descending Trango, we'd gazed across a two-mile-wide gulf toward Great Trango and watched Glenn and his team wandering across the snowy south flank. They looked like ants on a giant sugar cube as they searched for a place on the north wall to jump from. Their disregard for exposure made me uncomfortable as they trotted around the undercut fringe of an ice cliff riven with fractures. Beneath them was one of the most dizzying drops I'd seen, an awesome work of rock, tawny and streaked, bulging, ballooning, and smooth, and terminating in a shadowy gully of ice.

It was hard to look when they rappelled beneath the huge serac and set up their jump site. We flinched at their shouts of "one thousand, two thousand, three thousand," the mantra of BASE jumpers, yelled as Nic dropped rocks with streamers tied to them to time the fall. When I saw them lean over the vertiginous drop to aquaint themselves with the wall below, I felt queasy. The scene reminded me of a cartoon from the 1970s, drawn by Sheridan Anderson, in the climbing journal *Ascent*. Called "Madman offering himself to the brink of disaster," it showed a wild-eyed caricature of a climber leaning over a cliff, his body inclined at a ridiculous angle.

When Mark and I ambled back to base camp after our descent from our climb, we found a note from Irena inviting us to attend the first BASE jump of Great Trango, and the tallest one ever attempted. Like football fans marching to the stadium, we hiked around the mountain. On a sandy bench 100

Gliding toward the Dunge Glacier after free-falling down the Great Trango Tower.

feet wide and 500 feet long, we met Mandy, standing beside a cine-camera mounted with a 1,000mm lens, and Irena, calmly sunning herself while writing in her diary. Outwardly Irena seemed calm, unaffected by the fact that in a short time she would either be the wife of a very daring fellow, or a widow. But judging from how rapidly she was filling the pages of her diary with Russian Cyrillics, I guessed she was a bundle of nerves and that her writing came in screams and shudders.

"Do you know much about first aid?" Mandy asked me.

"Not much. Don't you have a doctor?"

"Yes," she chuckled, "but he's about to jump off that rather large cliff over there."

Mandy showed me a plastic barrel full of medical supplies. I sorted through splinting material for shattered bones, tourniquets to stop spurting blood and plasma to replace it, syringes to pump in morphine and antibiotics, and drugs to jump-start failing hearts. Glenn was a thorough planner, I saw. I assumed I'd find body bags if I dug deep enough.

Then the radio crackled to life. The countdown had commenced. Everybody aimed their cameras at the wall. I still held on to my belief that in the end sanity would prevail and they would call it off. I couldn't imagine how they could summon the pluck to jump off that horrible cliff, but then again, I was chicken-hearted when faced with the minifalls of sport climbing. My palms grew slick with sweat. I worried. Now I understood how my mother felt whenever I told her I was going climbing.

Then Mandy announced they were free-falling. The madmen were barely visible through my 200mm lens, but I saw a blur and tracked it down the wall.

"They're out of control," Mandy shouted. "Going head over heels."

Leo Dickinson, who was filming from a snowy platform at 18,000 feet on the mountain, came in on the radio: "Open your bloody chutes!" he screamed at them.

Events were crammed into seconds, yet to us their fall seemed to last forever. Fifteen hundred feet from their take-off point, their shapes showed clearly in my lens. They were tumbling like crash-test dummies. The weight of the cameras mounted on their helmets had made them tilt forward, and the thin atmosphere made it hard for them to get into a safe position to open up.

After 2,000 feet of head-over-heels, tumbling free fall, Glenn and Nic's speed had increased, and the air was thick enough to push against with their hands. They forced their bodies into flat, star-shaped positions. Two hundred feet above the bed of the icy couloir their hands released the pilot chutes and the main chutes ripped out of their packs. Mandy whooped as two yellow spots of parachute nylon burst open. Then everyone shut up as the chutes disappeared behind a massive buttress of rock. They seemed to linger back there for too long. The thought crossed my mind that they had collided with the wall. I looked at Irena. Her face was hard to read. She was hedging her emotions till the end. Then they emerged, and Mandy whooped again. Later, when asked how far he had missed the wall by, Glenn would answer, "By a bee's dick."

They traversed above the glacier and spiraled down. Behind them the Karakoram sky was blue and windless, with the white cap of Masherbrum framed at the head of the valley and the shark-tooth shapes of the Trango Towers bristling around us. A good day to fly. Glenn landed first, kicking up a spray of sand and then dropping to his knees as if in genuflection. The sound of his hyperventilating lungs reached me fifty feet away. Then Nic touched down and sprawled onto his chest. He stood up and erupted into a crow of birdlike laughter. Nothing seemed to faze him. Mark and I rushed over to them.

"Are you all right?" I asked Glenn. He wore the expression of someone who had eaten a plate of bad clams.

"Blurgh, blahh, urgh," he said. His lips twitched, and his eyes welled with tears. Then Irena was embracing him. "The *kasmat* is over," she said as they pressed themselves to each other.

Later that day, as we hoofed back to base camp, I thought about our days spent climbing Trango, clinging to the wall like geckoes, and of Nic and Glenn, bearing out Darwinism, evolving wings, and flying like raptors. Their notion to jump off Great Trango had at first struck me as a crazy stunt, a novel form of attempted suicide, but with little connection to climbing besides the fact that they had to climb a mountain to reach their launching pad. I had mistakenly written off their endeavor as a fine form of madness, but little more, until I thought of my own devotion to vertical pursuits and the puzzlement it causes anyone not attuned to climbing. On the recklessness scale, which was madder: spending days climbing up and down a huge wall, the whole time dodging rockfall and freezing your butt off, or scaling a peak and parachuting from its edge? Or what about big-wave surfing? Or speed-skiing? Or trans-ocean solo yachting? Or car racing? Or any activity in which the outcome is uncertain and the motive hard to fathom?

Seven decades earlier, an Englishman named George Leigh Mallory, who was en route to a fateful appointment with Mount Everest, had become flustered at a press conference by a reporter who demanded to know "why" Mallory was so hellbent on climbing Everest.

"Because it's there," Mallory finally blurted, frustrated at the world's inability to understand his desire to climb, and his own inability to explain it. And so it was for all of us on those freakish-looking granite shafts that summer of '92, whether we were there to climb or to fly.

Into the Cold:

Alaska, Canada,

and the French Alps

Two climbers drifting up a frozen rib, somewhere in Canada's Coast Range.

Souls on Ice

> *The Hollow-men live in solid rock and move about in the form of mobile caves or recesses. In ice they appear as bubbles in the shape of men. But they never venture out into the air, for the wind would blow them away.*
>
> *They have houses in the rock whose walls are made of emptiness, and tents in the ice whose fabric is of bubbles. During the day they stay in the stone, and at night they wander through the ice and dance during the full moon. But they never see the sun, or else they would burst.*
>
> *They eat only the void, such as the form of corpses; they get drunk on empty words and all the meaningless expressions we utter.*
>
> *Some people say they have always existed and will exist forever. Others say they are the dead. And others say that as a sword has its scabbard or a foot its imprint, every living man has in the mountain his Hollow-man, and in death they are reunited.*

So wrote the French metaphysician René Daumal some fifty years ago, in his quirky, unfinished fantasy, *Mount Analogue*, a slim fiction that regained popularity in the heady 1970s. Subtitled *A Novel of Symbolically Authentic Non-Euclidean Adventures in Mountain Climbing*, the story chronicles a hazardous journey by a group of alpinist-explorers to an uncharted and impossibly high mountain. For a decade and then some, my copy had gathered dust on a promenade of my bookshelf reserved for culturally dated yet indispensable volumes, such as Carlos Castaneda's *Tales of Power*. Nobody reads this stuff anymore, yet those who have (and what climber in the 1970s missed Daumal or Castaneda?) cannot forget the mystical routes that these books took us on. Back then, such fables were the blueprints of the climbing experience.

I recently found myself thinking of those bogeys of the ice world, the Hollow-men, so I dusted off *Mount Analogue* and reread Daumal's phantasmagoric pun on climbing. I had all but forgotten these spectral beings till one day in June 1994, while descending the West Ridge of Mount Hunter in the Alaska Range after a long ascent of a new route that became known as "The Wall of Shadows," I felt the snowy crust beneath me dissolve, and I dropped armpit-deep into a hidden crevasse.

It was a minor event on an Alaskan peak, de rigueur, I suppose. My partner, Michael Kennedy, and I had each plunged knee- to waist-deep into a half-dozen slots already that morning. Roped together for safety, we took evasive action to escape each gaping maw by rolling forward or backward and clawing crablike away from the darkness, hooking our ice tools into the snow. But at the crevasse in question—which I had straddled with my arms while my feet pedaled in the void below—I felt an urge to examine the mouth that had just tried to swallow me. So, after wriggling out, I gazed down its gullet. I saw two polished, parallel walls three feet apart shooting into a night-black deep. A cold breath from within the mountain sucked at my own panting lungs. I touched the crevasse wall. It was as glass-smooth as a lens, and bone dry. My glove froze fast to the ice. When I peeled my hand away, it made a sound like tearing paper. It was then that I saw it—staring out from the ice near the murky junction between black nowhere and the transluscent bluefish sparkle of day—a face, staring back. I stepped away, quickly, said nought to Michael, and resumed our punishing trudge—our ninth day on Hunter— down the ridge.

Of course, the mirrorlike crevasse wall had merely served up my own reflection, but the sight sent a tingle down my spine anyway and made me rifle my thoughts for a reference. And so I remembered Daumal's Hollow-men, sinister dwellers in the ice, watchers from within, waiting for us to join them.

Whether the Hollow-men are Doppelgängers, demons, or guardian angels, I am unsure, for Daumal died before completing *Mount Analogue*, leaving the Hollow-man concept tantalizingly sketchy. Maybe his inspiration for the idea came one day when he was rambling through the Alps, gazing into crevasses. The sight of his own reflection staring back from shadows and ice would probably have caused his heart to skip a beat, just as it did mine, for Daumal—writer, poet, linguist, surrealist, occultist, philosopher, and climber—penned *Mount Analogue* during the darkness of the Nazi occupation of France, and while slowly dying of tuberculosis.

Crevasses are high on the list of my phobias. I trace this fear back to a warm summer day in 1981, when I was strolling along the Mer de Glace above Chamonix, in France, with my wife, Salley, our Coloradoan friend Mark Wilford, and a British mentor of ours named Guy Lee, a veteran of Nordwands galore. Our objective was a petit granite aiguille, a day climb near a hut, and we carried sacks of baguettes, jam, and cheese, and thermoses of coffee. With me holding her hand to bolster her confidence, Salley stepped across her first crevasse, one of countless stretchmarks creasing the Mer de Glace.

"See," I told her, "It isn't dangerous, if you're careful." That was when we saw the tug-of-war ahead, and a happy day became a sad one.

A dozen or more French adolescents on a school outing gripped the end of a rope, which disappeared into a three-foot-wide crevasse. Beside the rope was a snowbridge that spanned the gap. It was pocked with a neat round hole, as if a mortar shell had pierced its surface. On either side of the hole were footprints. The kids pulled at the rope for all they were worth, trying to haul something out from the belly of the glacier, but whatever was in there was stuck tight.

Two guides and a teacher stood with the kids, with forlorn expressions haunting their faces. The guides shouted and raved. Alternately racing off and reappearing, they seemed torn between staying to help and hurrying down the glacier to raise a rescue. Two weary young British alpinists who happened along filled in the blanks for us: a young girl had broken through the snowbridge nearly an hour ago.

"Has anyone been down to check her out?" Guy spat out, as he rapidly uncoiled a rope.

"*Oui*," answered the teacher, who sat on his haunches, shivering, and blanketed by a red down coat. "They lowered me in. She spoke. We got a rope around her. She is fourteen. But even with all the children pulling we cannot move her." He drifted into a mood of stunned hopelessnes, his eyes welling with tears.

"We've been in, too," added one of the British lads. "She's in deep. Wedged like a cork. I couldn't reach her."

Everything would have been different if the children had been roped together; but they weren't, and lecturing or accusing wouldn't alter a thing. So, for the next hour we, like the French and the Brits ahead of us, tried to reverse the terrible situation. Roping down forty feet into the cold gut of the glacier, we had to hang upside down in our harnesses just to touch the girl's

Beware the surface of things: the crevasse, Mer de Glace, France.

blonde head. She didn't stir or speak. Her leg had twisted behind her when she slid in, so that her hiking shoe appeared sole-up beside her head, a silent statement of unspeakable anguish.

Back on the glacier surface, as night approached, we realized the girl would not live. The guides had left for help, and Salley began herding the children down the glacier, back toward Chamonix; better that they not see their schoolmate when we finally got her to the surface, she decided. In the afternoon twilight a helicopter flew up the valley, passing Salley and her flock as they scrambled up a loose moraine near the Montenvers railway station. The children, who were not fools, knew their friend was doomed, and many were crying. One of the children turned to look at the helicopter, slipped, and began skating down the slope. Salley stopped the child's fall, but lost her own balance, tumbled, and sprained her ankle. Limping now, Salley made her way to a bus waiting for the children, but in the confusion of the moment, for whatever reason, she was not allowed on the bus. She hobbled down under her own steam, arriving in Chamonix at midnight.

Back at the crevasse, two mountain gendarmes and a doctor stepped off the helicopter. Seasoned by a thousand rescues, they commanded us into a crew. We lowered one of them into the hole. Using a spray-gun filled with antifreeze, he quickly unlocked the crevasse's grip on the girl. We winched her out. The moment she hit the surface the doctor went through the motions of trying to revive her. There was a moment of hope as her small body quivered with jolts of current from the heart-starting machine, but her blood-drained pallor and sunken eyes told us that only her body would return from the crevasse.

Riding back to Chamonix in the helicopter, jammed beside the body bag, we were silent. After we landed in a green meadow, Mark turned to me, shaking his head sadly. "She had a gold ring on every finger. She was a kid," he said. We never learned her name. We never wanted to know it.

In Daumal's book, a character named Mo strikes a rock with his alpine pick to place a piton. His pick shatters a man-shaped cavity in the stone; " . . . torso, legs, arms and little tubes in the shape of fingers spread in terror. He has split the head with the blow of his pick. . . . An icy wind passes across the stone. Mo has killed a Hollow-man."

"Watch out for the Hollow-men," Mo's father warns him. "They will seek vengeance. They cannot enter our world, but they can come up to the surface of things. Beware the surface of things."

Next day, Mo's ice ax and his clothes are found at the foot of a cliff. The Hollow-men have ambushed him and dragged him into the mountain. Mo's brother, Ho, sets off to rescue his brother. Their father issues these instructions: "The Hollow-men have taken your brother and changed him into a Hollow-man. He will try to escape. He will go in search of light to the seracs of the Clear Glacier. . . . Go to him and strike at his head. Enter the form of his body, and Mo will live among us again. Do not fear to kill a dead man."

At the glacier, Ho looks into a blue serac and sees "silvery forms with arms and legs, like greased divers under water." Thousands of Hollow-men are chasing Mo, who eludes their clutches only by staying close to the bright surface of the ice, from which the Hollow-men cringe. Summoning all his courage, Ho aims his pick at the center of Mo's skull and cracks the ice. He steps into the serac and enters his brother's hollow form; then he steps back into the world of air, taking his brother with him. He becomes his brother, and his brother becomes him. They live on as one.

Mount Analogue is a fantasy, a trifle, and the climbing in it is just a stage for Daumal to mount his broader philosophies. In real life, frail flesh is seldom retrieved from the ice so bloodlessly, so beautifully. Nevertheless, we would do well to heed Daumal's warning of the icy underworld.

"Beware the surface of things."

Mountain travelers, this is your mantra.

Greg Collum and Steve Masceoli on the summit of Mount Combatant. Waddington rises behind.

Mortals on Combatant

We fly low up the Tiedemann Glacier, under a thick wad of cloud shrouding the steep southern buttresses of Mounts Tiedemann and Combatant. Looking out the windows of Mike King's Jet Ranger helicopter, we see Combatant's granite flanks shining slick after morning rain. Beneath the mountain, the glacial snows are streaked black with gravel and mottled pink with blooms of algae. Higher up, in the icefall separating Combatant from Mount Waddington, ice chunks lie about where rickety seracs have collapsed and, we soon find, will continue to collapse, thunderously loud and as regular as clockwork, all throughout our climb. It is late August, the dog days of the Indian summer of '94. The glaciers are tired, disheveled, ill-tempered; they itch for a cleansing blanket of snow and the brace of winter to make their bones strong again.

Chopper time is pricey; so when Mike lands his contraption on the glacier, I lend a hand to Greg Collum and Steve Masceoli, and we hurl our packs out of the machine, rough as airline baggage handlers. That finished, we hunker against a mini-tornado as Mike lifts the heli back into the air. In the time it takes to wipe the snow from my shades, the chopper becomes a speck against the clearing sky. It disappears over the jagged spine of the Serra Peaks, leaving us totally alone in this valley in the heart of British Columbia's Coast Range. And alone is a hard thing to find, these days.

Trying the first ascent of Combatant's south buttress was Greg Collum's brainchild. He'd attempted it a couple of years earlier with Andy Selters, but they only got a few pitches up the wall before the dreaded Coast Range weather engulfed them in a fug of rain, sleet, and snow and sent them packing. When Greg returned from that attempt he showed me a photo of the route and sang its praises: bigger than El Cap, perfect rock, and, in autumn, the likelihood—if you're lucky—of long spells of clear weather. That photo and the elusive promise of a wilderness adventure climb was all the persuasion Greg needed to get Steve and me into his road-worn Dodge van, driving north into Canada.

And now we were there, standing before a 4,500-foot obstacle course of a ridge, watching evaporating clouds twist and curl around the lower buttress like smoke from a dying fire. It was then that it became soberingly apparent to us that this climb would be no casual outing.

Combatant's south buttress is really a series of sharply sculpted and quite independent granite towers. The first spire, which Greg refers to as the Incisor, is a slender spike of flawless stone 2,000 feet tall; should geologic fate have placed this monolith in Yosemite Valley, its only rival in the beauty contest of rock would be the Lost Arrow Spire. Behind the Incisor, appearing out of the mist, we next see a tightrope-narrow ridge decorated with needlelike pinnacles. This long, complex traverse—which we dub the Jawbone—gains 1,000 feet of height in its 2,000-foot horizontal span. A scree ledge, acres broad, comes next, offering the certainty of a comfortable bivouac. Then, like an apparition materializing out of the ether, we see a second spire of tawny granite, 1,000 feet high. The final summit—a third tower topping out at over 12,000 feet above sea level—stands 500 feet higher again, at the end of another knife-edged traverse.

The wall is massive. Massive, too, are the loads at our feet. Stuffed into four bulging packs we have wads of storm clothing, hammocks, bivy sacks, sleeping bags, and a tiny tent; a stove, fuel, and food for two weeks; water jugs and sacks to collect snow for drinking water along the way; a radio transceiver to call Mike from the summit to tell him when to fly in and pick us up; mountain boots and rock shoes; crampons and ice tools for the descent; a weighty rack of biners, pitons, copperheads, hammers, nuts, cams, and a bolt kit; and a tangle of ropes and slings. Somehow, all this junk must be dragged up the Incisor, ferried along the Jawbone toward the summit, and then humped down to the col between Waddington and Combatant. We have tried to sift our gear down to a minimum, but the combination of big wall and alpine climbing that the route presents, and the need to be well provisioned in the event that a storm whips up and prevents Mike from choppering in, means fat loads.

As the sun burns off the mist and turns the glacial cul de sac into a cauldron, we enter the icefall, dragging, humping, and hand-hauling our loads into and out of a labyrinth of crevasses and ice barriers. Transporting the loads takes all day. We are steaming with sweat by the time we reach the foot of the Incisor, where Greg's previous attempt had started. He is amazed to find that the glacier has receded twenty feet, exposing a cliff that had been locked in deep freeze since a previous ice age. While Greg excavates a patio of flat stones on which we'll spend the night, Steve and I jam our hands into a crack and climb upward for 300 feet.

Two hours later, as we rappel to the ledge on the ropes, we see friendly looking cumulus sails becalmed in a crimson evening sky. We swing onto the bivouac ledge next to Greg and slip into our sleeping bags just as day turns to night. Later, as a midnight freeze sets in, the gurgle of water running through glacial plumbing abruptly stops. The silence, to our highway-noise-hardened city-dweller ears, is as jarring as crashing cymbals. The shock of it wakes us; then we roll over and return to our slumber and the vibrant, technicolor dreams that only seem possible under a blanket of sky.

LIKE GREG, I HAD ALSO BEEN HEREABOUTS IN THE PAST, in 1990, and I had seen our buttress on Combatant, as well as the Himalaya-like massif of the "Big Wad," as Canadians call Waddington, from ten miles distant. I had just returned from climbing K2 and had gotten an invitation to visit the set of the movie *K2*, in which Waddington was serving as a substitute for the world's second-highest mountain. The film's producer invited me as a sort of consultant to the stars, an advisor on the art of affecting an authentic high-altitude gasp, a convincing shiver, and an authentic boot-plod.

For three days I watched the filmic fantasy of *K2* unfold. I saw fiberglass walls fixed to the sides of a crevasse blasted off with explosives to collapse a ladder spanning the abyss and send stuntmen plunging to their make-believe doom. I hitched heli rides onto mountain tops to watch climbers and actors create the illusion of trudging out the last paces to summit glory. I saw scores of Haida native women made up with beards, turbans, and nose putty to resemble Balti porters and watched them march up a glacier carrying featherweight balsa-wood boxes. I marveled at the logistical monster of the movie set, a village of prefab huts that floated on a plywood raft on the glacier. There was a mess hall, a kitchen feeding a hundred people a day, and hot showers pumped in from a manmade lake on the ice that was fed by bucket-loads of water scooped out of a tarn and flown in by chopper. "That water costs us a dollar per gallon," the producer bragged to me. "Keep your showers quick."

It was all very Hollywood, but weirder than all that was the small-world encounter I experienced the moment I got out of the chopper at the movie set. Of all the people on Earth to greet me, there was Ali, brother of the Balti expedition cook Rasool. I had just been hanging out with Rasool for three months in the Chinese Karakoram. Ali, along with three other Balti porters I knew from expeditions, had been jetted from Pakistan to Canada to play authentic porters.

Relating more to the Balti tribe than to the Hollywood tribe, I shared their Quonset hut and heard Ali's broken-English account of their journey from their oil-lamp-lit, plumbingless, dirt-floored mud huts in the mountain hamlet of Hushe to the bright lights of Vancouver. En route, they'd seen astonishing sights: jets that flew higher than 8,000-meter mountains, a vast ocean, skyscrapers with walls made of mirrors, elevators and escalators, and supermarkets as big as a village. Of particular interest to these Moslem mountain men were the motives of the fishnet-stockinged and see-through-blouse-attired ladies of the night who strutted Vancouver's streets.

On my last morning on the set of *K2* I sat on a film crate soaking up the sun with Little Karim, a diminutive Balti who had climbed three 8,000-meter peaks. Behind us came the soft mutter of Ali, kneeling and prostrating on a foam pad, making his morning communion with Allah. Little Karim pointed to Waddington and told me he thought this mountain really looked like K2. Then he gazed the length of the glacier, nodded, and agreed that the Tiedemann resembled the Baltoro. Finally he pointed to Combatant.

"And that one, maybe a little like Trango Tower, yes?"

It was then that I noticed the immensity of the south buttress.

WE GAIN HEIGHT ON THE WALL ON THE SECOND DAY, following a line of flakes and fissures. Morning mist floats around us, evaporating by 10:00 A.M. About then, when the valley fills with sunshine, we hear the first whip cracks of avalanche. The rim of the ice-bound gap between Combatant and Waddington explodes into a cubist jumble that bounces toward our tracks from the previous day. Safe on the wall, though, we blithely watch from our hanging belays as hour by hour the serac remodels itself. By day's end it is whittled into a cigar-shaped ice pinnacle, so slender it defies the laws of physics. As we settle into our second bivouac, again on a flat ledge, again in bivy sacks, we hear a sharp snap and a roar in the night, and we know that the ice cigar has succumbed to gravity.

We find the technical crux of the route on the third day, in the vertical central section of the Incisor. We stuff our fingers into cracks till they bleed; then overhanging cracks take us on a six-pitch ride. In the afternoon, as Greg climbs around a small roof and launches up a groove, a cloud appears out of nowhere and spills a deluge of graupel onto Steve and me. Snow pellets bounce

Steve Masceoli belaying during our ascent of Mount Combatant.

down the wall like white ball bearings. When we reach Greg, he's standing on a small ledge, graupel lining the folds of his clothing. We pad out the ledge with ropes and a haulbag and rig the two-man tent to hang half-on, half-off the ledge. Packed inside it, like peas in a pod, we fire up the stove and eat soup and bagels while snow slides off the tent with a hiss like static.

There is no hint of the squall the next morning, and the warmth of the day soon becomes cloying. The terrain is less steep above, and we know that we'll crest the Incisor today. Hauling has been a bitch, so we reach an executive decision to lighten our load by eating the foot-long salami we've been toting. Salami for breakfast is hard work, but we force it down our necks. The sudden influx of pig grease into our bodies has the effect of Valium, and we climb slowly, queasily, up the tower. A nagging thirst from the salty hog-loaf soon scratches at our throats.

We've been fueling our need for water by scavenging from the rare snow patches along the route, but by afternoon on this fourth day our water bags are empty. We must reach the snow patch on top of the Incisor. In the meantime, Greg gets a sip of water while he jumars by using a tube of thin, flexible plastic to suck at trickles of water that ooze from mossy nooks. I watch him gravitate up the crack, poking his proboscis at soaks, slurping and sucking like some nectar-hunting insect.

An old hand at hanging out in the Coast Range, Greg is really the archetypal globetrotting climbing slacker. When not ferreting new routes out of the moss-plagued cliffs around Seattle, he is thumbing through his library of climbing books and maps, hunting down overlooked classics from the Yukon to Thailand to the Karakoram. As a professional investor, he has always set his own hours of work and leisure and has successfully avoided the curse of nine-to-five wage slavery. Consequently, the workday highway commute is anathema to Greg, as I found one morning at 8:00 A.M. as we inched along in a gridlock of traffic, on our way to a crag on the outskirts of Seattle.

"What's with all these cars?" Greg suddenly demanded.

"It's rush hour. These people are all going to work."

"What, all at the same time?"

THAT FOURTH AFTERNOON WE CREST THE INCISOR. Sharpened by eons of glaciation and storm, and case-hardened by lightning strikes, it is the perfect summit to straddle. Ahead of us, a hundred feet below and arching up in a craggy sweep, we see the Jawbone traverse, the next obstacle in our path. Clearly, there are a lot of days left in this ascent.

Just below the top of the Incisor we squeeze onto a series of small ledges for the night. I flush a cat-size raven from his perch and curl up on its roost, while Greg and Steve occupy a sliver of flatness fifty feet below me. The rock around us glows gold in the twilight. We look down at the wrinkled glacier and hear the thump of the icefall. A huge black cliff on Bravo Peak and a truck-size chunk of Waddington become victims of heat exhaustion and tumble onto the glacier. Sunset highlights a vein of smoke suspended in the air; then darkness is broken by a faint glow on the horizon: a forest fire raging near the town of Bella Coola.

The next morning—day five—we take a committing step by rappelling off the tip of the Incisor, onto the Jawbone traverse. We are confronted by a prickly serration of totemlike towers, some up to 100 feet tall. Unless we can skirt around them, it will take us days to negotiate the ridge. We are also starting to worry about the weather, not that the sky looks threatening, but because, having had so much good weather, we are paranoid that a big storm must be in our collective horoscope.

Steve seems particularly hesitant to pull the rope down from the Incisor. He's right to worry; if a storm hits while we are in the middle of the traverse, we'll be in a jam, as rappelling the thousand feet to the icefall, down loose cliffs and past the serac-ridden pocket glaciers that inhabit every cold dent in the mountain, will be a nightmare.

I'd MET STEVE, A QUIETLY PRAGMATIC CARPENTER, during the years he'd lived in Seattle, just before he'd moved to Iowa, a place he portrayed as a Siberian gulag of flatland servitude for a climber of his enthusiasm. But it was a place where Lisa, his wife, had a career and he could find work. Good-tempered and reticent by nature, Steve has a wealth of epic tales concerning his climbs in North America. For example, there was his ordeal by bear, in 1993, in Alaska.

On that trip he and his partner flew into the Tokositna Glacier to climb Huntington's west face. Coincidentally, Mike Kennedy and I had flown out the day before his arrival. Steve and his partner arrived in perfect weather, put up their tents, and set to lounging in their respective shelters. Steve was listening to his Walkman when something outside the tent slapped him hard on the side of the head. At first he assumed it was his buddy playing a joke, but then a ruckus coming from the haulbag got his attention. So Steve exited the tent and came face to face with a small but very hungry brown bear. It snorted rudely at Steve and then continued gulping down their bivy treats, packaging and all.

"As soon as I saw that bear I knew we were hosed," Steve told us, in his low-pitched, understated voice.

The next minutes were frantic as the climbers snatched up as much survival gear as possible. Retrieving a rope, ice axes, sleeping bags, and their radio, they commenced an hours-long running battle with the bear, which, to guard its newfound larder, repeatedly charged the two climbers, driving them up the glacier.

"By midnight things were desperate. The bear had us baled up against the slopes of Huntington. It kept coming up from the tents to chase us. I was sure we'd have to try to kill it with our ice axes. All the time I was radioing the base camp over on the Kahiltna Glacier, trying to get a plane to get us out of there. But there was no answer on the radio."

The bear kept up its skirmishes; then, suddenly, it wandered off to lap up a trickle of water running down a cliff. The climbers dashed back to their now-wrecked camp just as a plane landed on the glacier. Steve's SOS had been picked up. As the rifle-toting pilot stood watch, they bundled their gear into the plane and flew out. It was probably the shortest trip ever to attempt Huntington.

"I figure the bear had wandered up the glacier in early spring, when there was plenty of snow covering the crevasses," Steve concluded. "But its escape route had been cut off when the spring thaw revealed the crevasses. It was one sad bear, skinny and starving. It must have been lost for a long time. Last I saw of it, it was climbing up to the French ridge on Huntington, probably trying to get over to the Ruth Glacier to hassle some other poor climbers."

In the spring of the same year that Steve, Greg, and I made our climb of Combatant, I had run into Steve again in Alaska. Both of us were there with separate partners to climb routes on Mount Hunter's north face. To Steve, this wall of ice was the ultimate climb. During a blizzard at the Kahiltna landing strip camp, we spent days in a snow cave with a tribe of marooned climbers, pouring back a bottle of Jim Beam, cracking jokes, and telling tall tales. Steve spoke of how his wife and small son were never far from his thoughts, and he wondered aloud if family ties didn't hold him back from pulling out all the stops on the formidable climb of Mount Hunter. As it was, he didn't succeed on the mountain that year, and it was still a thorn in his side when we were on Combatant.

In 1997 Steve would return to Hunter with Alan Kearney to climb the Moonflower Buttress. Seventeen pitches up this wall of ice streaks and granite cliffs, a huge, tumbling ice block struck Steve and killed him instantly. No one who knew Steve could accept that a person of such integrity and enthusiasm, and with such a concern for safety, had been cut from the fabric of life.

STEVE PULLS THE RAPPEL ROPE DOWN from the tip of the Incisor and we make our way along the Jawbone, which drapes through the sky in a rocky arc, like a suspension bridge. We rig Tyrolean rope traverses to ferry the bags from pinnacle to pinnacle. Our ropes weave through the stony teeth like dental floss. The rock is a multicolored granitic meltdown, sometimes solid, sometimes loose. We kick blocks off as we climb, watching them tumble in sparky, Fourth-of-July-smelling showers into the shadowy gulf. On the nineteenth pitch Steve carefully dances around a choke of black diorite blocks wedged into a dihedral. As he brushes past one the size of a refrigerator, it topples, bouncing past me and Greg, barely missing our ropes. All along the Jawbone we contend with hazards like this, where the only way to make progress is to tread with delicacy, or to behave like a bull in a China shop and push the boulders off the ridge.

By that day's end we are ensconced in bivouac sacks on an eyrie atop a pinnacle. High clouds and cold air that night leave little doubt that the weather will change. Errant snowflakes blow into the opening of my bivy sack and touch my cheek on and off all night, making my sleep unsettled.

And change the weather does. On the sixth day the gray cloud cap lowers onto us. By afternoon we are climbing through wet snowflakes. With cold hands and soggy gloves we jam up a couple of cracks splitting a cliff at the end of the Jawbone; then we hike up a fog-shrouded yet easy-angled and wide scree terrace. Just before dark we pitch our tent on a roomy ledge. Then a snowstorm pelts down.

Mist and sleet conceal the final tower the next day, so we rest. It's been seven days since we started out, and we've become used to the routine of moving up the mountain. Around the tent we fashion Aztec-altar-like chairs and tables from flat stones and sit with our sleeping bags wrapped around us, reading torn-off sections of the sole book we have allowed ourselves to lug along, a copy of *Ancient Evenings*, by Norman Mailer.

Nothing in me wants the climb to end. I feel content to keep going for another seven days, and, maybe, another seven after that. I peer into the wafting mist and imagine a climb on which the summit is always somewhere above, in the infinite, hidden by cloud. You'd never reach this summit, and I wonder how long it would take before I'd get bored with my theoretical endless climb.

Hunger would probably dictate the parameters of a climb without end. A climber could never carry enough food, so a hunter-gatherer talent for grazing on mosses, lichens, and wildflowers, and for trapping bugs, birds, and rock rodents would be in order. Judicious cannabilism of one's partners might be tempting, too. Clothing would eventually wear out, so one would have to evolve skin as tough and hairy as goat hide, along with leathery, high-friction footpads. Gear would wear out also. Stone implements might suffice for a time, but eventually the specially adapted climber-to-forever would have to go for it solo, perhaps having developed suction-padded digits or prehensile appendages. In order for climbers to keep pushing along on their eternal route, they'd have to live and breed on the wall. There would be Machu Picchu–like stone castles on terraces like ours, and, on the wall, Anasazi-like huts and hanging, pod-shaped villages of woven feathers, grass, and butterfly wings, all interconnected with walkways of vines.

I pass the day mentally sketching out this culture of wall-dwelling mutants, mindlessly climbing toward some unattainable goal. A sun dog brightens the sky; the temperature warms and then chills by afternoon. We munch down a meager dinner of noodles, then sleep. Not a second of the day has been wasted, yet we've done nothing, perfect nothing.

On day eight we leave our final camp before sunrise. A starry sky is above. We quickly solo the first easy rocks; then verglas slows us. The sun arrives as we reach a steepening of the cliffs. We warm our blanched fingers and toes and break out the rope. Five pitches on hueco-pocked granite get us to the top of Toothless Tower, which we name in honor of Greg, who these past weeks has been sporting a gap in his front teeth after a tooth had departed his jaw.

We press on, traversing the final knife edge of perfect rock and scaling three pitches of cracks up a bone-white wall. Two hundred feet of scrambling on snow and boulders puts us on Combatant's summit by midafternoon. Thirty-six pitches and eight days of alpine roaming lay behind us. The view is dominated by winding Chamonix-like glaciers and Waddington's icy Nordwand.

Greg tunes his radio to Mike's frequency and aims the antenna toward the distant lake where the White Saddle Air Services helipad sits. If we don't contact Mike, we'll have a hungry three-day wait till our designated pickup, as we are now down to a few ounces of provisions. All thoughts have now turned to food. Even the appalling chew-and-spew fast-food restaurants along the Canadian highway seem enticing.

After we've spent some time eavesdropping on various citizens' phone calls in which matters ranging from alimony to wild parties are discussed, Mike's wife answers our call, and we arrange a pickup for the next afternoon on the col below us. We rappel into the night, down a buttress and then into an icy gully. It's midnight when we reach the tent.

The next morning, our packs are heavy as we traverse the rock-strewn terrace beneath the great southern buttresses of Combatant. We rappel over a bergschrund and onto the huge white expanse of the col, zigzag around some crevasses, and then unshoulder our packs and wait for the sound of the helicopter that will pluck us off this ice cap.

High cirrus flecks the sky. It looks as if we've finished the route just in time. Those last few hours on the ice we hunker in our bivy sacks, sharing our last morsels, a stale bagel and a Clif Bar. We sit there, tossing about names for our route, like proud parents; Greg finally settles on Belligerence, a pun on the combative name of our peak. But it hasn't been a belligerent climb at all. It's been a smooth ride, and a bargain to boot—a Trango Tower–scale route for the price of a twelve-hour drive from Seattle and a $900-helicopter ride, and all done in less than two weeks.

Then, while I look out the entrance slit of my bivy sack watching the play of light and shadow on the glacier, I see the chopper appear. Moments later we are in the sky, floating above an icefall, a forest, a river, a lake cradled halfway up a mountainside—gone from Combatant so quickly it's as if we'd never visited it.

Yosemite
and Other Walls

Half Dome in Yosemite Valley. Zenith ascends the pale rock on the right.

Whatever Happened to Luke Skywalker?

The dirtbag climbers from my past sometimes visit my dreams, like ghosts in the night, their faces, nicknames, and scurrility hovering against the granite backdrop of Yosemite Valley. They are the ones who stood in the shadows, never admitted into the scene because we real climbers could sniff the air and sense they were climber-impersonators and not the genuine article, and because they were weird and scary, characters beamed in from a Hunter S. Thompson story. Rascals and blatherskites, petty criminals and acid casualties, kooks and misfits, natural-born losers and sociopaths, they had enough experience on the rocks to masquerade as climbers, and they flocked to Yosemite's Camp 4, a.k.a. Sunnyside Campground.

I'm talking about the climbers' Yosemite of 1970-something, maybe the early 1980s, and I'm talking about an environment where being weird was fairly normal, where renegade behavior was fashionable among real climbers. Dirtbag climbers, however, were a cut below those of us who shared tent space with bubonic ground squirrels and scavenged the cafeteria leftovers of Japanese tourists. Dirtbags were predators, thieves, and con artists who disguised themselves as climbers and preyed on those of us who came to Yosemite with nothing but climbing in our hearts.

Luke Skywalker, where are you now? Stepping out of the shadows one week in 1980, he made a plausible facsimile of a climber at first, even trying an El Cap route or two, but his icy stare and his disjointed mutterings and crazed cackling while on belay freaked out his partners so badly that they signaled retreat after a few pitches. No, Luke was to climbing what decaffeinated is to Starbucks. He was ersatz. His real identity was forgotten when some wit nicknamed him after the intergalactic traveler from the then-popular movie *Star Wars*.

I met Luke on Half Dome. I had just humped a massive haulbag up slab and through forest to the foot of a route called Zenith when I heard a deranged-sounding scream from the cliffs above, followed by the ping of a dropped piton bouncing down the wall. My partners, a New Zealander whose nickname was The Dog and a Brit whose nickname was Egg, scattered for the shelter of rocks while the steel missile ricocheted into the woods.

"That must be Luke Skywalker up there," suggested Egg while balancing another cigarette on his lower lip and torching it with a Zippo lighter.

Luke, it was known, had taken to soloing big walls, or at least trying to, because no one would climb with him anymore. It was also suspected that Luke was in the habit of divesting climbers of their climbing gear, since his climbing rack seemed to expand with every wall he attempted, a peculiar anomaly for someone who left retreat anchors everywhere.

We'd been warned he'd been seen heading for Half Dome to solo the old Royal Robbins route, Tis-sa-sack, and there he was, swinging about in his aiders, in the 500-foot leaning corner above us called the Zebra, so named for the black stripes weeping over the white rock.

Luke swung his hammer around his head and flailed with his hands and screamed. Seeing us, 500 feet below, he yelled down something about a swarm of bees. Indeed, an eerie buzz did emanate from the wall. Farther down the valley, to the west, the afternoon sky was turning a strange shade of magenta and orange as smoke from a massive controlled-burn choked the sunset. Luke continued raving a few minutes more, then slid down the line of ropes he'd installed up to his high point. Near the ground he tossed his rack down with a loud clang and angrily damned it to hell.

"Out there," said The Dog. His real name was Nic Craddock, but we called him The Dog because of his studied scruffiness. Whenever he said, "Out there," it meant things were about to get weird. He was never wrong about this.

Luke marched toward us and greeted us like we were all old friends, though this was the first time we'd laid eyes on him. Only his reputation preceded him.

"Hey, man, I see a cigarette, got a spare? Thanks. Got any 'biners I can borrow? I'm kinda short. How are you guys set for food? I could really use a good meal before I set off tomorrow. Maybe I should hike down to the supermarket and bring up more munchies, I dunno, hey, you got five bucks you can lend me? Oh, man, you wouldn't believe the bees up there, I got swarmed, thought they were gonna sting me to death. Complete freak-out, had to rap off. Goddamn bugs. It was intense."

Luke spat all this and more out of his mouth in a machine-gun staccato. His eyes had a penetrating yet translucent quality; there was a jittery twitch to his facial expressions, the calling card of way too many acid trips. I felt uncomfortable in his presence, and a shiver went up my spine, as if someone were doing a jig on my grave. We slipped away from Luke and found a flat place to bivy, but he followed us, laying his sleeping bag beside ours, curling up like a stray pup at our feet.

"Out there," repeated The Dog with a whisper and a nod.

Around midnight a rustling sound from our haulbag woke me and Egg, so called because of his yolk-colored hair; his real name was Graham Everett. I expected to see a raccoon nosing into the bag, and I grabbed a stone to fling at it; but the moonlight revealed Luke digging through our possessions. Seeing us sit up in our sleeping bags, he froze. We stared at each other. Nothing was said. A long minute passed, and then Luke slowly replaced the things he'd removed from our haulbag and went back to his sleeping bag. Heightened by moonglow, Luke's Neanderthal gaze had a dangerous depth, full of awful possibility and stunted morality. He'd used it as a weapon, staring us down with his opaque glassy orbs, and he successfully put the frighteners on us. Egg lit a nervous cigarette and whispered something about getting our heads bashed in with a piton hammer while we slept. So we didn't sleep, but kept watch on Luke all night, at least till sunrise, when we dozed off and Luke disappeared up his ropes to do battle with Tis-sa-sack and the bees.

When we entered the bug zone that day, we found that the humming wasn't made by bees but by some harmless, lethargic, dronelike flies that had hatched in the millions, all of which were now looking for a home and a purpose, at an altitude a thousand feet above the base of Half Dome. We watched swallows and yellow jackets intercept the flies like fighter planes swooping through a squadron of bombers. But to Luke they were killer bees, and in a final fit of screaming he retreated, yelling the whole way down.

Zenith had been climbed the first time the previous summer by the big-wall maestros Jim Bridwell, Dale Bard, and Kim Schmitz. The rock on this climb is layered like onion skins: a mass of flakes stacked one over another, expanding, elastic, hollow. Most of the climbing is on aid placed behind these shaky flakes. It made for a creaky insecurity as you felt the piton or nut you

The Dog lowers off a steep pitch on Zenith.

hung from slip downward as the flake it was lodged behind flexed open a millimeter. The ultimate expanding formation on the route was dubbed the Space Flake—eighty feet long, thin as a cookie, guillotine sharp, and booming like a drum. We climbed this wild, diagonaling feature with nuts and cams and stacked pitons poked into its underside. It seemed that a mere fart would be enough to dislodge this scimitar of rock, the result of which would be the surgical removal of all traces of climbers from the wall. In recent years a large chunk of it has fallen off.

On the sixth day we climbed into the middle of the wall, where the rock was white and bleached like bone. Rain had never touched this overhung face, and not even lichen clung to the wall. Climbing a corner system, Egg was knocked backward onto the rope by the rush of thousands of flies exiting the crack he had shoved his hands into. They sheltered in there to escape the heat of the day, and the rush of musty air from their foul nest had the whiff of Beelzebub.

By the seventh day we were growing nerve-wracked and argumentative from the constant insecurity of pitch after pitch of expanding flakes. Even our bivouac that night was off a huge orange biscuit stuck to the wall. As we hung our porta-ledges from nuts, cams, and pitons all wedged behind the flake, The Dog lectured us about earthquakes, which, in California, have no manners and come when least expected. His information was not appreciated, causing us to conjure up a shared vision of our flake flapping in a quake, spitting out the anchor, and sending us to ground zero. Flying in formation down the wall on our porta-ledges, we would surely be bickering, each of us blaming the other for not adding a bolt to the belay.

We reached the top on the eighth day after nailing a toast-thick flake, then joining the final pitches of Tis-sa-sack. The next day we were back on the valley floor, drinking beers and inhaling sandwiches outside Degnan's Deli. Around us moved a procession of dirtbags, misfits, and oddballs. After our cozy solitude on Half Dome, contact with the human race was unappealing and we wanted out. We talked about going right back onto another wall and debated whether or not we seemed like dirtbags to the people around us. We agreed that we were dirty but not dirtbags, that we didn't fit into society at that point in our lives but we weren't misfits, that though we were oddities we weren't oddballs. And anyone could see just by looking that we weren't tourists. Climbers, we agreed after another six-pack, were as indigenous to Yosemite as bears, and we belonged there just as much as any Winnebago.

Budweiser-driven elitist climber drivel lolled off our tongues. Soon we had a crowd around us. They lapped up our wisdom and our tales of Zenith so long as we fed them beers. As the session wore on, I saw that several dirtbags and misfits had infiltrated the audience. There was the Bearded Lady, a poor girl who started off as a normal-enough climber but who suffered some hormonal tragedy that left her bereft of mind and gave her a swarthy five-o'clock shadow. She supported herself by stealing tips from tables in the restaurants. And there was the dude who pedaled his bike around the loop road morning, noon, and night, and had the habit of riding up to you, hitting his brakes, and then hopping off the bike and spinning his front wheel in front of your face. "Spinning," he'd say with a screw-loose smile, then scoot off. I saw that those around us were nodding in agreement with our diatribe against the dirtbags and unsavory elements who were spoiling Yosemite. They had no idea we were talking about them. I realized then that "dirtbag" is a relative term and that they didn't see themselves as lost souls at all.

"Did ya hear about Luke?" a passing climber asked us. Eagerly, we listened.

But some background first. All summer long, thieves had been stealing from climbers, out of tents, from cars, from packs left at the base of climbs. Even the walls were not safe (as we discovered when Luke raided our haulbag); someone was nocturnally jumaring the ropes of climbers fixing on El Cap and stealing the equipment from their high points. One fellow whom Luke hung out with had been fingered by a climber who stumbled across a dirtbag nest in the boulders behind Camp 4 and found said dirtbag sleeping on a piece of ornamental carpet that had been boosted from his van, along with everything else he owned. But the rangers let the dirtbag off, saying they had to have more than a ragged shred of carpet to justify an arrest; they had to have the loot. The dirtbags might have been dirtbags, but they had an efficient system for getting the gear out of Yosemite to the fence who sold it for them.

Now here's the punch line: some climbers decided to lure the thief with a sting, by leaving a fat rack at the end of a rope on El Cap and then waiting in the woods. It didn't take long till Luke turned up, jumared the rope, took the rack, and rappelled down. The vigilante climbers met him at the bottom of the wall with piton hammers in hand.

"I thought you guys left already," Luke said with a whimper.

Being locked up slowed Luke down for a few days, but he was soon out. Through some legal technicality, the charge didn't stick. A climber's word against a dirtbag apparently wasn't enough. People joked that Luke would have to murder someone to get thrown out of Yosemite, that the corpse would have to testify, and that no one would believe the corpse.

He did leave, though. On a rainy and frigid fall night, a Canadian hellion named Darryl Hatten (who would later be ousted from Yosemite for riding a bicycle through a restaurant and causing indigestion to many a tourist) visited Luke's abode—a plastic tarp draped over a picnic table. Darryl carried a knife and a bucket of cold water. He slit the tarp, doused Luke with the icy water, and threatened Luke with unspeakable atrocities. Darryl's threats had a convincing quality, even though he was really a gentle giant, and Luke fled Yosemite, shivering and wet.

Luke was gone, but other dirtbags replaced him. The climbers continued to climb; the dirtbags continued to steal. I seldom visited Yosemite after the mid-1980s. It seemed that the mood of the Valley had changed: too many people, too many rip-offs, rules, and rangers. Maybe it was I who had changed. But, on a rare visit to Yosemite a few years ago, while sitting around a campfire with an old wall partner and dredging up the past, I did hear an

105

update on Luke. The source, said my friend, was an L.A. newspaper that contained the grisly tale of a young man who beat his grandmother to death with a hammer when she refused to loan him money. He beheaded her and was apprehended while driving around with the corpse in his trunk. The photo of the murderer, my friend insisted, was Luke.

I thought of Luke's piercing eyes transfixing me that night below Zenith, and the suggestion of evil in that glare. A campfire chill rattled my bones. It had been a close call, but climbing is always full of close calls.

Steep country on
El Capitan.

The Denz Option

A small news item in a past issue of *Climbing* magazine, in a section titled "Screamer of the Month," recently caught my eye. It described the spectacular plummet of a climber named Steve Edwards on the second pitch of Wyoming Sheep Ranch, a very serious A5 route on El Capitan. He'd dislodged a massive block, fallen 150 feet, yet survived unscathed. I hadn't had cause to think about that stretch of rock for many years, but the tale of that lucky lad made me remember the cast of characters who were in on the first attempts on the Sheep Ranch, which, back in 1980 before anyone had climbed it, we called Heart of Darkness.

The first person to lead the pitch that nearly killed Edwards was a New Zealander by the name of Bill Denz. Denz was a good hand on mountains and walls, a solid alpinist with a penchant for soloing. He'd done hard things in the stormy New Zealand Alps, where he was regarded as a climber ahead of his time, willing to push himself to the limit. Even today, I'm told, there is a Denz pitch—a mixture of ice, rock, and aid, vintage 1979—on the south face of New Zealand's Mount Hicks that has resisted all attempts to repeat it. Denz was built short and chunky like a wombat and wore nerd-framed, Coke-bottle-thick glasses behind which he seemed eternally abstracted, and which acted as a wall that made him hard to know. The Bill Denz I recall was a man who was self-sufficient, stoic, complex, reticent, intense, ambitious, competitive, steel-willed, fiery, fearless, undemonstrative, and selfish. These are the attributes of the classic alpinist.

Denz, the Canadian Darryl Hatten, and I had figured out the meandering line of Heart of Darkness over the summer of 1980, and one autumn day we toted a sack of gear to El Cap. It was mostly Denz's gear, I recall, his inclusion in the team being largely because Hatten had sold everything but his harness for spending and drinking money, and my piton rack was thin after a summer on the walls.

I led the first pitch—an A3+ groove—in scorching heat, and I set an anchor. Denz jumared the rope, then started leading the second pitch, the one on which, fifteen years later, Edwards would dislodge the block he was nailing past, and fall, ripping out the copperheads that were fused into hairline water runnels, snapping off the rivets below that, and bouncing onto the pins and nuts in the initial expanding arch.

Denz started by skyhooking left from my hanging belay, then he entered the arch. The black stone was hot as a foundry, and my legs burned where they touched the wall. Strangely, from inside the moist crack of the arch, tiny frogs croaked. The day wore on, and when Denz, hot and thirsty, reached the end of the arch and found a blank face, he called down that he was going to bathook his way to a seam forty feet away that looked like it would take copperheads. Hatten, beerless and impatient on the ground, and I, on belay and fried, called up to Denz to forget the bathook idea and just whack in a few rivets.

Denz didn't like this idea and told us so. Separated by 100 feet of nylon, we began arguing. It was a crazy place to have an ethical debate, with Denz dangling under the arch, Hatten pacing around the scree grumbling for a hair-of-the-dog, and me hanging on belay, but yell about ethics we did.

"Bathooks are bullshit," Hatten yelled. "You have to drill a hole to place the bathook, so why not fill that hole with a rivet?"

"Because I want this pitch to be *real* A5," Denz retorted.

"But, Bill, you're making this pitch A5 in a totally artificial way. Every other route on El Cap uses rivets to get past blank rock. No one goes bathooking into no-man's-land like that," I said.

What we were gabbing about was the difference between bathooking (drilling a quarter-inch-diameter hole a quarter-inch into the rock, tapping a pointy-nosed hook into the hole, then standing in aiders on this tenuous rig) and riveting (tapping a short steel bolt like the ones you see holding your washing machine together into the same hole). Rivets, which hold little more than body weight, are scary enough, but at least they provide some security, whereas bathooks fall out when the climber moves past them. The Denz option guaranteed death-defying fall potential; if a bathook popped he would fly through the air for forty feet, hit the expanding arch, and maybe rip the gear back to the belay—and me. Denz, who was cool-headed enough to ride

The east face of Kichatna Spire. The Denz-Woollums route takes huge corners in the center of the tallest section of wall.

out the terrifying bathook journey, wanted the pitch to become a legend. Problem was, the other two members of his team couldn't agree with the premise of how he was going to create that legend.

Our carping led Denz to lower off, intending to discuss the matter and complete the pitch the next day. On the valley floor, Hatten infused himself with much-needed beer, and we set to talking. The mood degenerated fast. Denz called us cowards for not letting him finish the pitch, then took it back; Hatten threatened to remodel Denz's face with a piton hammer, then took it back; I quit the team, then took that back. We cooled down, shook hands, and got some sleep, but I knew this mix of people was like oil and water. I understood then that the three of us would never climb the wall, because we were of utterly different chemistries and had wildly different reasons for climbing.

Greg Child

In any case, the Denz option won out. The next day, Hatten belayed while Denz bathooked at the speed of continental drift. He drilled lots of holes to get through that forty feet of steep rock. Two comments that drifted down from the wall that day epitomized the relationship between my partners: "Put a rivet in, you maniac!" and "No!" When Denz eased onto a marginal copperhead with a death-fall's worth of unclipped rope swaying beneath him, I saw Hatten scrunch into a fetal ball and brace himself to hold the mother of all whippers. But Denz didn't fall. He got through the copperhead section and past the vibrating block and completed the pitch. It was an incredible lead, even though I disagreed with the premise.

By day's end, Hatten, moving like a storm, had added a third pitch. Nevertheless, he'd had it with Denz, and he quit the team that afternoon.

"He's got a death wish," Hatten said of Denz, and I nodded.

Without Hatten—my partner on the Pacific Ocean Wall and a one-day ascent of Sentinel West Face, and who I knew could lead any aid pitch he set his mind to, so long as I could keep him sober—I too, abandoned Denz.

"Look, I know I'm difficult, but can't we figure this out?" Denz begged, in the warmest show of feelings I'd seen since meeting him. I almost changed my mind.

Hatten quickly joined a team trying the Sea of Dreams—a notorious El Cap route, known at the time as the hardest big wall on the planet—but he didn't last. His drinking problem was out of control. He guzzled a flask of vodka several pitches up and, drunk as a lord, took a rope and rappelled off, bidding his partners farewell. Heading down, he appeared at the belay of some Frenchmen climbing the North America Wall. Terrified of the hammer-wielding, French-obscenity-babbling Canadian swarming over the belay, the Frenchmen cowered while Hatten rigged his rope and took off again, swinging wildly over to the ropes we'd temporarily left on Heart of Darkness.

As for Denz, he headed down to Patagonia and tried to solo Cerro Torre, where he had a grand epic of storms and granite. He was quiet about what he accomplished on that attempt, but he brought back a photo that showed that he reached—twice—the final ice mushroom, a few dozen feet below the summit. He failed only because the ice that season was rotten and prevented him from clawing his way off the rock and onto the final frozen cap. After Patagonia he drifted through South America, living by his wits and on traveler's check scams. A season or so later, in Nepal, he soloed a bold, unclimbed, and nightmarishly corniced ridge on Kusum Kanguru. He also crept across a high pass into Tibet for a permitless solo attempt on the then-unclimbed 23,000-foot peak Menlungtse. After that, one tale has it, he smuggled into Australia, inside his belly, a load of condoms stuffed with hash oil. This financed his climbing for some time.

IN 1982 I TRIED HEART OF DARKNESS AGAIN, with two Californians, Peter Mayfield and Auggie Klein. Arising from that attempt, a photo of us all on the now-infamous second pitch appeared in the *Wall Street Journal* and other papers of the day. That's because an L.A. advertising executive saw us racking up in the parking lot and enlisted us as models for an ad campaign for Bankers Trust Company. He gave us red tee shirts so we'd look like we were all in a team, paid us each two hundred dollars, and loaned us radios so they could coordinate our movements on the wall with photographers in the meadow.

The slow pace of a day of aid climbing was nearly too much for these fast-paced L.A. types, and they nearly gave up on us; but we had their radio. Finally, after Mayfield finished doing the dirty work with the drill and running roughshod with rivets over Denz's bathook path, they snapped their photos. This was the first time I had been paid for climbing, and I liked it.

Seven pitches up, we reached Calaveros Ledge and entered the black diorite of the North America–shaped blotch in the center of the east face. An easy pitch off the ledge got us to a loose black arch followed by a terrifying runout of skyhooking on small edges on hollow-sounding rock. The lead took me all day and totally taxed me mentally. I named the pitch Psycho Killer, called it A5, and realized with horror that above us were many similar pitches.

The next morning—our fourth on the wall—we awoke to a heat wave. Not enough water, not enough drill bits, not enough staying power for the many days ahead. We retreated, pledging to return another season. Before we began the descent, we made one of the last legal haulbag hurls from El Cap, before the National Park Service wisely outlawed climbers from tossing their bags back to the ground. We jettisoned two bags rigged with portaledge rainflies as parachutes. They suffered a bad landing. On the ground, a stink worthy of a tidal mudflat and the buzz of flies led us to our bags, which had exploded into a churned, pulpy mass of sleeping bags, pitons, and canned mackerel.

THIS SECOND FAILURE ON HEART OF DARKNESS was doubly galling to me because of an encounter I'd had with Denz a few months before, in the spring of 1982, on the Shadows Glacier in the Kichatna Spires Range of Alaska. I was there with New Zealander Paul Aubrey to try the first ascent of the 3,000-foot East Face of Kichatna Spire. Denz had heard we were going, hastily lined up a partner, and then phoned me while I was still packing my bags to say he was in Alaska already. "It's nothing personal, but I intend to beat you to it," he said quite coolly.

Sure enough, when Aubrey and I got out of the plane that landed us on the glacier, the first thing we saw was Denz and Scott Woollums, three-quarters of the way up the wall. After they finished and got down, Denz smugly entered our camp during a snowstorm to rub it in our faces that he'd aced us out of our prize. Aubrey and I were playing chess when he appeared, and we did our best to ignore him. When we finished playing, Denz challenged me to a game. I quickly checkmated him. He challenged me to another game, which I also won. Then he challenged me to another. He'd won on the mountain; now he wanted to beat me intellectually.

We played long into the Alaskan twilight. It was impossible not to laugh at this, a grudge match in nowhere, Alaska. The mood between us warmed. I recall some of our conversation that night: Denz told me that if he could choose another "career" besides climbing, he'd be in military intelligence, "to know what was going on, from the inside." And we talked about the thorn in our sides, Heart of Darkness. He said he knew he could have held the team together if he'd consented to use rivets, but he had to be stubborn. The episode had been an exercise in willpower—his will against ours, and against the rock. He couldn't give in because someday when he was soloing an alpine wall and part of him was saying "go down" and part of him was saying "go up," he might weaken and choose the easy way out. The Denz option always chose the hard way.

Finally Denz checkmated me. He shouted a victory war cry, and said goodnight.

IT WOULD BE NICE TO THINK THAT WE ARE BIG ENOUGH of character not to let something as venal as competition tarnish our climbing, but that isn't the way it is. If you take climbing seriously enough to climb new routes, you covet climbs as if they are your own. The climb becomes a part of you; you guard it like a dog guards his bone, and anyone who tries to steal your climb transgresses against your deepest self. Without realizing it back then, Denz and I had entered into one of those pissing contests that seem so important at the time, but which, later, seem infantile. He felt that I had stolen Heart of Darkness from him, so he took Kichatna Spire from me. But while Denz had seen success and resolution on Kichatna Spire, Heart of Darkness was still an unclimbed ambition for me. I wanted it bad.

Never got it, though. The next time I turned up in Yosemite, in 1984, with a carload of gear, I found I'd been beaten to the first ascent of Heart of Darkness by a week, by Rob Slater and John Barbella. They'd named the route Wyoming Sheep Ranch, renaming the Psycho Killer pitch Welcome to Wyoming, and adding a stack of mind-numbingly hard pitches above it.

Bill Denz, by this time, was gone. In 1983 he'd been descending the west ridge of Makalu in Nepal and had started a small slab avalanche. The current of moving snow took him over the ridge, and he fell to his death. Nic Craddock, who knew him well, told me that his friends were shocked to hear he'd died, but they weren't surprised. "He was always pushing himself," said Nic. "The feeling was, it was bound to happen sometime."

Death could have visited Denz many times, including the day in 1980 on El Cap when he first nailed past the loosely perched, refrigerator-size block that Steve Edwards eventually cut loose. If Denz had pulled the block off, he, like Edwards, may have survived unscathed, but I doubt that I would have, because, if my memory serves me right, I was on the ground, packing a haulbag right at the spot where it cratered.

Lynn Hill during her crash course in groveling, on Russian Tower in Kyrgyzstan.

Dawn to Dawn on Russian Tower with Lynn Hill

Lessons in the Art of Groveling

Any decent alpinist is familiar—no, skilled—in the art of groveling. I'm talking about the primal ability to claw, tooth and nail, over the moss, choss, and dross of alpine terrain. Of wending your way up china cabinets of rock glued together by the merest film of bug, bird, and bat shit. And of rappelling off creaky anchors down walls and into mud-choked gorges, through a no-man's-land where rocks ricochet past and explode in little blossoms of dust. Groveling is about curling up for the night, like a rat, on a bumpy ledge, and shivering without a sleeping bag. It's about being too hot, too cold, too hungry. About tent entrapment in rain and snow, and enduring your own and others' clammy, smelly, sweaty, fetid, bad-breathed bodies and biohazardous underwear. It's about eating kerosene-tainted food and smacking your lips for more. About wading through snot-slick, knee-deep snow, in pissing rain, bent over by a hernia-inducing load. About blistered feet, cracked lips, and gobied hands. Well, you get the picture.

   With Lynn Hill on the 3,000-foot wall of Russian Tower in the Alai Pamir Mountains of Kyrgyzstan, I learned that we have different talents. One difference between my climbing and hers is, approximately, the difference between a barroom brawl and the Bolshoi Ballet. Sure, Lynn can waltz 5.13

like a gazelle on cruise control, but to suggest that she has complete mastery of the steep would be erroneous, for on her mountaineering report card there is one skill for which she gets a B minus. That skill, I am sad to say, is the very foundation—the taproot, the DNA—of alpinism. That skill is the art of groveling.

Shaped like a Patagonian spire, Russian Tower stands above a river called the Kara-su in a craggy region called the Karavshin. By helicopter it is an hour and fifteen minutes east-northeast of Tashkent, the capital of Uzbekistan, which, like Kyrgyzstan, is another nation spawned from the collapse of communism.

When Lynn and I set off at 1:30 A.M. for Russian Tower in August 1995, we already had one big rock tower under our belts, Peak 3850, which had taken three days to ascend and descend. On Peak 3850 Lynn had grooved on the free climbing but had failed to appreciate the attendant groveling found along the way, including bivouacs in guano-filled caves and on sloping terraces with our feet stuffed into haulbags, and a full day of rappelling down a couloir where we became bowling pins to the stones that rolled around us.

"Is it always like this?" she had asked.

"You get used to it," I replied.

So this time we decided we'd blitz the wall in one continuous push, sans bivouacs. Having climbed the Nose free in a day two years previously, Lynn felt a one-day ascent of Russian Tower, via Perestroika Crack, a route established by Russians in 1988, was feasible even with me as her partner. It had been climbed free before, by French climbers, at 5.12b, but not in a day, and it had been climbed in a day, also by French, but not free. The French called it the "Astroman of Kyrgyzstan," a homage to a famous, long Yosemite route. We could do it in a day, swinging leads, Lynn was certain, with the stylish addition of the second climber free-climbing every pitch: an all-free, no-jumars ascent. It sounded good, but I packed one jumar anyway, just in case.

At 4:00 A.M. we slithered over the last of the boulders in the long talus-choked gully that led to the start of Perestroika Crack. A couple days earlier I'd watched a mudslide puke like lava out of this gully as afternoon sun cooked a snow patch in a high nook. In darkness, at the foot of the wall, we roped up and began liebacking up weirdly sculpted granite fins and grooves. In our pack we carried a small amount of food and water, headlamps, rain shells, and two bivy sacks (to use on the summit, of course).

At sunrise, after four pitches, we crested a pedestal and met Dan Osman and photographer Chris Noble, who had bivied there to get photos of us on the next section of the route, an impressive fracture diagonaling across   115 clean diorite. As Chris snapped away, Lynn and I swung leads up fist cracks for six 5.10 pitches. Our minds were blissfully full of solid rock until Lynn encountered a jigsaw of razor-sharp flakes. Progress slowed. She tried a crack, then down-climbed when it became too loose, tried another, and down-climbed again. Clearly, some master of choss had negotiated this rubble, but Lynn didn't dig it. Traversing with difficulty under a bulge to better rock, and adding several grades in the process, she pulled over a lip and made a belay. It was 3:15 P.M.

My lead was next. I squeezed into an off-width, gasped and moaned—and groveled. On a top rope, Lynn laybacked it. Swiftly. "Easier like that," she informed me instructively.

Late in the afternoon we reached the crux—a leaning 5.12 dihedral and finger crack. Lynn motored through this expeditiously and belayed; then I ground my fingers into the crack and battled on. Halfway up, I noticed we were surrounded by the amber light of the day's demise. Where had the hours gone?

At Lynn's belay we clipped headlamps to our helmets for the impending nocturnal performance. Without a word, she grabbed the rack and, at precisely 7:35 P.M., started up the next pitch, a steep, thin crack. It was an unspoken agreement: time was of the essence, she excels on this type of climbing, and besides, her knitting-needle-diameter fingers would better fit the next 5.12 crack. Wisely, we would save my strength for the less dignified climbing that lay ahead. She reached the end of her pitch just as a deep-sea dark engulfed us. It was a moonless night, as black as if a squid had squirted ink in our eyes.

By headlamp at that belay we studied the topo, a rough sketch a French friend of Lynn's had scribbled. "According to this, we've completed the sixteenth pitch. Only four to go," she said, optimistically.

I looked up. A vague silhouette of black rock against a black sky loomed far above. I mentally triangulated our position. "That's more than four pitches. The topo is wrong. We'll summit at sunrise," I said, ever the gloomy sage. Then I suggested we find a bivy ledge.

"No way! A couple hours at most! We're going to the summit!" So on we went.

I got lost in the Stygian dark of the next pitch and had to pendulum across the wall to get back on route. Lynn followed the pendulum free, padding across the slab like a suction-cup-footed gecko. Leading the next pitch, she headed up a soaring hand crack that by day would have produced squeals of joy but at midnight only made me want to spit up my lunch. Suddenly I had lost interest in the leader-and-second all-free ascent. Such ethics are a

Lynn Hill jamming and lie-backing the long fissure of Perestroika Crack.   117

nine-to-five luxury, I thought. I groveled up the rope, awkwardly using my single jumar backed up by a Sticht plate, and wishing I'd brought that second rope-ascending gadget.

When I reached Lynn's belay ledge I tried to convince her it would be nice to curl up and get some sleep right there, but she wouldn't have it. When she handed me the rack, I realized with crushing finality that there was no way I was going to get this girl to bed down tonight.

A hundred vertical feet later, I was frigging RP nuts into a fissure. Each nut seemed so bad that I stemmed a move higher up the corner to find a better placement. The promise of better pro turned out to be a ruse. Soon I had no good gear in, and I was miles up the corner, muttering, squawking, and hearing nuts pop out and tinkle down the rope. My legs wobbled at the thought of a huge fall. Then my headlamp clicked off just as Lynn, shivering at the belay, yelled something at me about hurrying up. So I did a series of blind slaps at the rock and somehow ended up at a stance, panting nervously. As I belayed her up, I noticed that she made the pitch look very easy.

We were now dozing off at each belay, jarring awake only when the leader tugged the rope for slack or when the shivering cold seeped bone-deep. I was jumaring Lynn's leads to save time, but she still followed my leads free, determined to make the first continuous free ascent of this peak. At some dim hour, there was an explosive crash of boulders thundering down an El Cap–size wall across the valley. Nebulae of spark-illuminated dust appeared and faded in their wake. The rockfall cleared our sleepy heads.

My last lead was a doozy. I struggled up a wide fissure until my head clunked against a ceiling. I twisted my body to gaze out from the underside of the roof. My headlamp revealed a wide crack dripping with water. I muttered something like "What have I done to deserve a wet off-width roof by torchlight at 2:00 A.M.?"

From the belay I heard muttered back, "Only you know the answer to that."

Lynn hauled herself over the top of Russian Tower at 5:00 A.M. When I jumared up that pitch—the twenty-fifth—and joined her, I was gibbering from cold. With daybreak a crisp wind had whipped up, blowing down from the ice cap up-valley. Stumbling toward her as club-footed and numb-skulled as Frankenstein's monster, I saw Lynn switch off her headlamp. "I guess you were right; we did top out at dawn," she said with a dry-lipped smile. We'd been on the move for twenty-eight hours, in rock shoes for twenty-four hours. When I pulled my Kaukulators off my feet, I saw something resembling two

bludgeoned corpses that Mafia hit men had dumped in a river. I gave my feet the last rites, then Lynn and I curled up on a flat shelf, slipped into our bivy sacks, and slept for three hours.

We woke at 10:00 A.M. to begin limping down the descent, a complex of gullies and rappels. The rubble underfoot was a strange gneissic scree. We slid onto our butts every second step. I managed to get a rhythm going by using my backside like a third leg. Sliding on my heels, then my butt, then up again, and rolling a move or two in a cloud of dust, I efficiently accelerated past Lynn, who observed my progress with an expression of distaste. To her it looked like I was out of control, but in fact I was reveling in my true element: groveling.

I tried to explain to her that the poise and control needed to climb 5.14 was a detriment to her future as an alpinist. She'd spent too long being grace-ful, resisting gravity to self-propel herself up impossibly steep cliffs. On the other hand, I, as a mountaineer, had learned to utilize gravity to aid my movements over this sort of wasteland. What looked to her like the oafish clumsiness of a big-booted troll clodhopping down a gully in a self-generated avalanche of scree and dust, was actually the product of careful training.

We arrived at a slab with water cascading over it, rigged a rappel, and headed down into an abyss. Mud and blocks clattered over the edge to either side of us. One rock hacked a bite out of the rope. "I don't know about this mountaineering stuff," Lynn said. "It's dangerous."

"Nonsense. You'll get used to it."

Heading on to prepare the next rappel, I skated down acres of dirt-covered slabs, hopped across streams, and waded through patches of rotten snow, leaving Lynn to pick her way through the debris. In a few days a rain-storm would descend on these mountains and this gully would become a cement mixer, running feet-thick with a roaring flood of mud. But today the sky was clear, and I groveled down happily, knowing with animal certainty that none of the rocks clattering around us had our numbers on them, enjoy-ing the feeling of being better than Lynn Hill at something.

Mark Wilford,
just before the
storm hit, 1989.

I Was a Trango Love Slave

Most people are slaves to one obsession or another. It's normal, I think, except that one of mine—to climb Trango Tower, a 20,470-foot peak in Pakistan's Karakoram Range—always seemed to land me at the brink of disaster whenever I tried to climb it. I would wind up clinging to rock and ice several thousand feet above ground with a creeping feeling that I'd like to take a very long nap.

And now it was happening again. For ten days we'd been following a maze of ice-choked cracks on Trango. We'd managed to scratch two-thirds of the way up the northeast wall, but as I hung suspended from a cluster of steel pitons hammered into a crack, tendrils of ink-black clouds circled the spire, and snow and sleet poured from the sky.

I zipped up my storm suit and waited for Mark Wilford, my partner, to finish his lead. He was clinging like a gecko to a seamless stretch of wall a hundred feet above me, hanging from tiny steel claws called skyhooks. If a hook lost its grip, he'd plummet fifty feet. But at least he was moving, keeping warm.

All I could do was wait, as slush began flooding the cracks and a fountain of ice water spurted out of the fissure into my face.

"It's a waterfall down here!" I shouted. "If I don't move soon I'm gonna freeze."

"Hold on," Mark called back. "I'm nearly at a place to stop."

A few minutes later I felt the temperature start to drop, and the wall froze into crystalline silence. Then Mark reached a crack, hammered in three pitons, and tied off the rope. "Come on up!" he shouted.

Ice coated me, creaking like rusty armor when I moved. I clamped my two ascenders onto the rope and started up. Under normal conditions these devices lock into nylon rope like a pit bull's jaws, preventing a climber from sliding backward but allowing him to scuttle easily upward. But, the 150-foot rope linking me to Mark had frozen into a slick cable. I got maybe ten feet and then slid back down with a jolt.

Hours passed as I struggled to climb a mere 100 feet. By the time I'd hauled my bones up to Mark it was dark, and powdery snow cascaded over us. We worked to unclog the joints of the porta-ledge, our make-do motel room for the duration of the storm, but as we shifted our full weight onto the shelf it collapsed, throwing us into the dark. Dangling from our harnesses, we screamed at the buckling contraption, the storm, the mountain, each other.

"We're gonna die up here," I moaned.

"Shut up," Mark said.

By midnight we had pieced the porta-ledge back together and were inside the fetid hanging cabana, festooned with ropes. Boots, spoons, pocketknives, headlamps, and sacks of food dangled from webbing loops on the nylon ceiling. We lay like mummies in a sarcophagus for three days, and our blood grew thick in our veins. Food and fuel dwindled to quarter rations. To blot out our fear, as well as the racket caused by falling ice, we concocted a nightly cocktail of sleeping pills, codeine, and an exotic French tablet called Ronikol that stimulated the circulation in our wooden feet.

On the fourth day, with snow still whiting the sky, our pills ran out.

"How much more of this can you take?" I asked Mark, feeling myself beginning to slip into the otherworldliness that accompanies hypothermia.

"As long as you can," he replied stoically.

"Well," I admitted, "if we don't get out of here right away, I have a feeling we'll never get down."

Until now, retreating had been unthinkable. The hardest climbing was behind us, and above us cracks shot to the summit like the express lane on a freeway. Easy going, more or less. Still, I had a feeling we'd overstayed our welcome. I chopped ice from the ropes and began the half-mile-long rappel back down. At one point I hammered in a piton and just dangled there, looking up. From a distance the porta-ledge looked like a car rammed into a snowdrift.

Ten hours later we staggered into base camp and flopped inside our tent, steam rising from our stinking clothes. Waiting for sleep to take us away, we stared out the tent door at the silhouette of Trango Tower: immense, beautiful, dangerous, a mountain turned on heaven's lathe.

"I hate to say this," I said as we lay there, "but we're going to have to come back someday."

TRANGO TOWER JUTS LIKE A STILETTO from the bouldery banks of the Baltoro Glacier. Its unusually slender shape had obsessed mountaineers since the 1950s, but for twenty years no one attempted to climb it. It was, they said, a project for the year 2000.

Then in 1975 a team of hard-boiled British alpinists, including Joe Brown, Martin Boysen, and Mo Anthoine, made an assault on the south face. They didn't get to the top, but I remember, as an infatuated teenage cragger, poring over Boysen's journal account of the attempt. The team was halfway up the tower wall when Boysen hammered a piton into a wide fissure, swung his leg into a crack, and flexed his knee to hoist himself up. The move worked well, but when Boysen tried to extract the knee, it wouldn't budge.

First he squirmed. Then, in a panic, he clawed at his pants. After an hour of tugging and pushing, he tried to hammer a bolt into the wall so that his belayer, Anthoine, could ascend the rope and help free him. But he dropped the hand drill. Three hours went by and the crack still gripped Boysen as tightly as a giant clam.

"I sank into a trancelike, painless oblivion," he later wrote. "My mind wandered aimlessly, picking out memories, seizing on trivia, until the anguish inside me welled up uncontrollably and forced itself into my unwilling consciousness. I choked out a single sob, the distillation of my despair."

Struggling against hypothermic inertia, Boysen had an idea. Like a blacksmith at an anvil, he fashioned a jagged saw-edge by hammering a piton against the wall. With this new tool he hacked at his knee, ripping through pants and flesh. Blood oozed from his thigh, greasing the crack, and the mangled knee slid out. The expedition, however, was finished. To this day, the crack is known as the Fissure Boysen.

Undaunted, the Brits returned to Trango in 1976, and Boysen shot past the fissure to summit with Anthoine, Brown, and Malcolm Howells. The climbing press proclaimed it the most difficult ascent ever made in the Himalaya.

Boysen's account of their two Trango expeditions had a grand effect on how I thought about mountains. One passage in particular spoke to my own youthful obsession with climbing improbable routes: "One of the curious things about climbing is that certain routes or mountains become tokens, built up in the imagination and imbued with an aura of mystery." Boysen's partner, Anthoine, had a more visceral way of describing the addictive tug of high-stakes climbing. He called it "feeding the rat."

By the time I made my first trip to Trango, in 1986, with climbing buddies Tom Hargis and Randy Leavitt, the rat had taken up residence somewhere inside me, too. Among us, we had a worthy resume that included big peaks from Aconcagua to Everest and new routes up steep Himalayan towers such as Shivling in India and Lobsang Spire, a neighbor of Trango. Randy and I had once dangled together for ten days on a state-of-the-art route on El Cap that we called Lost in America. We'd arrogantly joked that the thrill of climbing Yosemite's big walls had become passé; the real threat, we said, was of being run off the road by a Winnebago on the way into the park. Wanting a new challenge, we set our sights on Trango.

The trip was ill-conceived. A week before trekking to Trango's base we made the mistake of climbing a new route on 26,000-foot Gasherbrum IV. Weeks at altitude and a harrowing bivouac spent shivering in the snow near the summit had left us punch-drunk and scarecrow-thin. Our larder was down to potato powder, ketchup, and oatmeal. Our gums bled from vitamin deficiency; our fingers were frost-nipped. We were in lousy shape for Trango. After a week on the wall we retreated, having barely made it halfway.

Three years later I tried again, with Mark Wilford, but we were run off by that nasty blizzard. By the summer of 1992, when again I found myself in Pakistan, I'd spent nearly a year of my life in the Karakoram Range. Climbing K2, the world's second-highest peak, only fueled my obsession. As I sat oxygenless and blissed out at the 28,250-foot summit, I deliriously confused fear with enlightenment. Mountains, I thought, were temples. As soon as I got down from K2's flanks, I secured another climbing permit for Trango and, like a monk on a pilgrimage, embarked on my third try.

KAFKA COULD NOT HAVE CONCEIVED A MAZE MORE CONFOUNDING than the Ministry of Tourism in Islamabad. In this musty building, square one in the game that mountaineers play each summer in the Karakoram Range, I'd seen hardened alpinists reduced to nervous wrecks by a narcoleptic bureaucracy and an arcane little booklet titled *The Mountaineering Rules and Regulations of Pakistan.*

I was in the office of Zafarullah Siddiqui, Deputy Chief of Operations. Beside me sat Mark, back with me again, and Rob Slater, our third partner for the climb. Siddiqui was explaining that we had a problem.

"No expedition comprising less than four members shall be allowed to proceed into the mountains," Siddiqui parroted from the booklet, raising his head to look at us.

Mark Wilford, heading up our ropes during the first ascent of our 1992 route, which we named Run for Cover.

I protested, whining that I'd been assured there was no problem with three climbers, that Trango was steep and four was a crowd. Siddiqui shrugged. "No party comprising less than four members shall be allowed to proceed into the mountains," he repeated.

Overhead, a ceiling fan swished through the liquid heat, rustling mounds of papers on his desk. Pinned to the wall, sun-jaundiced postcards of Karakoram peaks fluttered. From behind them peeked geckoes the size of minnows. I glanced at Mark. He nodded and slid an envelope stuffed with rupees across the desk.

Siddiqui grinned. "We'll just say that your fourth member is delayed and will join you later," he said, then stamped our permit and escorted us to the door with vigorous handshakes and wishes of good luck.

Two weeks later we stood on a moraine, staring up at Trango Tower. I doled out more wads of rupees to our departing porters, tipping the poor soul who'd carried our 300 eggs, a third of which had broken and stained him with a sulfurous stench.

"Rasool," I asked our cook, "what does Trango mean?"

"Hair-oil bottle. Because of the shape."

I pointed to another spire: "How about that one—Uli Biaho?"

"Skinny chicken."

Nepalese and Tibetan peak names have meanings such as Mother Goddess of the Snows, but the Balti people are more pragmatic. Rasool liked to tell the story of a guide whose client had asked to know the names of some peaks in a remote valley. The peaks happened to be unnamed, but not wanting to disappoint his client, the guide proceeded to rattle off a few: Ali Peak, Fatima Peak, and so on, after the members of his family. The trekker noted the names, and they have since appeared on maps all over the world.

At the 13,000-foot base camp it was clear that the neighborhood had changed. In the six years since my first visit a host of climbers had picked at Trango like vultures at a carcass, adding seven new routes to the wall. The tents of Korean, Australian, British, Russian, and New Zealander climbers were clustered like mushrooms around a tree trunk. It looked, as Rob said, "like Yosemite on Memorial Day weekend."

We spent a week scanning the walls for a route untouched by human hands, finally settling on a jigsaw of cracks on the eastern margin of the south face. Two natural ledges, a grand terrace at 18,600 feet and an eagle's-nest perch at 20,000 feet, offered places to bivouac. Far to the left of our planned route lay the Fissure Boysen; 1,000 feet to its right was what we were calling the Fissure Child, where Mark and I had stalled out in 1989.

Originally we had hoped to attack the northeast wall, a less busy side of the mountain, but a few weeks before leaving home we'd learned that our route had been scooped by a tenacious Japanese climber named Takeyasu Minamiura. I was peeved that he'd beaten us to our intended route, but when I learned what happened to him—his parapente snagged on a rock spire after he jumped from the summit, stranding him on a ledge and leaving him to eat snow for nine days until his rescue—I didn't mind so much. He'd earned his route on Trango.

After two weeks and seventeen pitches, we reached a ledge we called the eagle's-nest, at 20,000 feet, having woven an intricate path. The ice-choked cracks we'd followed had a habit of ending abruptly; to link the gaps, we'd had to swing back and forth on our rope and then dive at the cracks like acrobats—a maneuver called a pendulum. That night we hunkered down in bivy sacks, planning the next day's climb to the summit. With only a few pitches left, success seemed a sure bet.

Of course, we were wrong. A blizzard blew in, and at dawn I peered out of my bivy sack to see our ledge shrouded in a foot of snow and the sky milky with boiling clouds. I was warm inside my sack, but I recognized those clouds. They were the kind that stay for weeks, coating everything with ice. They end expeditions. Twisting around, I faced Mark. He'd cinched the entrance to his bivy sack tight, like a knothole in a tree stump. One eye peered out.

"Déjà vu," he said.

Down we went. Without speaking, we rappelled into the white-out, waves of wind-driven snow washing over us. By this stage in our climbing careers, Mark and I were unfazed by stormy retreats. Rob, however, saw it differently. As we stumbled down the gully back to base camp, I noticed a familiar look on his face: fear. That, of course, is the expression one would expect after a brush with the Big Freeze, but we knew it also meant that Rob was probably through.

Rain fell in sheets during the week Mark, Rob, and I were stranded down in base camp. The Koreans had beaten the storm and completed their ascent, and other teams were beginning to empty out. Our liaison officer, provided by the Pakistani army, was bored to tears. He'd endured a month waiting for us to climb Trango with nothing to entertain him except a copy of *Cosmopolitan*, which in Pakistan is the nearest thing to a girlie magazine that money can buy.

On the morning of August 22 the storm evaporated, and we packed again for the climb. A chill in the air told us autumn storms would arrive any day, so we planned to move fast. With our ropes left in place from our previous sortie, we'd be able to climb to the ledge at 18,600 feet the first day.

After bivying there, we'd tag the summit the next day. We'd have to travel light; other than slings loaded with hardware, we'd carry only the clothes on our backs, a day's worth of energy bars and water, and our bivy sacks, which we stuffed into our pockets.

As the morning sun hit the cliffs above base camp, we heard the sound of falling debris. The storm had coated the walls with melon-size barnacles of ice, and now they were peeling loose and heading for Earth. Just getting to the mountain would be a little like running through a combat zone.

We were about to set off when Rob spoke up.

"I'm not going back up there," he said. "I don't want to end up buried in a shallow grave."

"Don't worry," Mark said. "We'll bury you nice and deep."

"I'm serious. I can't go back up."

I nodded. Over the past few days Rob had talked of selling his climbing gear, getting married, having kids. He calculated out loud how much this trip had cost him in lost broker's commissions. I'd seen mountains do this to people before; I'd seen them do it to me. We parted with a handshake, and Mark and I headed up the wall—a team of two again.

Rob somehow must have sensed what was going to happen next. We were standing on the ledge at 18,600 feet, and out of the blue sky, a boulder the size of a refrigerator was homing in on us. We scrambled for shelter, and the next instant the boulder slammed into the snow twenty-five yards to our right. Up on the rock face, a newly formed cavern was spilling stones and ice chunks, and we huddled against a boulder as errant meteors burst around us, creating blossoms of white powder. What were the odds that one of the falling rocks would find its target on our soft heads?

"Didn't you say you wanted to head up first, to take photos?" said Mark, with a slight grin.

I clamped my ascenders onto the rope and climbed as fast as I could slide them, as if speed alone would outsmart the gauntlet of stones. Fifty feet up, my ascenders jammed with ice, and swearing and scraping the ice with a piton, I slowed to a crawl. I tried not to look at anything but the rope in front of me as rocks kept raining nearby.

By midafternoon we reached the eagle's nest, where we'd bivouacked a week before. Trango's icy topknot was in sight, and we were above the rockfall. I breathed more easily.

The feeling lasted a moment. I felt the ledge beneath my feet shake. Then a sonic boom rent the air, dust rose up the wall, and a long rumble echoed through the valley as boulders avalanched down toward the Dunge Glacier. As I looked to my right, a 500-foot pillar of rock toppled like a skyscraper. The route we'd just climbed was obliterated.

We kept moving. Our feet and fists flailed against the slick verglas, and our lungs heaved. We passed a tangle of parachute cord on Minamiura's lonely ledge and arrived at the summit in the last pulse of twilight.

"This is it?" I asked.

"Yep," Mark said.

"Bit of an anticlimax, isn't it?"

"That's the way it goes."

I'd expected something loftier. Instead, we dangled uncomfortably from an old titanium piton, the calling card of some Slovene climbers, hammered into the final snowcapped block. We hung there and stared for a moment at a pitching sea of mountains. Nearby, Mustagh Tower and Masherbrum burned pink with alpenglow. Farther on, the jagged 8,000-meter peaks of the Himalaya fringed the horizon.

I could have looked at that panorama for hours, thinking back on the long journey that had led me there. Over the years I'd somehow walked away from my climbs with ten fingers and ten toes when other climbers lost theirs. I'd even watched a friend die on that dismal molar called Broad Peak. But I don't think I had fought so hard to climb a mountain before. Frankly, I felt mildly ridiculous on top of Trango Tower, like a pole-sitter trying for a spot in the record books.

I wished, for a moment, that we'd called off the climb a hundred feet below the summit. That way we would have been able to come back another year, and another, to keep feeding the rat.

Regarding

Mountains

On a pinnacle in the Coast Range of Canada.

Masters of Understatement

Recently I saw a lecture by the septuagenarian hero of Everest, Sir Edmund Hillary. He stood on the stage, smiling over the crowded auditorium like a friendly old bird of prey, and delivered his life-and-times address, a talk he has probably given more times than there are footsteps up Everest. Clicking through fading images of his youthful climbs in the New Zealand Alps, then dismissing Everest in about six slides, Sir Ed came to his Antarctic climbs and travels.

In 1958 he traveled in a convoy of tractors to the South Pole, a 1,000-mile journey over polar ice. Crevasses lurked beneath their cat-tracks all along the route, and the machines kept breaking through snowbridges spanning holes large enough to absorb a house. To illustrate this point, Sir Ed showed a picture of a Ferguson tractor, nose pointed skyward, its rear end eaten by a crevasse. The tractor, driven by Jim Bates, had been chugging along when the snow beneath it gave way, sending the machine sliding backward toward oblivion. It stopped only when its cabin jammed in the mouth of the slot.

"I walked to the edge of the crevasse and peered in," Sir Ed told the oohing and aahing auditorium, "and I saw Jim looking up through the cabin window."

"'Hello, Jim, how are you down there?' I said."

"'I'm okay,' Jim replied, 'but I don't like the view.'"

The tone in which Sir Ed delivered this punch line was a calm, droll, yet risible monotone. The audience laughed on cue, as he knew they would. Taken at face value, the story suggested that he and his pals were in complete control, that dodging crevasses was all in a subzero day's work, and that nearly losing tractor and driver to the frozen depths was a mere trifle.

Yet a waggish inflection in Sir Ed's voice hinted that there was more to this tale than he was divulging. In fact, there was, no doubt, stress, panic, and drama. But Sir Ed was too stately a gent to run around the stage flapping his arms and gushing about the near-death experiences of his Antarctic tractor boys. He let understatement carry the story instead and left his listeners to imagine the scene for themselves.

Understatement—the knack of intensifying the effect of a story by telling it with restraint and a trace of irony—is a time-honored tradition of the adventure raconteur. It is based on the principle of revealing less in order to tell more.

The origins of the understated adventure narrative go back to the nineteenth-century British explorers. Whether they were dying of thirst in a desert, freezing on a polar quest, or being attacked by headhunters, those upper-crust Brits always downplayed the experience in their accounts. Yes, they were proud, sometimes bombastic imperialists, but the likes of Sir Richard Francis Burton, who in the 1800s roamed uncharted Africa searching for the source of the Nile, or Sir Ernest Shackleton, who at the turn of the century led a rowboat full of men across ocean and ice after their ship was crushed in the southern icepack, had a gift for describing outrageous ordeals and awful privations with comparative humility.

After all, this was Victorian England, and when one stood before the fellows of the Royal Geographical Society to deliver an account of one's expedition, comportment was as compulsory as the top hat and tails that they wore. To be carried away by emotions was unseemly. Understatement was a code of behavior.

The writings of climbers of the early twentieth century—such as Eric Shipton, Bill Tilman, and the American Bradford Washburn—embraced the cult of understatement and the ethos of making light of the most harrowing circumstances. Modern incarnations of alpine understatement include "A Crawl Down the Ogre," Doug Scott's 1977 article from *Mountain*, about an epic on a Karakoram peak. The following exchange occurs between Scott and Chris Bonington, when Bonington rappels down from the 24,000-foot summit to find Scott has wrecked his legs:

"'What ho!,'" Chris said cheerily.

"'I've broken my right leg and smashed the left ankle,'" I said.

"'We'll just work on getting you down,'" he replied airily. "'Don't worry, you're a long way from death.'"

But times change. The 1990s are a decade of total disclosure. It is vogue to wear your heart on your sleeve, to let Geraldo and Oprah squeeze every gruesome detail out of your personal tragedy. In this atmosphere, the understater is an endangered species.

But not extinct. Check out the *American Alpine Journal,* the last refuge of the climbing understater. The 1994 *AAJ* contains a masterpiece of restraint, a story titled "Good Neighbor Peak."

This tightly worded two-page story describes a new route up the south spur of Mount Vancouver, a remote 15,979-foot peak in Alaska's St. Elias Range. The climbers are two Northwesterners, Bill Pilling and Carl Diedrich. Bill's tale begins like any other Alaskan climbing account, but the last three paragraphs betray a *Touching-the-Void*-scale saga when Bill plunges into a crevasse during the descent.

"Ten feet into the fall," he writes, "the frontpoints of my right crampon snagged on the wall of the crevasse, forcing the toes of my right foot upward and hyperextending my knee. Ligaments were torn, a major artery ruptured and muscles ripped. Forty feet down, the rope checked my fall."

With a miserly economy of words, Bill records his extraction from the crevasse and reveals the severity of his injuries: his leg is purple, swollen horribly, and he is in shock. After a bivouac the escape begins: "On May 19 I was just able to walk with an ice axe and north-wall hammer splinted together into a walking stick. Carl masterminded the 7000-foot descent to the Seward Glacier, carrying an extra-heavy load and lowering me down some 25 pitches. I was in severe pain and moaning and groaning."

The final paragraph tells us that they took nineteen hours to descend the rest of the mountain and three days to walk sixteen miles to base camp. Altogether, they were out for eleven days. During their foodless march along the glacier, Carl carried and dragged both packs while Bill guided them by compass through a white-out. The account ends plainly: "We were picked up by plane on the 26th as planned. It was a month before I walked again without crutches."

This tale of two men in deepest shit was a tale worthy of becoming a talk show tearjerker, a *Reader's Digest* potboiler, but instead the author had presented experience without introspection or anguish. But I couldn't resist—something in me wanted to hear the whole tale—so I persuaded the author to meet me at a Seattle tavern, where I planned to loosen his tongue with a few pints.

As Bill Pilling walked into the pub I detected a slight limp, even though a year-and-a-half had passed since the accident. With gray-flecked, close-cropped hair and thick-rimmed glasses, he looks more like a scholar than the archetypal American wilderness mountaineer that he is; his first ascents

A climber at 22,000 feet on K2's North Ridge.

include sea-to-summit climbs in the Fairweather and St. Elias Ranges and a big route on Devil's Thumb.

I ask how the leg is doing. "Good enough," he tells me, to plan a return to the mountains in 1995. Yet I sense it will be a long time before those grim days on Mount Vancouver are out of his system, as he says, "For a year after the accident I had dreams of crossing sparkling snowfields and suddenly breaking through."

I tell him that his article in the *AAJ* struck me as the epitome of understatement. He smiles, as if pleased. When I ask why he played down the enormity of his and Carl's ordeal, he replies enigmatically, "Understatement presents the truth by not presenting it."

To Bill, what counts in climbing is not what is written or said, but what the climber actually does in the mountains. Serious climbers who read the *AAJ* can read between the lines and understand what he and Carl experienced.

He does not regard climbing tales as "entertainment," and he dismisses the climbing and adventure magazines for shamelessly submerging into the swamp of commercialism. For him, the only climbing publication that matters is the *AAJ*, because it is *not* commercially motivated. All the recognition in the world doesn't amount to a hill of beans to this climber.

Bill expresses his beliefs with conviction, yet he is not strident. Then he lets his guard down and describes what happened on Mount Vancouver.

"It started on the sixth day of the climb, during the descent from the summit plateau. We'd given up the final 400 feet because of bad weather, and because of a cough I suspected was edema. Carl was in front, I was following, when I saw a little crack in the snow. The next instant I broke through into a crevasse. My crampon points snagged right away. The leg bent back. There was so much pain that my mind blanked out. I screamed the whole way down."

The force of the fall dragged Carl backward about twenty feet. When Bill stopped he was forty feet down, flipped over and suffocating under a forty-five-pound pack.

"The pain felt like boiling water was pouring into my leg. That was the internal bleeding, the broken popliteal artery emptying a pint of blood into my leg. Calf muscle torn almost in half. Ligaments ripped. My lower leg swollen to twice its normal size."

I wince at the concept of so much pain in such an austere place. Then Bill goes on.

"I knew that staying alive was going to be so much work that for a few minutes I didn't know if I wanted to bother. I just wanted to go to sleep. But I knew my family would be unhappy if I died, and that Carl would be in a jam, so I told myself, 'Okay, I'm gonna live.'"

Bill swung onto an ice block jammed beside him in the crevasse and stood on his good leg while Carl hauled out his pack.

"Hey, Bill, how're you doin' down there?" yelled Carl, peering over the edge.

"Not so good. I've injured my leg."

"Hang tight, I'll get ya out," Carl called back.

"Later he told me he was thinking 'we're totally fucked,'" says Bill, his tone turning serious.

"Carl gave me a tension belay and I climbed out using my ice axes and my good foot. I had to chop through a cornice at the top. He dragged me over the lip. I lay on the snow, writhing, screaming, leg cramping, seeing colors, shivering, verging on shock."

While Bill thrashed around in agony Carl set up the tent; then he took

Bill's boot off and got him into his sleeping bag. Every move was agony.

The next morning, their seventh day out, they took inventory of their gear, food, fuel, and painkillers—"to see where the edges of our world were." They figured it would take five days to reach base camp. They had four days of food, five Tylenol per day, and a few codeine pills.

Their radio was at base camp, so rescue was impossible. The weather was bad. They were at 12,000 feet. Carl considered descending to base camp alone to get help, but, says Bill, "who gets the stove, who gets the tent?" And the glacier was heavily crevassed. No, splitting up was out. "So I tried moving and found I could walk on my heel. We lashed my ice axes together for a walking stick and set off. Some of the way I walked; some of the way Carl towed me along on the rope and I slid through the snow. I kept hitting my leg and nearly blacking out with pain."

At a steep slope Carl began lowering Bill. Then they did "the Joe Simpson number," and Carl lowered Bill over a cornice and into a big crevasse.

"I was hanging free on the rope, spinning around," says Bill. "Carl couldn't hear me and kept lowering me into the gaping maw. Fifteen feet into the hole I found a false floor and stopped. Carl climbed to the edge and looked in, shouting, 'What are you doing down there? You poor fucker!' I didn't like being pitiable."

On the eighth day they struck steep ice. Carl lowered Bill again, from a metal picket he had hammered into the slope.

Then they traversed, which for Bill was painfully awkward. "I kept hitting my leg. The pain made me somersault backward. I had to self-arrest to stop sliding over a cliff."

Later Bill broke through another crevasse. He screamed, utterly terrified of crevasses.

Composure had now totally gone. "Carl was repeating over and over, 'Gotta get off, gotta get off, gotta get off,'" says Bill. "He was going mad from the stress." Since the accident, he'd been doing everything: making camp, cooking, dressing and undressing Bill, getting Bill's boots on and off, breaking trail, lowering him, dragging him, carrying everything.

They reached the upper Seward Glacier at 1:00 A.M. and camped behind a block of ice that had fallen from a serac. Bill finally took some codeine. He hadn't taken any till then since he needed a clear head. They laughed together for the first time that night.

They slept late that ninth day. Carl shouldered a heavy load, while Bill sat on his pack and was dragged along the glacier on the rope. Their food was down to soup and candy bars now, but Carl was "still strong as an animal. Amazing guy. This was his first trip to Alaska. He's from a German family.

Quiet guy, a Deadhead, spent a lot of time hanging out in the Guatemalan jungle in native Indian villages that have since been destroyed by the Guatemalan army."

As the day wore on, they weaved about crevasses and waded through deep, wet snow. Bill was moaning, and, he says, Carl finally shouted, "'Will you shut the fuck up?' Then I stopped whining."

Fog rolled in that afternoon, so they navigated by a compass bearing. They reached base camp on the eleventh day, in perfect weather.

"I felt really unhappy on the walk to base camp because I couldn't appreciate the silent beauty of this glacier. I learned what pain can do to a body: it felt like a hole had been punched in my emotional gas tank. When we radioed the bush pilot for a pickup, we didn't tell him what had happened. Didn't want to alarm him."

Bill finishes his tale and sips his beer. I knew the rest of the story: painful weeks of crawling around his apartment to get from the couch to the kitchen, physical therapy, and then a gradual return to walking and work.

The contrast between his account in the *AAJ* and the story he told me was like night and day. Few climbers—myself included—could resist the temptation to bare their soul and turn such a tale into a personal story. When I suggest this, Bill just shrugs, and, with a smile that tells me the discussion has ended, says, "Modesty becomes a gentleman."

Hi Mum! The author losing brain cells atop the second highest peak on Earth.

Gunning for Second Best

If you have stood atop an Alaskan or Himalayan peak and have gazed across a seemingly infinite carpet of summits stretching toward the curve of the Earth, you will think it balderdash when I suggest that a day will come when all those peaks and all the routes have been climbed.

Imagine such a future: every last bump on the maps of the ranges surmounted, and, on all of those bumps, every ridge, face, and couloir climbed. No more first ascents left anywhere. Even on the crowded crags in the valleys below the mountains—where a route rated 5.15 will, no doubt, be a trade route—there won't be an untouched finger-edge to be found; there won't even be room to squeeze in a variation between variants.

Add this to the scenario: the enchainments and traverses of the great peaks all linked, the precipices all BASE-jumped or parapented, the first solos soloed, ski descents skied, speed ascents maxed out. Imagine once-legend feats of climbing so commonplace that in any restaurant in any city, you'll be able to call out, "Hands up, those who have scaled all the 8,000-meter peaks," and half the diners, a waiter, and maybe even the chef will salute.

That may sound like a laughable proposition in an era when there appear to be as many untrodden dots on the maps as stars in the night sky, but as rich as our galaxy of mountains may appear, it has a boundary. With nothing new left, with no thresholds to shatter, what would happen to climbing? Would the sport die?

Instinct tells me that people would find the challenge of the first ascent

Greg Mortimer and Steve Swenson plod out the agonizing final hours to K2's summit, 1990.

recyclable. Even in a climbed-out world, I suspect that climbers would reinvent, again and again, the Last Great Challenge.

All hail, the Last Great Challenge! Perpetual yet ever-changing, it punctuates the history of climbing like a glory list of wars and battles. There has always been a LGC, and there always will be one.

What, you ask, is an LGC? It's nothing more than a new yet undone feat in climbing, a "first" to which climbers can aspire, a record to break, a frontier to explore. Simple as that may sound, the LGC is also the breast that nurtures our climbing culture. Without it, climbers would be without direction.

To qualify for LGC status, a climb should be some kind of milestone achievement; but it must also have entertainment value, and it should be sexy, too. Take, for example, the list of LGCs generated by just one mountain: Everest. Highest peak of all, it has reigned as the Empress of Last Great Challenges ever since climbers began hurling themselves at it in the 1920s. The quest to be first to its summit was a singular struggle, but even after Tenzing Norgay and Edmund Hillary settled that score in 1953, climbers continued to worship Everest as numero uno LGC.

The "Big E" has given climbers a total of twenty-three individual routes and many more variants, as well as a host of first national ascents. During the 1970s mastering the mountain without the support of bottled oxygen— "by fair means"—was the great adventure, and it was Reinhold Messner and Peter Habeler who scooped that one, in 1978. Women broke barriers, too. Junko Tabei of Japan made the first woman's ascent in 1975, Sharon Wood did it first for Canada in 1986, and Stacey Alison, in 1988, was the first American woman up Everest. The first female oxygenless ascent was by Lydia Bradey of New Zealand, in 1988. The same year, a Frenchman, Jean Marc Boivin, paraglided from Everest's apex, touching down on the Khumbu Glacier eleven minutes later. But one of climbing's tours de force came in 1990, when Australian climber Tim Macartney-Snape became the first to climb every vertical inch of Everest's 29,028-foot rise by hiking 1,500 miles from the Bay of Bengal at sea level to the summit. Forsaking all forms of mechanized transport, Tim even swam across the great, gray, greasy Ganges River. Naturally, he did it all "by fair means." Beat that!

Everest may or may not be the zenith of climbing, but this sampler of the LGCs it has spawned shows that to get the spotlight in climbing, you have to be creative.

Climbers invented the LGC to give climbing a sense of order, because, let's face it, climbing is a disorderly pursuit, played on an untidy field of mountains, glaciers, and cliffs. Lacking the coherent black-and-white rules of spectator sports such as baseball, climbing is incomprehensible to everyone except climbers. The desperate need to make sense of climbing to ourselves, and the desire to legitimize it to the world, led to the creation of the LGC. The hope was that by cloaking certain ascents in a special mystique, climbers as well as nonclimbers could gather around the banner of a single adventure, and by celebrating it we would celebrate all of climbing.

But popularizing the LGC proved to be problematic. For one thing, the media inevitably distorts climbing. Regardless of attempts by climbers to codify our actions on the vertical, TV producers and print journalists always turn their films and reports on climbing into something more like Muzak than music. Just look at big-budget movies such as *Cliffhanger* or *K2*. Nevertheless, media involvement and big sponsorship are essential parts of an LGC, because these days the new frontiers all seem to be located in Nowheresville, and getting to Nowheresville is expensive.

The recipe for cooking an LGC is as follows: first, select an objective. It might be a climbing feat of great ferocity, a rugged journey, or a daring stunt. Avoid objectives with unpronounceable names. No matter how impressive it may be to climb Bojohagur Duanasir, a peak in Pakistan, it will never become a household name or have the cachet of a McKinley, a K2, or an Everest.

The next step is crucial to the marketability of your LGC: get a publicist or an agent to groom your image as a suitable representative of a master race of thrill seekers. Your publicist will then alert the media. With remorseless repetition, you must hammer out the message that your mission is the Mother of All Last Great Challenges. Portray yourself and your climbing team as icons of human endeavor. It helps to be good-looking, for after all, this is a beauty contest. When the aforementioned pieces are in place, the effect is as unstoppable as a runaway train. The climb and the climbers are shot out of the cannon of fame, and legends are born.

Craft your LGC from the following categories:

1. THE ROUTE

A good, hard route is the most honest form of LGC, but these days we've seen so many good, hard routes that mere difficulty is passé. A gimmick is essential. See categories 2 through 13 for suggestions.

2. HIGHEST PEAK DU JOUR

The only easy thing about this category is that it gets lower every year. Until recently, the world's highest unclimbed peak was Ultar (24,240 feet), in Pakistan. Japanese teams spent years, and lost a few climbers' lives in the process, to bag this rubbly pile, till success struck in 1996. Whatever the next highest peak is, it's sure to be cheaper than Ultar's predecessor in this category, Namcha Barwa (25,531 feet), which was climbed in 1992 by a Japanese team that paid a million bucks to China for the privilege. The funny thing about making an LGC of the highest unclimbed peak of the day is that almost without exception they are downright ugly and dangerous mountains. As an LGC, this class scrapes the bottom of the barrel.

3. HUNTING AND COLLECTING

For the list-oriented climber. Premier in this category was the "quest" (some called it a race) to climb all the 8,000-meter mountains by the high-altitude hardmen Reinhold Messner and Jerzy Kukuczka. Messner did it first, in 1986, beating his Polish counterpart by just a few months. Nobody doubts the excellence of getting up all fourteen of the 8,000-meter mountains, but it does seem a bit silly when a measurement system determines a mountain's importance. What if, instead of talking about the 8,000-meter peaks metrically, we talked about them in feet? Would we call them the "higher than 26,246-footers?" Or would we round out that clumsy tag and call them the "twenty-six-thousanders," in which case there would be twenty mountains in this group for climbers to collect?

Another famous collectible is the Seven Summits. The mission to climb the highest peak on each continent was fulfilled separately in 1985 by Texas oilman Dick Bass and Canadian photographer Pat Morrow. The ex-Soviets have their own collector's badge, the honor of becoming a Snow Leopard—one who has summited the five 7,000-meter peaks in the far-eastern ranges. More modest LGCs were created for those unable to jet about the world. Climbing all fifty-three of Colorado's 14,000-foot peaks is coveted by some, while "Munro bagging" is still popular in Great Britain. (Hugh Munro chronicled Britain's 543 high points and 276 mountains above 3,000 feet. "Munro baggers" are those who scale them.)

4. THE NOBLE CAUSE

This is the ulterior motive climb. Climbs for world peace, for the disadvantaged, and for cleaning up Everest are good examples. Doesn't anyone just go climbing anymore?

5. THE STUNT

J. M. Boivin's "Extreme Dream," as he called his Everest flight, is a hard act to follow, and a perilous one. He was killed a couple of years later while BASE-jumping off Angel Falls in Venezuela.

6. THE FIRST (FILL IN YOUR GENDER, NATIONALITY, STAR SIGN, SEXUAL PREFERENCE, ETC., HERE)

Is it really a measure of anything to make the first dyslexic Taiwanese ascent of a mountain with a tongue-tying name such as Gyachung Kang? Try a bit harder!

7. THE FIRSTEST

This includes first free ascent, first solo, first winter climb, first naked ascent in roller skates. Lynn Hill certainly scored a biggie in this category by becoming the first human to free all the moves on the Nose of El Cap in 1993. It was a nice plus that she happened to be a woman.

8. THE FASTEST

Pure speed. Stopwatch essential. Classics include the first one-day ascent of El Cap by Jim Bridwell, John Long, and Billy Westbay in 1975; in 1992 Peter Croft and Hans Florin did the route in an astounding four hours and twenty-two minutes. The late Frenchman Benoit Chamoux's twenty-two-hour sprint up K2 in 1986 wasn't too shabby either, even if he was following the tracks and fixed ropes of other climbers.

9. THE BIGGEST

Get out your tape measures. The biggest unclimbed rock wall, geologists say, is an 8,000-foot granite prow on Mount Dickey, in the Alaska Range. The bad news is that more than 3,000 feet of it are buried below glacial ice.

10. TOUGHER THAN A TWO-DOLLAR STEAK

Hard, harder, hardest—the big technical grades in free climbing, aid, and ice. The late Wolfgang Gullich's Action Direct (8c/9a, or 5.14d) in the Frankenjura region of Germany has seen many failed attempts and might be the hardest sport climb on Earth, but a repeat ascent will decide that. The tendon-searing push toward 5.15 continues.

11. THE GREAT JOURNEY

Epic trudges, such as traversing ice caps or peaks, or horribly long approach marches. Leeches, mosquitoes, tropical diseases, and dying of thirst are hallmarks of this category.

12. THE RACE

Makes for good copy in magazines. The idea is to have climbers compete for the same goal. A good tactic is to eavesdrop on the plans of other climbers and then sneak in to steal their LGC. Take your boxing gloves.

13. THE MOST MISERABLE CLIMB

A most popular category. The grand contender must be the Japanese team that suffered through fierce winds and -45°C cold to climb one of Everest's hardest routes, the Southwest Face, in the winter of 1993.

And now an exclusive scoop. . . . Announcing the latest LGC! I challenge all comers to a race for the Seven Second-highest Summits. Having already climbed Asia's second-tallest, K2 (28,250 feet), I have a nice edge on this project. The other peaks in this collection are Mount Logan on the Canadian-U.S. border, which, at 19,855 feet, is North America's second-highest; Ojos del Salado (22,539 feet), in Chile, South America's number two; Mount Kenya (17,063 feet), in Kenya, Africa's; Mount Tyree (16,289 feet), Antarctica's; and Dykh-Tau (17,070 feet), in the war-ravaged, ex-Soviet Republic of Georgia, Europe's second-highest.

As for Oceania, that agglomeration of lands Down Under, geographers are yet to determine the official second-highest peak there. Is it Carstenz Timor (16,010 feet), a subsidiary bump of Carstenz Pyramid (which is a contender for Oceania's highest), in Irian Jaya? Or, should we decree that subsidiary summits are unlawful and nominate Mount Wilhelm, (14,796 feet), in the jungle of Papua New Guinea? But if Australia is the true continental land mass of Oceania, the objective will be Mount Townsend, a wallaby-infested 7,250-foot hill in the Snowy Mountains.

But wait, I hear my fax machine spitting out a message. Perhaps it is my publicist. Maybe a big corporate sponsor wants to invest in my challenge to be second best. Ladies and gentlemen, start your engines and count up your frequent flyer miles. The race for the LGC has begun!

Jim Wickwire thumbing through the book brought down from K2; Abruzzi Ridge.

What Goes Up Might Come Down

The strangest artifact I ever saw on a mountain summit was a 100-pound steel cross. It was jammed into the top of the appropriately named Cerro Cathedral, a steep spire in the Bariloche area of Chilean Patagonia. Rusting and battered by lightning strikes, and guyed down with twisted cables, the cross vibrated in the wind like a hummingbird's wings as it overlooked a deep valley and the dormant volcano El Tronador, from which hellish sulfur sporadically fumes.

This cross is an example of the extraordinary lengths to which people will go in the fetish some of us have for decorating mountain summits. The Andes and the Alps bristle with crosses, crucifixes, and Madonnas. On certain summits of the Chinese empire, zinc busts of Mao can still be found, while in the former Soviet Union, the much-photographed heads of Lenin that once adorned the summits of the Caucasus Range have followed the fall of communism, booted into the abyss or stolen.

Last time I looked, Everest's crown resembled a ham-radio operator's installation, bristling with poles and cables set up by a recent expedition that remeasured its height. But this won't last long; like the tripod left there by the Chinese in 1975, this pile of junk will blow away or disappear under a layer of ice in a few years. Elsewhere in the Himalaya, on the now-forbidden mountain Nanda Devi, rumors persist that in 1966 an American expedition planted a beeping black box—a "spy" device to monitor Chinese nuclear missile launches—near the top. The rumor also says that the box was avalanched off the mountain, that it and its radioactive power source are slowly filtering into the headwaters of the Ganges River, and that shortly after, a similar device was successfully installed on the Indian peak Nanda Kot.

Usually, though, things left on summits are innocent mementos. Summit registers stuffed into tin boxes and jars dot the North American high country, from the Canadian and Colorado Rockies and the Black Hills to the Southwest desert spires to the Sierra Nevada and Cascade Ranges. Atop their mountains, climbers scribble their names on these scrolls and nostalgically thumb through the entries. Water-soaked and time-worn, these messages-in-a-bottle are the climbers' free press. They give vent to grand poems, tripped-out raves, and inspired essays. They also record the nuts-and-bolts details of who climbed what route and when, how hard it was, the speed of the ascent, and the weather on that day. These time capsules reflect the thoughts of the generations who chose to spend their time in the hills rather than in cities. Climb for enough years and you'll probably revisit some summit from your past, and confront your younger self.

Tomfoolery can dictate what is left on summits. Plastic flamingos have been toted up Everest. In Australia, the Totem Pole, a 300-foot tall, 10-foot square sea stack on the coast of Tasmania, has a "No Parking" sign fixed to its summit. Also Down Under, on a cliffline of dolerite columns and pinnacles called the Organ Pipes, above the city of Hobart, I once encountered a concrete lawn cockatoo, with wings outstretched, roosting atop a spire.

Given enough time, objects left on summits may become collectible, historic, even valuable. In 1986, when I was rappelling off the top of Gasherbrum IV in the Karakoram Range, and my partner, Tim Macartney-Snape, yelled down that he'd found an old piton hammered into the summit blocks, I shouted back to Tim, "Get it!" Apart from us, only Carlo Mauri and Walter Bonatti, who had made the first ascent in 1958, had visited that summit. Even at 26,000 feet I had dollar signs in my eyes; I figured we could sell it for a small fortune to some wealthy Italian gear freak. But Tim's hammering didn't budge the steel spike, and it stayed in place. Along with the sling we looped around a chockstone, it remains booty for future scavengers, for what goes up might eventually come down.

Jim Wickwire, a Seattle climber who reached the top of K2 in 1978, has a strange collection of artifacts brought up and down from high peaks. They include a slice of compact metamorphic rock, a small red plastic capsule, and a weathered-looking book, all of which once decorated the flanks of the world's second-highest mountain.

When Jim, Lou Reichardt, Rick Ridgeway, and John Roskelley climbed K2, Jim carried a number of small objects to the summit. One item was a sheet of microfiche film containing the names of 3,000 of the expedition's sponsors. Another was a small red plastic capsule, which he'd loaded with a wad of business cards from several friends. Also in the capsule was a gold wrist chain that had belonged to the deceased father of another of Jim's friends. Jim had pledged to the owners of these items that he'd leave them on top of K2, and his last act before leaving the summit was to ram the objects deep into the snow with the end of his ice ax.

When Jim rejoined the other summiters at the highest camp, Ridgeway handed him a chunk of rock that he'd pried from a boulder that juts out of K2's icy summit dome. Rocks from the highest summits are prized souvenirs among many climbers. Perhaps that's because climbers feel that they leave a part of themselves on their mountains, so by taking a small shard of stone they are enacting a fair trade with the mountain. This seems true in the case of Jim: by the time he struggled back to base camp, he was frostbitten and would eventually lose parts of his toes, and he had severe lung damage from a harrowing forced bivouac he'd spent near the summit.

While Jim mended back in Seattle, he had his summit stone sliced in half. One half he kept. The other he sent to a climber whom he admired, another man who had grappled with K2: Dr. Charles Houston, who in 1953 had tried to make the mountain's first ascent, via the southeast ridge (now called the Abruzzi Ridge). The attempt by Houston's small team had been audacious for the era, and they had climbed high; but a storm and the illness of one member, Art Gilkey, had turned them around. The descent, in which most of the team began an uncontrolled fall but were safely held by one man's flawless execution of an ice ax belay, and in which Gilkey disappeared in an avalanche, became a legend in American high-altitude climbing history.

Jim's motive for sending Houston the rock was straightforward: "I wanted Charlie to have something from the summit because I know that in '53 he had wanted to get there very badly."

Not long after he sent the rock, Jim received a package from Houston. It contained a neatly crafted applewood box, which housed an old book. Its cover torn away, its leaves yellowed as parchment and brittle as autumn leaves, the book is filled with essays by distinguished men of letters, including Francis Bacon, William Hazlitt, Robert Louis Stevenson, and A. A. Milne, all English and all writers of the 1800s. A note from Houston explained that the book, like the summit stone, had come out of the snows of K2.

The book had been sent to Houston after Ardito Desio's 1954 Italian expedition had succeeded in climbing K2 via the route Houston had twice

Descending from the summit of Everest. The rock patch near the lower climber has provided many souvenir stones for ascenders of the North Ridge.

tried. Desio sent the book with a note: "My dear Charlie," it began, "The little book of English essays that I sent you was found in Camp 3 or 4 of the Abruzzi Ridge. I thought it was one of your books or of your partners. If it is not, (then) I cannot know who may be the old owner, but in any case (it was) one of the climbers of K2 indeed."

In fact, the book had been abandoned by Houston's team in 1953, but, Houston wrote in a letter to Jim, "Just whose the book was I don't recall, but we all read and shared it during bad days in camp . . ." Houston sent it to Jim feeling that he might value the memento, and indeed, it is one of the most prized items in Jim's collection of mountaineering esoterica. He may value it even more than the red capsule that followed him across mountain and ocean to and from the summit of K2.

In 1979, a year after Jim's climb, Reinhold Messner and Michl Dacher made an ascent of K2's Abruzzi Ridge. When Jim saw a translation of the tale of Reinhold's climb, in the German magazine *Der Spiegel*, he read, "Messner found a capsule that the Americans had left on the summit. Instead of leaving something at the top of K2, Messner decided to take something with him, the capsule the Americans had left the year before with the names of the people who had donated money to the expedition . . ."

Jim immediately wrote to Reinhold: "I would appreciate it if you would return the capsule and its contents and I in turn will give the contents back to my friends. Returning these items is entirely up to you as I left them on the summit without any thought of ever seeing them again. Perhaps all of this is a good lesson in not leaving things on high mountains."

Reinhold mailed Jim the capsule—now faded by the elements to a translucent pink, and punctured by crampon points—with a letter saying that he'd discovered it lying precariously perched on the edge of a fracture in the summit snowfield. Evidently, the wind had carved a foot of elevation off K2's snowcap in the year since Jim had been there.

The return of the capsule and its contents allowed Jim to ceremoniously present his friends with their business cards, now seasoned for a year at 28,250 feet on K2. It also reunited the piece of jewelry with its owner. "My friend was overcome with emotion when I handed back his father's gold wrist chain," Jim recalls. "He'd subsequently regretted sending the memento to K2 and was glad to have it again."

Jim's lump of faded plastic had circled the globe. Born in the mold of a Korean plastics plant and shipped to Seattle, it had then traveled in Jim's pocket to Pakistan and to the summit of K2 via the northeast ridge. Rescued from the brink of the abyss by Reinhold, it continued its journey, traversing K2 by descending the Abruzzi Ridge and then heading on to Europe. Finally, it had flown in a mailbag across the Atlantic back to Seattle.

Sitting in Jim's home, I turn the fragile pages of the book of essays and rub the K2 stone for good luck. Then I ask to see the legendary and well-traveled red capsule.

"Ah. There is a footnote to the red capsule story," Jim informs me.

In 1991 Jim pocketed the capsule and boarded a flight for Tokyo, where he planned to meet Reinhold at a conference. Jim thought he might have some fun by presenting Reinhold with the capsule, but this was destined never to be: Reinhold didn't make it to Tokyo, and somewhere in that teeming city, Jim lost the fabled artefact. As best as he can ascertain, the red plastic capsule has ended its journey in a Japanese landfill.

Scandals at

Altitude

A Yugoslav postage stamp commemorating Tomo Česen's alleged solo ascent of Lhotse's south face.

Burden of Proof

The Tomo Česen Affair

I was nervous as I dialed the international code for Slovenia, a nation carved out of the former Yugoslavia, and punched in the number for Tomo Česen's house in Kranj. After all, not only was I about to speak to the man pegged as the world's greatest alpinist, but I was, in essence, going to ask him if he had lied about the 1990 climb that had made him famous—the first ascent, solo, of the 12,000-foot south wall of Lhotse, in Nepal—because that was what the European press was saying in 1993.

Lhotse rises immediately south of Everest and is the fourth-highest peak on Earth. Its 27,892-foot summit was climbed first in 1956 by a Swiss team, who efficiently dispatched the western slope above the Khumbu Ice-fall. Nothing was easy about the south face, though. Its avalanche-raked barricade of crumbling black cliffs and ice chutes had defeated thirteen expeditions since 1973. A hundred alpinists had pitted themselves against it, including Europe's finest, such as Pierre Beghin, Christophe Profit, Marc Batard, Kryzystof Wielicki, and Reinhold Messner. The wall consumed four of Europe's best, too, among them Poland's Jerzy Kukuczka, the only man apart from Messner to climb all the 8,000-meter peaks. Kukuczka fell from near the summit when a rope snapped on a 1989 attempt.

By 1990 Lhotse's south wall had earned the title "Last Great Problem of the Himalaya." Whoever overcame its evil-looking geology was destined to enter history as the dragonslayer of alpinism. Then thirty-one-year-old

Tomo Česen claimed a solo first ascent of the wall in a sixty-four-hour round trip in the spring of that year.

The speed, endurance, skill, and damned good luck needed to execute the climb were phenomenal. Messner called it "the climbing event of the decade," and indeed it was light-years ahead of any alpine achievement in recent memory. Measured against Česen, even the best alpinists were primitives. Mentally and physically, he had to be a superman.

Lhotse brought Česen fame, though almost immediately his lack of witnesses, his sketchy story, and questions about his photographic proof raised doubts. In 1991 he was accused of fabricating the ascent, and European magazines became a battleground for angry letters between Česen and his detractors. Notable alpinists such as Pierre Beghin sided with Česen, though, and briefly stilled the doubts. They believed him because they wanted to believe that Česen had taken alpinism into the future, and that a climber's word can be trusted. Climbing has always worked on the honor system. When climbers failed, they admitted failure; when they succeeded, they got kudos, regardless of proof.

But the doubts that erupted in 1993—based upon the revelation that photographs Česen used to prove his ascent do not belong to him—have been impossible to ignore. In the wake of this discovery, Česen has lost many believers. Even Messner, who awarded Česen the $10,000 Snow Lion Prize in 1989 for his climb of Jannu and who dedicated a chapter to Česen in his autobiography, has recanted his support, saying petulantly, "If Česen cannot prove his Lhotse climb, he will not be in my books about Himalayan climbing, and I will remove the chapter about him from *Free Spirit.*"

Nevertheless, Česen insists he climbed Lhotse.

As the clicks and whirs of satellite telephone language gave way to a ringing sound in Slovenia, I considered hanging up. I admired Česen's achievements and always believed that he had climbed Lhotse. Now, I wasn't sure. If his ascent was a hoax, then it was a con as cynical as if NASA's moon missions had been staged with smoke and mirrors. But what if the ascent was genuine? That was a possibility, too. Sifting out truth from rumor would not be easy.

Česen picked up the phone. I introduced myself and asked if we could speak about "the situation." He paused and then said, "Sure, okay." I was surprised. I expected him to hang up or shout a stream of Slovenian insults at me for being another bloodsucking reporter hounding him.

THE ROAD TO LHOTSE

By all appearances, Česen certainly had the credentials to solo Lhotse. His rise to prominence began in Europe in winter 1986 with the Alpine

Trilogy, a continuous linkup of the north faces of the Eiger, Grandes Jorasses, and Matterhorn, which he soloed in four days, acing Christophe Profit by one day to the coveted enchainment. Profit, who was filmed for television, linked the peaks by helicopter; Češen, with more humble means, connected them by car and ski lift. Harder than that though, in 1987 Češen soloed No Siesta, a serious ice route on the Grandes Jorasses.

Češen's Himalayan initiation began in 1985, on the first ascent of 27,903-foot Yalung Kang, a subsidiary peak of Kangchenjunga. Češen was a member of a large Slovenian team that tackled the mountain in traditional expedition style, fixing ropes and establishing four camps with Sherpa support. After reaching the summit (Češen used oxygen to do so), his partner, Borut Bergrant, literally gave up and dropped off the mountain while descending. Češen survived a freezing bivouac by pacing back and forth on a ledge. The experience ravaged him—he lost thirty-five pounds—but it showed him he could survive ordeals of altitude.

A nineteen-hour solo of the regular route on 26,400-foot Broad Peak in 1986 was followed by an impressive solo attempt on K2, where he climbed 8,500 feet in seventeen hours before halting at about 26,000 feet. In 1987 he tried Lhotse Shar, beside Lhotse's south wall, with a big team. Afterward he always soloed his big routes. "If I'm aware that everything depends on me and only me, I can concentrate 100 percent," he said in a 1991 interview for the book *Beyond Risk*. "And if I have 100 percent concentration I can pull out of myself all the power and strength I have."

Winter 1989 saw him solo more desperates in Europe—the Red Pillar of the Brouillard on Mont Blanc and Modern Times, a 2,500-foot free route on the Marmolada, in the Dolomites. In the spring he went to Jannu's north face, an oft-tried flank of a 25,294-foot Nepalese tusk. This solo involved hard ice and verglassed 5.11 rock up an 8,000-foot wall. The skill and self-reliance it called for was staggering, as was Češen's speed: he bagged the route in a twenty-three-hour push, just a week after he reached base camp.

Češen said, in the 1991 *American Alpine Journal*, that "the limits of risk and impossibility are very different for different people." He was ready for Lhotse.

ČEŠEN'S LHOTSE ACCOUNT

The following is the story according to Češen's published accounts, which have been translated into several languages. He decided to climb the south wall by a variation of a route tried in 1981 by a force of twenty-two Yugoslavs, led by Ales Kunaver. On that team was Viki Groselj, and before Češen left for Lhotse, he had sat in Groselj's house, looking at his slides, and plotting a route.

The 1981 attempt had reached 26,740 feet. In 1985 Frenchmen Michel Fauquet and Vincent Fine got to 24,300 feet, alpine style, which convinced Česen that he could solo the route. He had studied it from Lhotse Shar in 1987, and he knew that survival depended on speed and on avoiding the daytime hours, when snowstorms engulf the face and avalanches thunder down. Indeed, in 1980, Nicolas Jaeger, a Frenchman, had disappeared on Lhotse Shar when an eight-day storm hit him after he had soloed to 26,500 feet.

Base camp was reached on April 15; then Česen sprang up Lhotse Shar four times, to 23,600 feet, to acclimatize. On April 22 he set off into the frozen night. He carried a forty-pound pack containing, according to his own report, a sleeping bag, bivouac sack, seven ice screws, ten pitons, 300 feet of six-millimeter rope, extra gloves, socks, and goggles, camera, two-way radio, food, and three liters of coffee—his only liquid. He took no stove.

Česen climbed for fifteen hours on 60-degree snowfields to the left of the 1981 route and then bivouacked at 24,600 feet as dawn lit the wall and rocks started ricocheting down. Early the next afternoon he continued up a couloir flanked by canyonlike walls and then bivouacked again at 26,900 feet. Above loomed the huge, loose cliff that had halted the 1981 team. On April 24 he started again at 5:00 A.M. in good weather. In the 1991 *American Alpine Journal* he described this section: "A snowy ramp led to a vertical step, mostly rock but covered here and there by snow and dubious ice. This would have been fine at 5000 meters but at 8000 meters it needed superhuman strength. It took a good three hours to gain some 60 m, some with artificial aid. . . . I fixed a part of my rope at the top of the step in preparation for the descent."

Next came "a snowy step, then a long traverse." Deep snow, wind, and storm hampered him. Finally the clouds parted, revealing the South Col and Everest, and Cho Oyu farther west. To the south was a sea of clouds. He described the last section by writing: "I had to dip a bit into a saddle and then up to the very top. It was 2:20 P.M. I called Camp on the walkie-talkie."

Below were Dr. Jankl Kokalj and Tomaz Ravnihar, who was making a film about Česen. Clouds prevented them from seeing Česen, but Ravnihar recalls his broadcast: "There's nowhere else to go! It seems that I've reached the summit!" Česen had blitzed the wall in forty-six hours.

Česen had previously decided to descend his route rather than escape down the easier, yet, for him, unknown west face and the notorious Khumbu Icefall, and had left his gear at his second bivouac. He reversed the crux rapidly and gives no details in any of his published accounts of the climbing from the summit back down to 25,600 feet. Amid worsening avalanche conditions, he located the piton anchors left from 1981 and rappelled into the night. His third bivouac was at 23,950 feet. Again he radioed camp, to check the weather. The forecast was for clearing skies, though Lhotse was engulfed in clouds and trembling from avalanches. "They say I'm cool headed but in that third bivouac my nerves nearly cracked," Česen wrote in the *AAJ* of his terror of being swept away. At midnight stars appeared and he continued down, reaching the bottom at 8:00 A.M. on April 25.

"I know that Lhotse has captured part of my soul, the part that yearns for uncertainty and true adventure," his article concluded. "It is a road where decisions have to be made and carried out constantly, a road similar to life, but where everything is happening on the very edge of life, an edge so sharp that it is often difficult to sense whether you are on the right side. For better or worse, from mountain tops you can see so much further, and the true limit is infinity. A man throws a rock—his desire—into the unknown, into the mist, and then he follows it."

THE HOMECOMING

Jannu had put Česen on the map, letting him quit his job as a steeplejack to become a professional climber, but Lhotse made him. It earned him a Slovenian national medal, and Messner nominated him for another $10,000 Snow Lion Prize. This amounted to a sizable sum when viewed in terms of the Slovenian economy. The Italian gear companies Scarpa, Great Escapes, and Camp hired him for technical advice and to endorse their products. His climbing club gave him a job organizing sport-climbing competitions. Česen also wrote a newspaper sports column, appeared on sports shows, made a climbing documentary in the United States, and authored a glossy book about his career.

Journalists flocked to Česen, too. When the American writer David Roberts visited his home in the foothills of the Julian Alps in 1990 to write the article "Sweetheart of the Himalaya" for *Outside*, he found Česen exuding "confidence and serenity," and he described him as "movie star handsome: six feet tall, lean but muscular." Writing for the British press, climber Stephen Venables found Česen "reserved, dour and intense," yet "quite genuine." Nicholas O'Connell, author of *Beyond Risk*, a book of interviews with climbers, met Česen shortly after Slovenia had violently expelled the Serbian and Croat armies and declared independence. O'Connell found he was "one of the best-known people in Slovenia." His generosity and his "Mr. Mum" devotion to his children, wife, and parents impressed O'Connell, as did his climbing talent (O'Connell watched him nearly flash a 5.13c sport route). Echoing many who know Česen, O'Connell remarked,

"He's the kind of person you'd never imagine could lie."

THE DOUBTS BEGIN

Gossip that Česen's ascents were fakes started in the alpine huts and bars of Chamonix soon after his return from Lhotse. Some people couldn't accept that Česen could climb so fast, so hard, so high, so alone, and get so famous without proof. Who had seen him do the Alpine Trilogy or his other solos in the Alps, they asked? Where was the photographic proof?

On Jannu his camera had frozen, and no one from base camp saw him on top. (Despite many inquiries by mail, phone, and fax, Dr. Kokalj was not available to answer my questions.) On K2 he had soloed the south face to the Abruzzi Ridge and then descended that route on a day when many climbers were going up and down, yet none saw Česen. As for Lhotse, aside from some unremarkable photographs showing hard-to-pinpoint views taken on the wall, and a summit photo showing Everest and the icy basin called the Western Cwm, published in July 1990 in the French magazine *Vertical*, his only proof was his word.

The wheels of doubt turned further. In Italy's *AlpiRando*, interviewer Mario Colonel asked Česen about Lhotse: "Your friends, did they see you reach the summit?" Caught off guard, Česen bridled, saying, "You ask as if you considered there was some doubt in the matter."

Within the skepticism ran more than a thread of envy. Česen's big routes were mostly climbs coveted by Frenchmen. The French take their alpinism seriously. Perhaps Česen's habit of snatching prizes from them was getting to be too much. "They don't like it when they're not the best . . . unfortunately," Česen jabbed.

He remained aloof from the speculators. "I know what I have done. I have always climbed for myself. It doesn't matter to me if you believe me, or if you don't," he said defiantly in a 1991 interview with *Vertical.*

THE RUSSIAN ASCENT OF LHOTSE

Doubts increased in November 1990 after a Russian team climbed the south face via a direct line to the summit. The Russian route was to the right of Česen's climb. Harder and steeper than Česen's line, it was done in heavy style: it took twenty-five men, two months of climbing, seven camps linked by thousands of feet of rope, and the use of oxygen above 23,000 feet to place Sergei Bershov and a severely frostbitten Vladimir Karatajev on top. After a press conference in Kathmandu, European magazines carried the news that the Russians had dropped a bombshell on Česen by claiming the first ascent of the wall.

155

An incredulous Pierre Beghin, France's most respected Himalayan al-pinist, who was there to try the wall that winter, reportedly exclaimed, "But what about Česen?"

"He didn't get to the summit," came the reply.

"But what about his photo of the Western Cwm?"

"You can't see the Western Cwm from the summit of Lhotse."

The photo to which Beghin referred had appeared in *Vertical* in the article "The Ascent of Tomo." Its caption read: "On the summit Tomo had just enough time to photograph the western cwm of Everest to authenticate his ascent." Surely the fact that Česen possessed this picture proved he had surmounted the south wall? For only from the top of Lhotse can one look north and see Everest. The Russians were said to have noted that between the point where Česen's route hit the summit crest and the actual summit was a 1,000-foot corniced ridge, an obstacle they doubted Česen had climbed, and something barely mentioned in Česen's published accounts.

Bershov was cagey about accusing Česen of lying, saying at the press conference, "I don't say he did not reach the top, but if he did he is a super-man." (Bershov repeated this comment to me during a phone interview, aided by an interpreter, in 1993.) In addition to Lhotse, Bershov has climbed a new route on Everest and has traversed Kangchenjunga, the world's third-highest peak—all in the company of big teams. He remains adamant about what he saw from Lhotse's summit: Everest's southern faces and tents on the South Col. He didn't see the icy basin of the Western Cwm, which from Lhotse's summit, he says, is blocked by the curvature of Lhotse's west face.

As for the traverse, I was surprised when Česen told me that he nego-tiated the ridge by climbing below its crest, on the south face, to escape the savage wind. I had photographed this ridge in 1988, through a telephoto lens, from Makalu base camp, and I saw a steep and fluted snow wall, over-hung by house-size cornices. Everything I've learned in the mountains has told me to avoid climbing beneath cornices or on slopes on the lee side of the prevailing winds; such areas are prone to windslab avalanches and are often covered in deep, soft snow. But that is where Česen says he climbed, rather than taking on the hard-packed snow on top of the ridge. The difficulties on the traverse were "trivial," Česen told me.

THE ACCUSER

In September 1990, when Česen was nominated for membership in the exclusive French climbing club, the Groupe de Haute Montagne (GHM), several members blocked his entry over the matter of proof. The most vociferous doubter was Ivano Ghirardini, a leading alpine soloist in the

1970s and early 1980s. He made the first Alpine Trilogy (spread over a winter), and his solos included the south face of Aconcagua and the first ascent of Mitre Peak in the Karakoram. He tried K2 and Makalu alone, then quit Himalayan climbing, disillusioned by the Asian bureaucracies that require permits for climbing mountains and that assign military liaison officers to accompany expeditions.

Prompted by the Russians' remarks, Ghirardini wrote a scathing polemic that appeared in *Vertical* in January 1991. "Alpinism in Perdition" berated Europe's glitzy mountaineering scene, with its televised and helicopter-supported ascents, sponsored climbers, and media-created heroes. Ghirardini argued that new routes were no longer done for the love of climbing, but were motivated by commercial pressures. So distrustful was he of the integrity of modern climbers that he proposed the creation of an international verifying organization for alpinism that would be "independent of sponsors, specialized magazines, and other commercial interests." The main thrust of the diatribe, though, was the accusation that Česen had lied about Lhotse and other solos for material gain.

"I always take the trouble," Ghirardini wrote, "to carry two simple cameras and several films with me on all my important solo climbs around the world. Then I can produce pictures for anyone who asks. I don't believe Česen is the poor, innocent Yugoslav climber he is made out to be. He is, above all, a professional alpinist, sponsored and sustained by manufacturers and newspapers. And as such, he is obliged to be irreproachable in the matter of his proof."

Ghirardini concluded that "without precise photos, close-ups that show him on the slope between 8000 meters and the summit, I don't believe in his climb."

Stephen Venables called Ghirardini's diatribe "the sour grapes of a bitter man who never quite made the top grade." Michael Kennedy, editor of *Climbing*, remembers trekking up the Baltoro Glacier in 1980, hearing rumors from porters of a fiery Frenchman up the valley who had battled with his porters, dismissed his liaison officer, and planned an illegal solo of K2. It was Ghirardini. Kennedy met him and recalls a "haunted, nervous figure." Soon after the meeting, Ghirardini came to blows with another liaison officer, who Ghirardini accused of indecently propositioning his wife. Was a firebrand like Ghirardini a reliable critic of Česen?

In February 1991 Česen defended himself against Ghirardini's attack in a letter in *Vertical*. "Mr. Ghirardini, you have gone too far," Česen began. He scoffed at Ghirardini's verifying commission and created a hilarious image of Ghirardini as president, following Česen by helicopter into the mountains

Viki Groselj's photo taken in 1981 on Lhotse's south face. Česen used this photo to support his claim to have soloed the route. A furor erupted when Groselj confronted the world with the news that the photo wasn't Česen's.

to spy on him. On a more serious note he rebuked the Russians' doubts by saying that they had no comprehension of modern alpinism, and that their old-style ascent represented "a step backward in Himalayan climbing." He implied that their criticisms were based on envy, since it took twenty-five Russians to climb a wall that he had soloed.

Česen also suggested that they might not have been able to see into the Western Cwm because, in autumn, a snow mushroom might cling to the summit, blocking the view; in spring, Česen said, this mushroom didn't exist. He also asked that since the Russians reportedly reached the summit at night, how could they have seen anything?

Bershov's book about Lhotse, *Let the Avalanche Go Around You*, seems to answer this question by showing a photo of Everest glowing with twilight. The caption states that the shot was taken 150 feet below Lhotse's summit.

Imprinted on the photo is the time signature: 4:16 P.M. The Western Cwm is not visible.

About his own ascent Česen was emphatic: "Before climbing the south face of Lhotse," he wrote in the letter, "I knew that if I succeeded there would be someone who would contest the ascent, judged to be almost impossible. That is why I spent a lot of energy taking photos on the route and on the summit." He also claimed "there are traces of my route because I left all my pitons."

Those words, printed in many magazines, would later return to haunt him.

DEFENDERS OF THE FAITH

Beghin, with Christophe Profit, failed on Lhotse in winter 1990. Rather than trashing Česen, though, they defended him. "I know the south wall of Lhotse," said Profit. "I've tried it three times. And I am convinced Česen climbed it—to the summit."

They had other climbs in common with Česen; Profit had been his "rival" for the Alpine Trilogy, and Beghin had tried Jannu's north face, but was beaten by cold and great difficulty. Beghin was familiar with big Himalayan solos, too, having climbed Kangchenjunga alone.

Beghin (killed in 1992 on Annapurna I) spoke for the conscience of climbing. In the French magazine *Montagne* he decried Ghirardini's attack: "I always believed that one of the golden rules of alpinism was respect for the word of other people. Everyone presumed innocent until proven guilty—as in law. Will we in the future have to produce proof of our achievements? If we, as alpinists, allow suspicion to intrude among ourselves, then we lose part of our soul. Alpinism will pass into the hands of the codifiers, the verifiers and all the other standardizers . . . You say Tomo Česen never got to the summit of Lhotse? Well, I would like to know who saw Hermann Buhl on top of Nanga Parbat, or Reinhold Messner on Everest after his solo climb of the north face? . . . It is my absolute conviction that on the dawn of 25 April 1990 he returned to the foot of Lhotse having accomplished one of the most beautiful exploits of contemporary alpinism."

The controversy was fed by European climbing magazines and even mainstream newspapers, such as the French daily *L'Equipe*, which covered the dispute. Ultimately, it became an embarrassment to French alpinism even though Česen was being defended by French climbers as well as being attacked by them. Quipped the noted Swiss climber Jean Troillet, a Česen supporter at the time, "Ah, the French . . . so good they are at slinging shit!"

The affair fizzled out in mid-1992. Česen was voted into the GHM, 159

Vertical's editor, Jean-Michel Asselin, declared in an editorial " Česen is no liar," and the troublemaking Ghirardini skulked back to the sidelines.

MESSNER'S DOUBTS

In summer 1992 Česen gave a lecture in Vienna to an audience of 1,000 admirers. He narrated slides, showed the film Ravnihar had made of him on Lhotse, and fielded questions. The host and interpreter was Reinhold Messner, who had nominated Česen for another $10,000 Snow Lion Prize. Although Messner was arguably Česen's greatest fan, this was their first meeting. It went badly for Česen.

Messner detected strange inconsistencies in Česen's tale of Lhotse. He showed photos of perfect weather, yet spoke of storms. Ravnihar's film (described by Stephen Venables as "a farce, like a propaganda film") showed no climbing on Lhotse. Few pictures showed landmarks on the face, or Česen climbing. Messner suspected that some photos came from Česen's 1987 attempt on Lhotse Shar.

Messner was baffled when Česen said he had left no pitons on the wall above 27,000 feet, either for ascending or descending. "I could not imagine descending this cliff without belays," Messner said later. In earlier statements, Česen had said he had left his pitons behind as anchors. When the audience asked Česen how he acclimatized so quickly (he summited nine days after reaching base camp, while most alpinists need a month to adapt to 8,000 meters), Česen said he had been in Tibet earlier. Messner later learned that Česen has never visited Tibet.

But a film clip of Česen returning to camp after the climb troubled Messner the most. "I've never seen a climber so fresh after an 8,000-meter peak," Messner told me in autumn 1993. "You can see in the eyes and face when someone has done something difficult at high altitude. Here I saw a fresh young man coming down a hill."

After the lecture Messner suggested to Česen that he could escape all the doubts about his ascent by climbing a major route with partners, "to show the world you can do it." Česen replied, "Nobody [else] can do these things. I must do them alone."

"From all his answers I had the feeling there was something wrong," Messner says now. He decided not to award Česen the Snow Lion Prize.

THE LHOTSE PHOTOS

With ten 8,000-meter peaks under his belt (as of 1994), Viki Groselj may soon join the handful of people to have climbed the fourteen highest peaks. In February 1993 he was preparing an exhibit of climbing literature for his climbing club when he came across the three-year-old *Vertical*, featuring Česen's Lhotse article. Groselj hadn't seen this issue before. Slovenians, he said, look to German and English magazines for information.

Groselj was surprised to see the Lhotse photographs because when Česen returned to Slovenia in 1990 he publicly announced that he had none. "My word is my only proof," he said, and, being a national hero, he was believed. Accordingly, no meaningful photographs from Lhotse ever appeared in Slovenia—not even in Česen's autobiography, *Solo*. This book shows only what appear to be staged shots of Česen climbing the glacier near base camp and telephoto shots of him very low on an unidentifiable, easy-looking couloir. Since the wall is brightly sunlit and the snow is suncupped in these photos, while he embarked on his climbs late in the day, when the wall is shadowed, it seems to me unlikely that these are from his Lhotse climb. Furthermore, Česen is lightly dressed, carrying only a small pack; he is not even wearing gaiters. In fact, most of the climbing pictures of Česen in circulation at the time were staged shots for advertising and promotional purposes. By comparison, photos from the Lhotse attempt by Beghin and Profit show a terrifyingly steep wall.

Groselj, who regarded Česen as "the genius child of mountaineering," knew that Česen had told journalists at the time of Ghirardini's attack that he had taken photos, but trusting Česen, Groselj had never probed this apparent contradiction. He experienced a feeling of déjà vu about the photos in *Vertical*, though. At home, he sorted through his slides and made an astonishing discovery: Two slides attributed to Česen were his. "I nearly fell down," Groselj told me.

One photo showed a fog-shrouded cliff at 27,000 feet, snapped by Groselj on the 1981 south face attempt. The other was the shot of the Western Cwm. *Vertical* had accidentally printed this image in reverse. "I took this picture," said Groselj, "500 feet below the summit, on April 30, 1989, when I climbed the west face [of Lhotse]."

How did Česen get the photographs? Groselj told me that two days after Česen returned from Nepal in 1990 he borrowed them from Groselj's wife, Cveta, while Groselj was climbing in Russia. Česen wanted them to show his Italian sponsors where his route went, he said to Cveta. At no time did he suggest to her that he would present the slides as his own.

"Since I trusted him as a good acquaintance of our family, I let him choose whatever he required. He returned them a few days later," said Cveta.

Now Groselj's faith in Česen was shattered. He also suspected that a third photo, of a cornice described by Česen as being at 24,600 feet, did not belong to Česen.

"It isn't my photo, but I am sure that Tomo got it from one of the other 1981 expedition members," Groselj told me.

Groselj had taken an identical shot on the south face, 1,500 feet lower. He found it inconceivable that this lump of snow had not changed shape in nine years. He also noted that Česen had described his route as being 150 feet left of Ales Kunaver's 1981 attempt, meaning that he could not have photographed the cornice from the position implied in the image. "This means that Tomo doesn't have any photo that is his, above 23,000 feet on Lhotse," says Groselj.

(After publication of this article, I received a letter from the wife of the late Ales Kunaver. Mrs. Kunaver berated me for smearing Česen and, by extension, all Slovenian climbers, and she told me that she had found Česen so trustworthy that before he went to Lhotse she had opened up her husband's enormous collection of slides from Lhotse and let Tomo "borrow what he wanted." Could this explain how Česen came by the unexplained image from high on Lhotse?)

GROSELJ, THE WHISTLE-BLOWER

Groselj confronted Česen and demanded an explanation. Česen admitted he had borrowed the photos, but he maintained that he had never claimed them as his own. Česen blamed *Vertical*'s editors for wrongly attributing Česen's name to the pictures. Why did he submit the photos to *Vertical* without Groselj's permission in the first place? And, if it was a mistake, why didn't he alert anyone when they appeared in *Vertical*? He had excuses—the same ones he would soon tell others—but they did not convince Groselj.

Groselj told his climbing club of his discovery, but his compatriots urged him to keep quiet. Česen was the unofficial climbing ambassador of Slovenia, and embarrassing him would, again, shame all Slovenian climbers. Still, despite the criticism of his club, Groselj went public with the story in April 1993, prior to his own departure to climb K2.

Česen had to respond. In newspapers, on TV, and in a letter to the Slovenian Mountaineering Union, he denied any foul play regarding his ascent or the use of Groselj's photos. He told the Slovenian public "I have no photographs from the summit. I have said clearly from the beginning that I don't possess any."

Česen had indeed told Slovenian climbers that in 1990, but some people remembered his defense against Ghirardini and the Russians in 1991. In *Vertical*, as well as the *Indian Mountaineer*, Italy's *Revista de la Montagne*, in Slovenian newspapers, and in *Beyond Risk*, he referred to a summit photo (now known to be Groselj's) that he said proved his ascent. "Many people have seen this photograph," Cesen told an interviewer in *Vertical*. "It poses no problem, it is at the disposal of all who wish to examine it . . ."

One of the few to see Cesen's photos was Stephen Venables, who visited Cesen's house in 1990 after Lhotse. Venables recalls that Cesen showed him about twenty slides taken on the Lhotse trip. None were action shots of him climbing. Venables remembers that Cesen was "very vague" about the final day of climbing, but when he produced a photo looking into the Western Cwm, Venables assumed "he must have topped out from the wall." Throughout 1991, in Britain's *High* magazine, Venables defended Cesen against his detractors. Venables had no idea that Cesen had announced in Slovenia that he had no photos from Lhotse, or that the summit photo would become so controversial.

ENTER *VERTICAL*

Dominique Vulliamy, a production assistant at *Vertical*, recalls Cesen as being distraught when he visited her home in Grenoble in summer 1993. He had driven from Slovenia in the hope of clearing up the mess he was in by persuading Vulliamy that the fault lay with her. The problem was, he said, a "misunderstanding due to the language barrier," and he offered Vulliamy a complex scenario. In 1989, after Jannu, he had proposed to her an article about Slovenian climbing. One climber he suggested writing about was Viki Groselj. Cesen never wrote the article, but he said that Vulliamy had phoned him after Lhotse and asked him to come to France with photos from his ascent, as well as photos for the story about Slovenian alpinists, in which she remained interested. That was why he submitted Groselj's slides. He blamed Vulliamy for accidentally "mixing" them with his own.

Vulliamy regards that account as a smokescreen: "The photos were never presented as being Groselj's. His name was not on them. And we never discussed, at that time, any other articles. How could it happen that the only photos he gave us by Groselj were from high on Lhotse?"

Vertical's editor, Jean-Michel Asselin, also found Cesen's explanation hard to swallow. In January 1991—six months after the controversial photos were published and at the height of Ghirardini's attacks—Asselin had quizzed Cesen about an inconsistency in his Lhotse article: Cesen had reported fog on the summit, begging the question: how could he have photographed the Western Cwm? Cesen, Asselin says, explained that fog shrouded only the south side, and not Everest, "so I could take that photo." In Asselin's opinion, this would have been an opportunity to inform *Vertical* of the mistaken use of Groselj's photo. But Cesen raised no alarms, rather he implied ownership of the photo.

Another thing troubled Asselin. In 1990, when he noticed that the summit shot was a duplicate, he had asked Česen for the original. Česen told Asselin it was "stolen at a lecture in Milan." Yet after the revelation by Groselj, Česen told *Vertical* that the lost photo was not the Groselj photo, but another one, which Česen took just below the summit.

Ironically, *Vertical*, which more than any magazine had built Česen into a star, has now adopted the position that Česen attempted Lhotse but did not reach the summit. "Knowing the challenge of the wall," said Vulliamy, "he decided to play his cards as well as he could, by using someone else's photos to prove an ascent he did not make."

THE DOSSIER

Summer 1993 got worse for Česen. In June, Messner announced that he no longer believed him, that he was retracting Česen's Snow Lion Prize, and that he planned to "erase his name" from his books. Then, in July, a dossier of evidence against Česen, stamped with the seal of a legal interpreter appointed by Slovenia's Secretariat for Justice and General Administration, began circulating throughout Europe. Its author was Viki Groselj.

The dossier compares Česen's conflicting comments between 1990 and 1993. Citing numerous print and TV sources, Groselj shows that in 1991 in France and elsewhere Česen had said he "spent much energy taking photographs on the face and on the summit." In 1993, however—after the outbreak of the controversy over the photographs—Česen denied ever taking summit photos. In an interview with the Slovenian sports magazine *Ekipa*, Česen was asked, "You did have a camera with you, why didn't you take photographs?" He replied, "I could go on explaining for an hour why not . . . but I simply didn't." Recall that in Slovenia in 1990 he had told the press he had no camera.

"He is getting mixed up into new lies," said Cveta Groselj, who, with her husband, has considered making an official submission of the dossier to the UIAA, the influential pan-European climbing association.

GHIRARDINI RETURNS

Česen's plight inspired Ghirardini to pen a blistering I-told-you-so attack on Česen, in September 1993 in *Vertical*, in which he charged that Česen had also lied about the Alpine Trilogy and K2. Ghirardini claimed that the weather was bad on the dates when Česen claimed he soloed the Eiger and Matterhorn, and he did not believe he could make such rapid solos at night under such conditions. He also said that Česen had altered his story about the times and circumstances of the routes. As for K2, Ghirardini regarded it "totally unlikely" that he could have eluded the many climbers ascending and descending the Abruzzi Ridge.

Ghirardini accused Česen and his sponsors of profiting from fraud. Česen should be "placed in the hands of the Slovenian police," Ghirardini said, and any photos he has from Lhotse should be "examined by a criminal laboratory" to check the frame numbers against the sequence of events. He further charged that Česen is accountable for the lives of less experienced climbers who try to emulate his alleged feats and get into trouble.

While Ghirardini's questions about the Alpine Trilogy deserve answers, Česen did provide an alibi for K2. Tomaz Jamnick, co-leader of Česen's K2 expedition, confirmed to me on the phone that he saw Česen reach the Abruzzi Ridge on K2 on August 4 and spoke with him by radio.

ČESEN'S LAST STAND

With support for him lagging and the press turning against him even in Slovenia, Česen raised his last defense in his claim of climbing Lhotse in the form of an entry in the 1993 *American Alpine Journal*. A month after Česen's ascent, Americans Wally Berg and Scott Fischer had climbed Lhotse's west face. Afterward, in Kathmandu, Berg was interviewed by Elizabeth Hawley, a Reuters correspondent. The meeting led Berg to write a "personal note," not for publication, to *AAJ* editor H. Adams Carter, but Carter published it anyway.

The note says that after the interview with Hawley, "we verified that Česen had reached the summit of Lhotse. As I recall, we were sure he had been there based on his description of the summit area, which Liz related to us a few days after she had interviewed him. Among other things, he described seeing an old orange oxygen bottle on a small platform just below the summit, which is a small snow cone." Berg also noted that the final snow cone was so precarious that he and Fischer belayed each other up it. Česen had told Hawley that he had decided against standing on top of it, which Berg thought was a smart move for someone without a rope.

Česen says Berg's observations prove his ascent. *Vertical* called it "good news for Česen." Messner dismisses it: "There have been fifty ascents of Lhotse. Česen could have asked someone what was on top. Why didn't he take a photo of the oxygen bottle?"

Unfortunately for Česen, neither Fischer, Berg, nor Hawley kept notes of those conversations about the summit, and at the time of my interview their memories were hazy. Fischer (who died on Everest in 1996) no longer recalled seeing any oxygen bottle at all. The Americans' summit photos don't show the oxygen bottle, either. Bershov, who followed Česen's final 150 feet to the summit six months later, says he did not see an oxygen bottle.

Berg stands by his original statement, though, saying in October 1993, "I recall walking out of the conversation with Liz Hawley feeling I had confirmed Česen's ascent." And Carter, who visited Česen in Kranj in 1990 after Lhotse and saw his photos, said that despite the controversy since then, he still had great faith in Česen's integrity. "I have known him from well before the time he became famous," said Carter. "He made a bad mistake using Groselj's photos, but I think he completed the Lhotse climb." (While researching this story in 1993, I loaned Carter all my reference material and this manuscript. Said Carter, after examining it, "I'm not putting a thing about this in the *AAJ*." It seemed to me that Carter did not want to sully the pages of the *AAJ* with this controversy, despite its importance. Moreover, it was clear that he personally liked Česen.)

ČESEN SPEAKS

When I spoke with Česen in October his tone was calm, although he had endured weeks of bad press. He spoke convincingly, though his version of events holds that many people I had interviewed are involved in a conspiracy to discredit him.

When I asked him to explain how Groselj's photos had ended up in *Vertical* with his name on them, he repeated his story of being asked by Dominique Vulliamy to bring some slides of Groselj's to illustrate an article separate from Česen's Lhotse piece. Česen claims he told Cveta Groselj precisely the same thing at the same time. He took the slides "to help Groselj" get published in *Vertical*. He also says the slides were marked with Groselj's name. Whatever happened next was due to mistakes by *Vertical*, which, Česen says, the staff refuses to admit.

Asked why it took three years before he admitted that *Vertical* had erroneously included Groselj's pictures with his article, he said, "this was my mistake," and explained that at the time he was worried by Ghirardini's accusations and thought it would look bad if he raised the matter then. Did he take photos from the top of Lhotse? He answered no, then added, "not directly from the top."

As for Messner's statement that Česen had told him in Vienna that he'd acclimatized in Tibet, Česen replied, "I never said this. I have never been to Tibet." Česen explained his spectacular speed on Lhotse and his ability to acclimatize from base camp to 8,000 meters in only nine days to rigorous training, which, he says, most alpinists don't do. His acclimatization technique is, in fact, somewhat supported by other ascents. Viki Groselj himself reached the 26,398-foot summit of Shishapangma in Tibet just twelve days after reaching base camp. However, the comparison between the two peaks must end there; the additional 1,500 feet of height to Lhotse's summit, and Lhotse's more difficult terrain, make it an infinitely harder climb.

Česen was enigmatic about the origin of the 1993 controversy, blaming it on "the fact that I don't have a good relationship with the expeditions commission in Slovenia." He says the trouble began when he appeared on a TV sports show and criticized Groselj's plan to climb all the 8,000-meter peaks by saying it was not at the forefront of alpinism. Česen suggested to me that Groselj and Slovenian Mountaineering Union President Tone Skarja, who are big wheels in the expeditions commission, have a mafia-like monopoly on the funding of Slovenian expeditions, and that Groselj was trying to silence Česen by publicly accusing him of stealing his slides and faking his ascent. "I think that these guys are trying to make something together," Česen said mysteriously.

As for the burden of proof, Česen says, "I'm satisfied with this," citing Berg's letter in the *AAJ*. Otherwise, he says, "the future will show I climbed Lhotse."

ASSUMPTIVE REALITIES

Tomo Česen is not the first climber to be accused—rightly or wrongly—of lying. The more I explored this affair, the more it reminded me of the controversy surrounding Cesare Maestri, the Italian who claimed the first ascent of Patagonia's Cerro Torre in 1959. Climbers have long contested this climb, and subsequent expeditions have found no traces of Maestri's ascent. In fact, on a subsequent ascent of the lower part of Maestri's route, American climber Jim Donini and his partners found masses of equipment and fixed ropes a few pitches off the ground, but thereafter signs of an ascent ended.

Nevertheless, Maestri still insists that he and Toni Egger battled their way up and down a futuristic route on the north face of that wind-lashed Patagonian tower. Like Česen, Maestri lacks witnesses and photos, as Egger disappeared in an avalanche during the descent taking the camera with him. Maestri cannot prove he climbed Cerro Torre, nor can anyone categorically prove he didn't. Maybe, for Maestri, the ascent has entered the realm of assumptive reality—he has said he climbed Cerro Torre for so long that he believes it, regardless of what the truth is.

Closer to home, I remembered the case of a friend who became caught in a web of deception. He and another climber got high on a Himalayan peak, yet did not make the summit. Afterward they decided it would enhance their careers to say they had succeeded.

167

This tormented my friend's conscience, but once the lie was uttered publicly, there was no turning back. When they published photographs, they added a shot of them standing gloriously on the summit of a peak not in the Himalaya, but in the Alps. People sensed something was amiss and asked questions. Finally my friend admitted to his wife—he had lied even to her—that the claim was a fiction. Although there was a flap at the time, few people remember the incident now.

But what about Tomo Česen? Did it matter if he was a fraud? If he had claimed any climb other than Lhotse's south wall, it probably didn't, but great climbers had died vying for it. Messner had dubbed the wall "a climb for the year 2000," and *Vertical* had termed the awaited ascent "an orgiastic highpoint in the history of alpinism."

Tomaz Ravnihar, the filmmaker at Lhotse base camp, who, it has been suggested, is part of a pro-Česen conspiracy to fake the ascent, explained away the scandal by saying in a letter to me that "Tomo's success was too enormous and this is the reason why mountaineering has suddenly become a matter of business and the reason Česen needs evidence."

Climbing has changed since Maestri and my friend told their stories. Back then, only honor was at stake. Today, climbing is more commercial. Reputations must be sustained to impress sponsors. For a handful of climbers, there is money and glory to be had. It may not be much money, and the glory is fleeting, but it can mean the difference between climbing for a living or digging ditches.

AFTER THE STORM

By the time the Tomo Česen affair played itself out in late 1993 the players were tired from a long feud. *Fokus* magazine in Slovenia had called Česen's climb "a swindle." The BBC had reported it as a potential hoax. Yet Česen remained adamant that he had made his climbs. "I really don't care anymore," he sighed. "If people don't believe me, that's their problem."

Groselj was frustrated that the Slovenian Mountaineering Union was blaming *Vertical* for an editorial error and had exonerated Česen of intentional wrongdoing. "I feel I am in a lonely place," Groselj said, wondering if the criticism he had endured for trying to topple Slovenia's icon of alpinism was worth it.

There are four possibilities in the Tomo Česen affair. Maybe Česen summited on Lhotse and, fearing that his lack of proof would undermine his claim, tried to pass other people's photos as his own. Or maybe he got high on the wall, backed off it, yet made the claim anyway. Or maybe he sat behind a rock beneath Lhotse and tricked his friends at base camp with a false radio message. Or maybe an elaborate conspiracy is afoot. I have to admit, the two men who were at base camp—one to document the ascent on film— have not advanced any information or provided any film or photos that show Česen doing anything on Lhotse. There really is no way of knowing, short of climbing that awesome wall and searching for the pitons Česen told me he left above 27,000 feet. And I'll be damned if I'm going to do that.

As this book was going to press, the May 1998 issue of *Climbing* reported that two very capable French alpinists, François Marsigny and Olivier Larios "took three days to repeat No Siesta (VII- 6a A2), a serious 38-pitch, 3900-foot route on the north face of the Grandes Jorasses near Chamonix. Prior to this No Siesta had only two reported ascents. The first, a three-day push by the Slovakians Jan Provaznik and Stanislav Gledjura in 1986; the second by Česen, who said he soloed it the following year in 14 hours. According to Marsigny, No Siesta has lots of hard climbing, bad rock, poor protection . . . . After taking seven hours to climb the last four pitches, however, he was convinced that no one could solo the route at the rate—22 minutes per pitch—Česen claimed in 1987."

Everest from the south.

Stealing Everest

The Fall and Rise of Lydia Bradey

The last time I saw Lydia Bradey we were stumbling through a Kathmandu alleyway, pursued by a fleet of fare-hopeful rickshaws that had tailed us from the Rum Doodle Tavern, where we and a throng of alpinists had been indulging in the pre-expedition ritual of imbibing the technicolored cocktails unique to that city. It was 1988. She was on her way to Everest; I was on my way to Makalu. Heading back to our hotels, we lamented the hangovers we were in for and joked that the hazy mental aftermath of this drunken night would be good training for her audacious high-altitude mission: to become the first woman to climb Everest without bottled oxygen.

In the decade after Reinhold Messner's and Peter Habeler's first oxygen-less ascent in 1978, twenty-four men had climbed *au naturel* to the 29,028-foot summit. Of those, four had died while descending. If Bradey survived her climb, she stood to become, arguably, the greatest female alpinist of all time. After six Himalayan expeditions, Bradey had the know-how, and coming to Everest fresh from unsuccessfully attempting K2, the world's second-highest peak, her body was honed to climbing in rarified air. If self-confidence was a measure of climbing prowess, then Bradey, a brash, twenty-seven-year-old New Zealander with a mane of bleached dreadlocks and a sapphire embedded Hindu-style on the side of her nose, left little doubt in those around her that she had the pluck to climb the Big E.

But the oxygenless, witnessless, solo she subsequently claimed was dismissed as a hoax by her teammates and the New Zealand press. That in-dignity, and a two-year ban from expeditioning in the Himalayan kingdom by Nepal's Ministry of Tourism, ended her high-altitude career at the height of her powers. Bradey's struggle to convince the world that she did climb Everest, and her argument with her teammates—dubbed Lydiagate by alpin-ists—remains one of climbing's great controversies.

Lydiagate, and Lydia Bradey, had fascinated me for several years. Did she lie about reaching Everest's summit, as her teammates claimed? Or, as Bradey claims, was she framed by her male counterparts because they were jealous that she succeeded where they had failed? Even today, only one woman has matched her alleged feat: Britain's Alison Hargreaves, who climbed Everest oxygenless in 1995, but died a few weeks later while descending from K2's summit. Alison became famous in Britain after making what is generally re-garded as the second female oxygenless ascent of Everest, but the first that can be confirmed. (Alison affirmed to me, in Tibet, that she "strongly felt" that Lydia had reached Everest's summit). Ironically, though, in the case of Lydia Bradey, the woman who claimed female alpinism's biggest leap for-ward got nothing but agony and acrimony for her trouble.

I caught up with Bradey, then thirty-four, in a cafe in Boulder, Colo-rado, in 1994 while she was visiting America. The terms of our meeting were different from that night of bar-hopping in Kathmandu. This time, a tape re-corder instead of a Rum Doodle cocktail sat between us. It seemed like a good time to interview her. With many climbing historians suddenly supporting her climb, based on important new evidence, she feels vindicated at last.

These days, her dreadlocks are replaced with a tomboy haircut, and the sapphire in her nose is gone, though her taste in fashion remains punkish. She resides in Auckland, New Zealand, and, at the time of our meeting, was living with a climber/engineer and rock climbing on weekends while finish-ing a physical therapy degree—deep roots for a woman whose appetite for climbing kept her living out of a rucksack and inside tents pitched beneath the world's ranges throughout the 1980s.

"I never really gave up climbing," she says, stirring a latte while ex-plaining her shift to academia. "I just channeled my energy into something else." She talks of her future, which includes graduation from physio school, a comeback to Himalayan climbing after a long hiatus, and maybe even an-other stab at K2.

But it's the past I want to talk about, and I steer the chat to Everest. Bluntly, I ask her if she really climbed it. Her "yes" is abrupt, final. I switch on the tape recorder, and she begins describing her controversial climb to Everest's summit.

Greg Child

IT WAS 2:00 A.M. ON OCTOBER 14, 1988, when Bradey emerged from a storm-battered tent on Everest's South Col. Wincing against the cold, she clipped crampons to her boots, swung on her backpack, and headed alone toward the apogee of the Earth's crust, 3,153 feet above her.

Her route—the Southeast Ridge—had been pioneered in 1953 by her countryman, Edmund Hillary, and Sherpa Tenzing Norgay. If all went well, she would become Everest's 240th summiter, and the first Kiwi woman to the top. There was, however, a glitch in Bradey's bold plan: she didn't have a permit for the route she was climbing.

Days before, climbing without Bradey, her New Zealand teammates—Rob Hall, Gary Ball, and Bill Atkinson, who had a permit for the Southwest Face, yet were attempting the South Pillar (a route for which they had no permit)—had quit their climb, unsuccessful. But, still feeling fit, and having fallen out with the three men, Bradey headed onto the Southeast Ridge—the so-called easiest way up Everest, called the "yak route" by Sherpas. Technically, both parties were violating a decree of the Ministry of Tourism in Kathmandu forbidding climbers from attempting routes they haven't paid a fee for, and from switching routes during an expedition. In 1987 Bradey had gotten away with an illegal ascent in Pakistan. This was nothing new; climbers often make "under the table" ascents. In her rebellious alpine philosophy, mountaineering permits were just bits of paper, and the bureaucrats who made the rules were corrupt stuffed-shirts who knew zip about climbing. Everest's summit was close, and she believed she wouldn't be bothering anyone by stealing onto the Southeast Ridge.

Starglow bouncing off the snows guided her through a junkyard of spent oxygen bottles and the skeletal wreckage of tents flapping in a subzero wind gusting out of Tibet. Three hundred feet from her camp she met four Spaniards, four Sherpas, and a Frenchman emerging from tents and plugging their face masks into oxygen bottles.

"Hey, mate," she said in a cheery Kiwi twang, "do ya mind if I tag along?"

Baffled by her unexpected arrival, they stared, until Ang Rita, a Sherpa, answered, "No problem."

The climbers headed up in single file. Unaided by oxygen, Bradey lagged behind. She passed tattered ropes, bucket-size bootsteps, even holes to slot her ice ax into. These were the leftovers of a season of record-breaking feats: Frenchman Jean Marc Boivin had parapented from summit to glacier in eleven minutes, and Marc Batard had blitzed the Southeast Ridge in twenty-four hours, while Stacey Alison, using oxygen, had become America's first woman atop Everest.

172

At 4:30 A.M. the Frenchman and two Sherpas hurried by her, shouting, "We go down." Minutes later she discovered what had alarmed them: the corpse of one of two Sherpas, either Lhakpa Sonam or Pasang, who had disappeared a day earlier. Judging by his twisted body, Bradey assumed he had slipped near the south summit, 2,000 feet above. "There's nothing I can do for him," she thought, and climbed on.

Wind increased with daybreak. She took her camera from her pack to snap the Himalayan sunrise, but when she pressed the button, the shutter jammed, frozen. Later she would wish she had carried a functioning camera.

Wading through an atmosphere containing a quarter the oxygen of sea level, Bradey watched morning turn to afternoon; then, at 2:30 P.M. she surmounted the south summit, a subsidiary bump on the ridge 354 feet below Everest's apex. There she remet the Spaniards. Jeronimo Lopez, Nil Bohigas, Luis Giver, and Sherpas Nima Rita and Ang Rita had summited at 12:45 P.M. Now they were jammed onto the south summit, making a rope stretcher to lower Sergio Martinez, who, feeling ill, had waited on the south summit while his partners summited. When they returned, he rasped, "I am dying," and slumped into an altitude-induced coma.

Squatting in the snow, Bradey watched the Spaniards mount the rescue. Amid the babble of Spanish being shouted into a radio, she heard Lopez mention her name.

"Say nothing about me," she told him, aware that the less said about her illegal ascent, the better. But Lopez had already broadcast her arrival at the south summit to base camp, and everyone down there knew Lydia Bradey was within gunshot of Everest's crown. Before Lopez left, he advised Bradey that the hour—3:00 P.M.—was late. To be overtaken by night would be fatal. Putting his face near hers, he shouted over the pummeling wind, "You will die if you keep going!"

Bradey eyed the obstacles ahead: a sharp ridge followed by the Hillary Step, a forty-foot cliff. It looked daunting, "like a separate mountain." The snail-like pace and dreamy mental state of oxygenless climbing worried her. No woman had been this high without "juice." She was breaking new ground. But, she knew, too, that success was only an hour or two away. "I go on," she announced.

After the Spaniards departed, she crossed a ridge so narrow that daylight filtered through the row of footsteps left by the thirty summiters who had preceded her that season. She recalls a thin rope dangling over the Hillary Step, steps kicked into the snow beside it, and then a gasping plod along a ridge. The six-by-three-foot summit, which she says she reached between 4:30 P.M. and 5:30 P.M. (she was unsure, having lost her watch), was an austere snowdome. In the wind-raked minute she spent on top, she saw Makalu and Cho Oyu poking through a morass of cumulus. "I've done it," she thought. "It's a fact."

Lydia Bradey had stolen the summit of Everest.

BUT 10,000 FEET BELOW, AT EVEREST BASE CAMP, Bradey's erstwhile team members were mad as hell. They had been monitoring the Spaniards' radio all day, hoping she would abandon her illegal summit bid.

Rob Hall, a lanky mountain guide with a bespectacled, professorial appearance, was chief of Bradey's group. They shared their Southwest Face permit with seven Slovaks, of whom Ivan Fiala was supreme leader. It was a symbiotic arrangement: the Slovaks needed dollars; the Kiwis needed a shoe-in on crowded Everest. But, admits Hall, his men and the Slovaks had bickered endlessly and nearly brawled over finances. Exhausted after their failed summit attempt and weary from haggling, Hall's men were anxious to leave.

From the outset, only the Slovaks planned to tackle the Southwest Face. Hall's group felt they stood little chance on a wall so difficult that, for the first ascent in 1976, it required the muscle of seventy-eight Brits and Sherpas using 180 bottles of oxygen and 6,000 feet of rope. So, Hall's group had moved to the South Pillar, a few hundred feet to the left of the Southeast Ridge. Like Bradey, they didn't have permission to change routes, but the Korean team who had fixed ropes up the start of the South Pillar did not challenge them about it. In reality, the Koreans had not climbed the South Pillar at all—more accurately, they had used its start to traverse onto the Southeast Ridge at a point just above the South Col, at 25,600 feet. Bradey insists that Hall and Ball, too, "were aiming to repeat this route." Hall disagreed when I interviewed him, calling her accusation that he also was involved in an "illegal" climb a "red herring." He said his climb was strictly on the Southwest Face and he "had no intention of sneaking onto the Hillary route."

Hair-splitting aside, since Kathmandu officials had rejected Hall's earlier request to switch to the Southeast Ridge, and since expeditions already at grips with that route had, said Hall, complained about Bradey's uninvited presence there, Hall regarded Bradey's choice to splinter from his group as an act of mutiny. Nor could his group stop her. "Short of tying her up with a rope and dragging her from the mountain against her will, there was little we could do to make her come down," said Gary Ball. As for the Spaniards, their permit was for the West Ridge, but at the last minute they'd bought their way onto the Southeast Ridge by paying Kathmandu authorities an additional peak fee.

To Hall, the translation he heard of Lopez's 2:30 P.M. radio broadcast—which, Hall claimed to me, said that Bradey was below the south summit, but was climbing higher despite being exhausted—meant trouble. That night, when the radio reported her back on the South Col, claiming to have summited, he didn't feel the elation an expedition leader experiences when a team member succeeds. New Zealanders regard Everest as their own, thanks to Hillary's ascent, and Hall's trip had received national support and media coverage. He feared that Nepalese authorities would blame him for her rogue ascent and ban him from other Everest bids for ten years—a risk he was unwilling to take.

With that in mind, he decided to apply drastic spin control and hotfoot it to Kathmandu. There, he would issue a statement describing a very different scenario about Bradey's climb, with a set of times that made it impossible for her to have summited.

And so began the bitter saga of Lydiagate.

THE DAY THAT BRADEY DESCENDED FROM THE SOUTH COL, Geoff Tabin, an American who had summited two weeks earlier, encountered Hall, Ball, and Atkinson as they were decamping.

"I thought it was ridiculous," recalls Tabin. "I said, 'What if Lydia needs a rescue?' They replied, 'It's not our responsibility. If she gets into trouble, it's her fault.'"

When she reached base camp on October 16, Bradey found that the New Zealanders had departed, leaving no message, and had taken most of the remaining expedition cash. Though she was disturbed that they had "abandoned" her before she was off the mountain—which, in the minds of some climbers, is to break an unwritten, yet cardinal rule of alpinism—Bradey was not totally surprised.

Relations between Bradey and Hall and Ball had been souring for weeks. Among the baggage they brought to Everest from K2, the expedition's first goal, was a rift that began over a "passionate affair" Bradey had had with a member of another K2 expedition. When she started climbing with her lover's team on K2, she believes Hall and Ball felt jilted, and they in turn had spurned her. On Everest, the mood between her and the men had become so polarized that she felt it was impossible to climb with them. Her choice to climb the Southeast Ridge, against Hall's wishes, scuttled the last shred of camaraderie between them.

But these squabbles quickly paled to insignificance. At base camp, Ivan Fiala, the Slovak leader, congratulated Bradey on her ascent and then told her that Dusan Becik, Jaroslav Jasko, Peter Bozik, and Jozef Just—her "soul mates" at base camp—were in dire trouble on the Southwest Face.

The Slovaks, climbing in a virtually gearless, all-or-nothing alpine-style mode, had slowed to a crawl at the difficult rock band at 26,250 feet and had had to bivouac in the open. On October 17, Just radioed base camp that he had summited and that the group was now struggling down the ridge that Bradey had earlier climbed. All were weak; some were blind from their extended exposure to extreme altitude. After a last call from another gearless bivy at 27,200 feet, hurricane winds hit Everest. The men were never heard from again. Their deaths brought the season's fatalities on Everest to nine. It was a sad finale to Bradey's grand tour of the Himalaya's highest. Forty-eight hours earlier, on the South Col, she had basked in pride when a Sherpa watching her walk into the tent encampment declared, "Strong woman." Now, though, the exhiliration of her climb was quickly fading. The following day she tearfully packed her tent to begin the trek home. Only then did she begin to consider what trouble might lie ahead for her.

WHEN BRADEY REACHED KATHMANDU TWO WEEKS LATER, Hall was already in New Zealand. At her hotel, the phone rang incessantly. Journalists from New Zealand and Europe badgered her with questions.

"They asked, 'Did you really get to the summit?' 'At what time?' 'What did you see up there?'"

Bradey sensed that the reporters didn't believe her. Then a sympathetic journalist faxed her a front-page story from the *Christchurch Star*. In it, Hall said, "It was simply not possible that she made it to the summit." He described weather conditions during her climb as "horrendous" and said she "could not prove her claim because her camera had apparently frozen."

Bradey was stunned. She expected controversy over climbing the mountain without the technical permission she needed, but she could not fathom how Hall could doubt her since he hadn't been on the mountain while she climbed it. That afternoon she taxied by motorized rickshaw to the Ministry of Tourism to check on the fallout. There, the head of mountaineering, Mr. D. Shresta, showed her a statement written by Hall. "It has come to my attention that a member of my team has been responsible for some misconduct on Mount Everest," the statement began. It concluded: "I do not believe that she made the summit of Mount Everest as the reports given by the Spanish group indicate that she was in very poor condition and the times that she is quoting simply do not add up."

"I said, 'Faaar out!' when I saw that," said Bradey. By now she was acutely aware that if she affirmed her illegal ascent to the Nepalese, she and her entire team might be banned from Nepal, but if she chose to avoid trouble by retracting her unofficial claim—which Hall had denounced—she would look like a liar. Without photos or witnesses her only proof was her word.

And her word, she found, did not count for much in New Zealand. During the next week at least fourteen stories about Bradey appeared in four New Zealand newspapers. Few of them supported her ascent. Bradey characterizes the stories as a deliberate campaign of disinformation spread by Hall.

One headline—"Nepalese Impound Passport of 'Everest Conqueror'"— had her held under virtual house arrest by local authorities. Another story, titled "Climber May Have Hallucinated," stated that two Americans had found her crawling down Everest, hallucinating. The story proposed that she was so intoxicated by oxygen deprivation that she had imagined the south summit was the main one. (In fact, while descending on October 15, Bradey did meet two Americans: John Petroske and Steve Ruoss of Seattle. Petroske still recalls the meeting: "She had cracked goggles and mismatched mittens, and she looked tired," he told me in 1994, "but she seemed no more wasted than the Spaniards. She said, 'The views are bloody marvelous. Go for it!'" Petroske says neither he nor Ruoss ever spoke to reporters, or to Hall, about Bradey, and they never said she was hallucinating or crawling.)

Another story, "Doubt Lingers on Climber's Claim," proposed that when the Spaniards met her at 2:30 P.M. she was not on the south summit, but 300 feet below it, crawling helplessly. Other newspapers reported the Spaniards saying she was back on the South Col an hour after appearing on the south summit—a time frame that made a summit bid impossible.

Lopez, who I interviewed in 1994, is mystified as to how his team could have been quoted in any newspaper, since no journalist questioned his expedition about Bradey until two years later, when Richard Cowper, a writer for the *Financial Times* of London, urged Lopez's team to check their journals and audiotapes of the radio broadcasts from their summit day (they were making a TV film and recorded their climb on video and audiotape and in writing). Ultimately, the Spaniards confirmed meeting Bradey on the south summit at 2:30 P.M.; that Lopez remet her just after dark, at 8:30 P.M. at 26,900 feet during her descent, while they were lowering Martinez, and that she reached the South Col at 9:00 P.M.—not between 4:00 P.M. and 7:00 P.M. as newspapers variously reported.

The difference was crucial support for Bradey's claim. Based on the Spaniards' times, she had six hours to go from the south summit to the top and then back down to the point where Lopez remet her—a plausible performance. But those revelations did not surface till 1990. In the meantime, few seemed willing to accept that Bradey had accomplished her feat.

I asked Lopez if he believed Bradey's Everest claim. He replied, "Her physical condition on the south summit was not a disaster. She was not crawling. Only she knows for certain if she summited, but she had enough time; so I must give her the benefit of the doubt. Anyway, if she didn't go to the top, what was she doing up there for so many hours?" Lopez also says that Cowper and I are the only writers to interview him about Bradey. No New Zealand journalists ever contacted Lopez, even though he was a key witness in Lydiagate.

Cowper's article appeared in England in November 1990, and it turned the tide of belief for Bradey. By 1991 the New Zealand media were largely supporting her claim, as were Himalayan chroniclers such as Xavier Eguskitza in England and Liz Hawley, who now describes Hall's actions in Kathmandu as being intended "to cover his arse." Even Gary Ball, who had portrayed Bradey as "willing to say anything to grasp the title of 'household name,'" distanced himself from the issue, revising his stance on Lydiagate to "I never said she didn't reach the top of Everest, though I'm not sure if Lydia knows that either." (Tragically, in 1993, Ball died of pulmonary edema while climbing Dhaulagiri in Nepal. He'd had serious altitude problems before, necessitating his rescue from a second attempt on K2 in 1993. Then, in 1996 Hall died on Everest when a storm caught him and a client he was guiding near the Hillary Step. Twelve people would die in that storm, and the episode would focus enormous media attention on climbing.)

Until the swing in public opinion, Hall and Ball had been heroic figures in New Zealand, but with magazine headlines like "The Woman Who Climbed Everest—The Men Who Doubted," they found themselves momentarily characterized as envy-ridden sexists who were conspiring to rob Bradey of her place in alpine history. Even so, Hall was unmoved by these accusations.

"I wish I could believe that Lydia did climb Everest," he told me by fax (faxed answers to written questions were the only way he or Ball would discuss Lydiagate with me), "but having climbed over that terrain four times, I just can't see how it would have been possible in the time she claimed."

It was 1994, and he had just returned from achieving a major Himalayan first, by climbing three of the world's four highest peaks—Everest, Lhotse, and K2—in a single season. It was his fourth oxygen-assisted climb to Everest's summit, to which he was regularly taking paying clients for a $50,000 fee. Far from being a villain, Hall was one of New Zealand's most respected climbers, the recipient of an MBE (Member of the British Empire, an honor bestowed on outstanding achievers of the Commonwealth by the Queen of England) for his services to mountaineering.

Hall claimed that the times at which Bradey says she reached the south summit and returned to the South Col are different from those he heard broadcast over the Spaniards' radio on October 14, 1988, and that the Spaniards, for reasons he does not understand, have doctored their story to create a more plausible case for Bradey's success.

THERE ARE TOUGHER AND MORE SHAPELY MOUNTAINS than Everest, but in the world of alpinism nothing is a better reputation builder than standing atop the highest point on Earth. Because Everest's summit symbolizes, rightly or wrongly, the zenith of human achievement, its "conquerors" have a chance to go professional and earn a living from product endorsements, speaking engagements, and guiding. These temptations bring out the best and worst in climbers. Ego and ambition are essential traits, in moderation, in the risky game of Himalayan climbing, but too much of them can lure climbers into disaster. They may also prod climbers to stretch the bounds of truth or resort to treachery.

A clue as to whether Lydia Bradey was capable of climbing Everest, or whether she would fabricate the feat, may exist in her past. An only child, she was born in a lower-middle-class section of Christchurch on New Zealand's South Island. Her father—she describes him as "immature"—left the family when Bradey was three. She tried to meet him at age sixteen, phoning him to suggest that they go skiing together. He refused, and she did not see him until age nineteen, on the eve of her departure from New Zealand for four years of climbing. John Bradey never paid child support, pursuing instead a life of sailing and "living beyond his means," while Bradey and her mother, Royce, a teacher, shared a one-room flat. Bradey remembers such cash-poor times that neither she nor her mother owned a watch, or even a simple clock for the house.

Bradey did well academically, but she hated team sports. She didn't date much during high school, spending her time climbing instead, from age fifteen. One of her teenage climbing and hiking pals was Rob Hall. "Rob was always sweet on me in a brotherly way," she recalls. "He was sensitive, too. I could talk to him about feelings and women's issues." She met Gary Ball, a charismatic guide with a gift for telling rousing stories and bawdy jokes, when he tested her on her alpine-guide course in New Zealand. He so admired "her attitude of determined self-sufficiency and her ambition to be the world's best-known woman climber" that he penned a flattering article about her for a New Zealand magazine.

By eighteen Bradey had climbed Mount Cook, New Zealand's highest peak, twice. At nineteen she tried McKinley in Alaska and then went to

Yosemite, where she hung out with the wall rats of Camp 4 and made ascents of El Capitan's multiday routes. Her large-boned physique suited the pack-hauling of alpinism, but her country-girl looks were charming enough to land her occasional modeling work. She checked in at rock-climbing ports such as Arapiles, in Australia, and Sheffield, in England, and she left broken hearts in every place. Invariably, the men in her past say it was Bradey who controlled relationships. "I used to drop boyfriends like books," she admits, preferring to escape relationships at the first sign of decline—as her parents had.

Bradey tried new routes on Asian peaks, including Gangkar Punsum and Cho Oyu. On each expedition she was the token woman, but frequently she bettered the men at altitude. On Kedarnath, a 22,770-foot peak in India, she and Australian Jon Muir survived the Himalaya at its meanest, when, hit by a storm near the summit, they roamed lost in a white-out for days, sheltering in snow caves, being hit by avalanches, and running out of food. She found dark appeal in tightrope-walking through uncertainty. She calls it "James Bond climbing."

Her alpine-style ascent of Gasherbrum II (26,363 feet), in Pakistan in 1987, established two things for Bradey: she could penetrate the 8,000-meter barrier and she was not about to let rules stand between her and success. Bradey and an Australian boyfriend, Geoff Little, climbed Gasherbrum II illegally after dangerous snows forced them to quit the adjacent Gasherbrum I, for which they had permission. Her performance on Gasherbrum II impressed Little: "No one who has climbed with Lydia could question her strength at altitude. I'm convinced she climbed Everest."

Gary Ball describes the flip side of this illegal climb: "Lydia returned to New Zealand a heroine from Gasherbrum II, but [bribes] had to be paid to officials there so the team wouldn't be banned from Pakistan."

When Hall invited her on his well-funded K2-Everest expedition for 1988, he found himself defending her against New Zealand Alpine Club members who wanted Bradey dropped because of her maverick behavior on Gasherbrum II. "I gave those people my personal assurance that there would be no repeat of the Gasherbrum incident, but she let us down."

To which Bradey retorts, "Lots of people break the rules. I felt you paid the peak fee and climbed whatever was possible." She points out that praise has been heaped on male climbers who have made illegal ascents: the Slovene Tomo Česen (till his name was tarnished by accusations that he invented some of his climbs) was lionized for a fast, permitless, solo attempt of K2 in 1986, and Voytek Kurtyka of Poland has climbed Broad Peak and many others on the sly. Bradey thinks she landed in trouble because alpinism, especially in New Zealand, is a domain in which a man's word has more clout than a woman's, and because the world in 1988 was not ready to believe that a woman was strong enough to solo Everest without oxygen.

But is there any hard evidence that she endured the ultimate aerobic pump and covered the final 350 feet to Everest's summit after the Spaniards met her? Geoff Tabin, the first person she met when she returned to base camp from the summit, believes there is.

"When I'd been on top," Tabin says, "there was an oxygen tank jammed in the snow, left by a French climber. When I quizzed Lydia about the summit I thought it was incredible when she said that even the oxygen tank had been blown away since I was there, but the Spanish later confirmed that the summit was bare. They said they had not discussed the summit with Lydia. If she were lying, she would surely have agreed with me that the oxygen tank was on top."

Lydia Bradey's case is unusual not so much for her lack of a summit photo or witnesses, but for the vehemence with which her partners counter her claim. Traditionally, climbers have been on their honor to tell the truth, and many ascents lacking definitive proof have been accepted at their word by the alpine community. Said Sir Edmund Hillary about Lydiagate, "I think, on the whole, if someone says they got to the top, unless there is strong evidence to the contrary, you take it that they probably did."

Despite Bradey's plausible scenario of events, as I sat in that Boulder cafe hearing her out, I began to find it somewhat incredible that the world press and her team had ganged up to discredit her. Only when she shows me a thick wad of newspaper clippings do I understand why the press and even some of her friends disbelieved her. They describe a confusing backflip she made while in Kathmandu in 1988: the public retraction of her summit claim.

AGONIZING OVER WHAT TO SAY ABOUT HER CLIMB in her official statement to the Ministry of Tourism, Bradey roamed the Nepalese capital from the Hindu funeral pyres on one side of town to the monkey-infested Buddhist temples on the other. The acrimonious outcome of her expedition, the deaths of the Slovaks, and the trouble she faced, had reduced her to an emotional shambles. In desperation, she sought the advice of Liz Hawley, the Reuters correspondent in Kathmandu and the doyen of Everest journalism. Unbeknown to Bradey, Hawley had reported Hall's statement to the media services, including the tidbits about Bradey supposedly hallucinating and crawling below the south summit.

Hawley, a matronly, no-nonsense journalist, seemed doubtful about Bradey, a dreadlocked punkette. She produced a photo of Everest and asked

Bradey to describe her route. Bradey had climbed the south side, but the photo showed the northeast walls of Everest and neighboring Lhotse—a view of the mountain that was unfamiliar to Bradey.

"Liz was confused," remembers Bradey, "and so was I." No climber herself, Hawley had never trekked to Everest, nor had she seen it from close quarters. Mistaking Lhotse for Everest, Hawley pointed to what she thought was the south summit and said skeptically, "Look, it's a long way to the top."

"I was almost crying," said Bradey. "I thought that being a woman, Liz would be understanding, but she was hard as nails." Liz Hawley has no recollection of this aspect of their meeting.

On November 2, Bradey issued a statement to the Ministry of Tourism: "I was just taking photographs and I accidentally went too high. I don't know whether I got to the top or not." Today, Bradey shrugs off the naivete of her statement, but her expedition's Nepalese liaison officer had told her there would be fines and bans if she stuck to her claim. Nepal subsequently took such a dim view of illegal ascents that in 1993 a British Everest team was fined $100,000 for permit violations. (The Brits negotiated the fine to a lesser penalty.)

Bradey's retraction fueled more bad press in New Zealand. "Climber Withdraws Everest Claim" headlined the *Star*. "Confusion Over Conquering Climb Conundrum Continues" ran the *Evening Post*. In "Topping Everest—Was It All A Dream?" a columnist wrote: "They say fame is a bubble which often comes from blowing your own horn and I am starting to wonder if Lydia Bradey is going to become famous by this method . . . I gather that Lydia is a bit of a rebel and is not too good at observing the strict disciplines involved in climbing the high stuff. Apparently she is a firm believer that girls can do anything and taking off on her own to scale Mount Everest was just her way of proving it."

Few of these journalists had ever met her.

WHILE ALL THIS WAS HAPPENING, I returned to Kathmandu after a botched try on Makalu. Though Bradey was still trekking in from Everest, she was nevertheless the talk of the town. At the Bat Tavern one night, I overheard a conversation between several climbers close to the heart of Lydiagate; Rob Hall and Gary Ball were among them. I recall snatches of talk: "She's ruthless." "Too ambitious." "She'd say anything to get famous."

I wasn't surprised to hear such gossip about the bad girl of the New Zealand Alps. Long before Everest I'd heard a rumor that painted Bradey as a ghoulish opportunist who had stolen the gear from a dead climber lying on Mount Cook. The truth was, she later told me, neither she nor anyone else ever found the missing climber's body. She did find his Sony Walkman in a hut, though. Telling those around her she was borrowing it for her climb, she went to Cook's summit and then returned the Walkman to the authorities. She and her companions also took great personal risks earlier, by climbing under an ice cliff to search for the missing climber.

But the fiction about Bradey robbing the dead is the one that stuck.

When Bradey arrived at Christchurch airport in mid-November 1988, a customs officer recognized her from the newspapers. He said, "You're Lydia, eh? There's a lot of press outside. We could smuggle you into a van and into the city, if you like."

But she decided to face the music. Television cameras, photographers, and journalists zeroed in on her outside customs. The manager of a trek that had accompanied her expedition took her aside and told her he had to make a statement for TV. What should he say?

"I don't care what you say, but don't say I was hallucinating. It isn't true," she told him. That night, viewers of the evening news heard the trek manager report that Bradey may have hallucinated her ascent.

Lydiagate raged for two more years as Bradey tried to make a confused public believe that she had really climbed Everest and that she had renounced her claim only to hedge trouble while in Kathmandu. Nevertheless, Nepal slapped a two-year ban on her, and the New Zealand Alpine Club rubbed salt into the wound by supporting it and refusing to endorse her on overseas expeditions during that period. Her only encounter with Hall was a screaming match. The embarrassing publicity winnowed her friendships to a loyal core. Finally, Bradey quit talking to reporters and "withdrew from climbing."

Still, she remained an abrasive fixture in New Zealand alpinism. At a slide show she gave after Everest, she asserted her claim on the summit and then dissed New Zealand climbers for being "miles behind the rest of the world in Himalayan climbing" and for "still regarding Everest ascents done in Hillary style, with Sherpas and oxygen, as significant international achievements." Chiding Kiwi climbers for "viewing risk in mountaineering as purely objective and not subjective," she praised the commitment that had gotten her Slovak friends up, but not down, the toughest route on Everest.

"The audience was speechless," remembered Geoff Gabites, a New Zealand Alpine Club stalwart.

Presented with this tale at our meeting in Boulder, Bradey grins. "Yeah," she says, "I was pretty obnoxious back then."

Meanwhile, after two more bouts with Everest, Hall and Ball summited,   183 using oxygen, in 1990. They racked up the Seven Summits (the highest peak on each continent) in seven months—all to carefully orchestrated media attention that made them even bigger celebrities in New Zealand. In 1991 they formed a lucrative business, Hall and Ball Adventure Consultants. By 1995 Hall's company had successfully put thirty-nine people on top of Everest. Many of them paid Hall $65,000 to be guided there.

WHEN MY LAST TAPE RUNS OUT, Bradey suggests that we leave the cafe and drive into the hills behind Boulder for a run. "I've got a lot of catch-up to do if I ever want to get fit enough to return to 8,000 meters," she explains jokingly. Jogging an uphill trail, we keep apace of each other for a while; then finally the winter air and the Rockies' altitude halt us, and we stand wheezing and steaming.

As we rest, I ask myself whether I have been convinced that Lydia Bradey summited Everest that day in 1988, and, like the Spaniard Lopez, I find myself giving her the benefit of the doubt. I think back on my own Himalayan expeditions and ponder my summit evidence. Aside from the word of my teammates, my main proof that we reached K2's summit in 1990, for example, is a self-timer photo of me sitting on a snowy crest. The sky is a milk-white backdrop of impending storm; the mountains behind are cloud-engulfed. Although my other photos show a few rocks that only a K2 summiter could recognize, the photo might have been taken on a poxy day at a ski resort—except, perhaps, for the smile on my face, the look in my eyes. Those things cannot be faked, and, I note, Bradey's eyes had never avoided mine, no matter how thorny the questioning got during the interview.

Whatever the histories of Everest conclude, doubts will always cloud Lydia Bradey's claim. But Bradey is a tough individual. She says she has put Lydiagate behind her and that she has personally forgiven Hall and Ball. "Life is too short to waste with fighting over who was first up a mountain, or whether they can prove it or not," she says. Still, describing those down-and-out days in Kathmandu and New Zealand had, for a moment during the interview, brought her to tears. She had found her composure quickly though, and her tone had become iron-hard. "I was a victim of sexual politics," she had said. "Did my teammates have a permit for the South Pillar? No. Did they get criticized for abandoning me on the mountain? No. Is there proof that I didn't do it? No. The heart of the matter is that I got up Everest and they didn't."

And, perhaps, it is as simple as that.

Everest,

Of Course

The north wall of Everest from Rongbuk monastery. The North Ridge runs to the left of the summit.

How I (Almost) Didn't Climb Everest

Fifty feet ahead of me and a hundred feet below the summit of Everest, a Sherpa named Ang Babu grunts and pushes at the butt of some French geezer who is tugging with all his might on an old hank of rope hanging over a short cliff. With a mighty heave the Sherpa shoulders his client onto the summit ridge; then they begin the easy home stretch to the top of the world.

It's a windless, cloudless morning near the apex of the North Ridge. On one side of this 2.5-mile fin of ice and rock, starkly backlit clouds lap at Nepalese peaks; on the other, tawny Tibetan hills stretch into a soft, heliotropic haze. I pause to take in the view, then realizing that in a few minutes I'll be on the highest place on Earth, I start sniffling with emotion. Or is it that bloody cold that's been dogging me for weeks?

Wiping my frosted goggles and freeing my oxygen mask of a golfball-size ice cube of drool, I look up at the Frenchman and his Sherpa guide. They move side by side until, after a few paces, the Sherpa inadvertently overtakes his client by a stride—and is sternly stopped by a French mitten backhanded against his chest. The Frenchman has paid a boodle of cash to be escorted up Everest, and he'll be damned if anyone else is going to beat him to this coveted summit.

This display of inverted camaraderie and French neocolonialism squeezes a weary laugh out of me (actually, through my oxygen mask, it sounds more like a dog barking in a rubber echo chamber). Karsang, the Sherpa beside me, drops his mask from his face and gives me an expression that crosses borders of language and says, "Can you believe that arsehole?" But we humor the Frenchman, and the remaining six of us on the ridge that day—a polyglot group made up from two expeditions—fall into rank behind the imaginary line he has drawn in the snow.

I share those last steps with Bob, a Nebraskan who ropes steers for a hobby, and who, like the Frenchman, is a member of a commercial Everest trip. Unlike the get-there-first Frenchman, who creeps ahead with excruciating slowness, Bob is just happy to be where he is. Bob's summit fantasy includes twirling a lariat to become the world's highest trick roper. When we passed through Lhasa he did rope tricks on a street corner—jumping in and out of the lariat, and lassoing a cheering Tibetan bystander—till Chinese soldiers broke up the crowd. Yeah, Bob is a nice guy, which is why I find it upsetting when he slips on the skating-rink-hard slope, pivots upside down and then slides forty feet to disappear over the 10,000-foot North Face.

It happens lightning quick, a blur to the eyes and the imagination. Aside from my lame shout of "Stop!" he is gone without a sound. I turn toward Karsang, partly to gauge from his expression whether I have hallucinated all this, but he, too, gapes toward the claw marks of Bob's slide to oblivion.

I gather what wits I can muster at nearly 29,000 feet and crampon toward the precipice. Foolishly I call Bob's name—what's the point, he's a croaker for sure—then I hear a cry for help.

"Dammit," I think to myself, now imagining the epic of extricating a mangled Bob from the cliffs below the Big One's crown. "Looks like I won't climb this tit of a hill after all."

I HAD ALWAYS SNEERED AT EVEREST, snubbed invitations to join expeditions to it, pooh-poohed it as an overrated, overclimbed status symbol. "Just because it is the biggest shitpile on Earth doesn't mean it is the best shitpile on Earth," I used to say. But in 1995 I went to the mountain Tibetans call Goddess Mother of Earth. Maybe I went because I was tired of making excuses as to why I had climbed so many Himalayan peaks, but not Everest. Maybe a crack at Everest is just inevitable for anyone silly enough to dub themselves a "Himalayan climber." Whatever the reason, as the departure date for Tibet neared, I did feel a growing fascination—okay, call it a dose of Everest fever—to stand on the Earth's highest point. Mostly though, I just wanted to get the bloody mountain off my back.

187

Greg Child

Shortly before I left for Everest I visited Steve Swenson, a friend who'd climbed the North Ridge in 1994. We'd climbed K2 together five years earlier, and he'd soloed Everest without oxygen. He described the route, showed me slides, and told me about the scene at base camp. "Expect lots of people, all types of people—a lot of them guided, a lot of them people you or I wouldn't classify as climbers—swarming all over the mountain," he warned. During his Everest season there had been six ascents and four deaths amid a near-constant climate of hurricane wind and cold. "Anyway," he said in conclusion, "you'll come away with good material for a story."

I justified selling out my No-Everest principles because I had a project up there: to make a film about climbing the North Ridge with an old friend who is an amputee. Tom Whittaker is a loquacious Brit I had met in Yosemite in 1978 while I was crawling out of a dumpster and he was crawling in. I was scavenging for pop cans stamped with the magic nickel-deposit seal, to cash in so I could buy a new rope. He had two legs back then, and he talked me into climbing the Nose on El Cap with him. Seventeen years later, and after he'd lost his right foot in a car smash with a drunk driver on Thanksgiving night in 1979, he phoned me to suggest another climb. This time I would help him become the first amputee up Everest. "Why would I want to climb with a one-legged man, Tom?" I asked him bluntly. "Because it will make us both very sexy," he replied.

To launch the expedition we needed money, and the best way to get the money was to make a documentary of Tom's attempt. So I faxed Leo Dickinson, the British adventure filmmaker, who, among his seventy films, had made a film about ballooning over Everest and crash-landing in Tibet. Leo got on board and persuaded a British TV station to finance the film. After we secured the film deal, The North Face helped underwrite the expedition, and we bought into a trip to Everest's Tibetan side. Before we knew it, we were at base camp.

And so were about 500 other people whose eleven base camps dotted the snout of the East Rongbuk Glacier. About half these people were support members, cooks, bottle-washers, and Chinese liaison officers. The rest—some 180 of them—had their eyes on the summit of Everest. Aside from a behemoth Japanese/Sherpa team on the Northeast Ridge, the bulk of traffic was on the North Ridge.

Why the North Ridge? Because it was a climber's bargain, with a peak fee of $15,000 and no limit on team size, as opposed to the $50,000 minimum royalty demanded by the Nepalese for a team of five climbers. It also allowed the four commercial operators on the North Ridge to offer middle-class Everest wannabes packages priced from $18,000 to $25,000. By contrast, a guided ascent of Nepal's South Col route sported the tony price tag of $65,000.

Everesting has always been a separate sport from the rest of climbing. For a certain breed of climber, it is the only mountain they'll ever try, and they'll pay big bucks for the big tick. To quote David Breashears, who has climbed Everest several times and recently made an IMAX film of an ascent, "Everest is the ultimate feather in the pseudomountaineer's cap."

"Doing Everest" became possible for people with disposable income in the 1990s, when a few climbers started guiding on the mountain. A cheaper deal than the "guided ascent" emerged with the advent of the "commercial trip," on which a team of lead climbers and Sherpas outfit the mountain with camps, oxygen, and fixed ropes and let the punters have at it without a guide. This is the ultimate high-adventure package tour, and the ultimate blind date, as you don't meet your partners till you reach Kathmandu. In my opinion, letting inexperienced people loose on an 8,000-meter peak is like giving a drunk an Uzi with a full clip, but it is astonishing how many people have gotten to the top, either guided or on commercial trips, and have survived the experience. These days, it is also sobering to tally up the number of ingenues who have died on Everest.

ALTITUDE-ADDLED FROM THE DRIVE TO BASE CAMP AT 17,000 FEET, I fairly fell out of the jeep. Everest loomed in the distance. The long sweep of the North and Northeast Ridge routes formed the left skyline, the West Ridge the right, and the Great Couloir and Hornbein Couloir formed gashes up the center. I was surprised at how rocky the mountain was—"black as a snake's arse," the wild-haired Aussie climber Jon Muir had quipped when we'd flown past it, en route to Lhasa.

Through binoculars I scoped the landmarks of the North Ridge route. Above the highest campsite, at 27,000 feet, were the crumbling cliffs of the Yellow Band; I'd read that around there, in 1933, the British climber Frank Smythe had been so discombobulated by altitude he had offered a bite of his lunch to an imaginary partner. Above that, protruding from the ridge, were two rocky humps, the First Step and the Second Step. The Second Step—a stack of rocks culminating in a fifteen-foot vertical cliff—is the technical crux of the route. Here the Englishmen George Leigh Mallory and Andrew Irvine were last sighted during a summit bid on June 8, 1924. Some climbers believe those two summited and beat Hillary and Norgay to Everest's first ascent by nearly three decades, but until their bodies are found and the film in the cameras they carried is restored, the matter of whether or not they summited will always be conjecture. The Second Step is also where Chinese

Trudging to Camp One, at 23,000 feet, on the North Ridge.

climbers, on the second ascent of the ridge in 1975 (Chinese made the first ascent of it, too, in 1960, but Western observers doubted the claim at the time), erected a ten-foot aluminum ladder to overcome this rocky obstacle.

Rumor had it around base camp that in 1994 some wise guy had cut the ropes securing this rickety old ladder to the wall and hurled it off the mountain. Some climbers in camp looked forward to the challenge of climbing the Second Step by "fair means"; others were mortified that the aid had been eliminated. Our team considered issuing a spoof press release to the climbing media saying we'd bolted the Second Step—just to piss off the traditionalists.

It was also on the North Face, on the slopes below the curve of the ridge, that Reinhold Messner made his tour de force in 1980 by soloing a new route without oxygen. He had been the only climber on the entire Tibetan side of Everest. His only companion at base camp was his girlfriend. Never again would a climber experience such solitude on Everest.

BY EARLY MAY THE EXPEDITIONS HAD MARCHED THE FIFTEEN MILES up the East Rongbuk Glacier to establish Advance Base Camp (ABC) a 200-tent ghetto jammed onto a moraine strip at 21,000 feet, below Everest's bleak, black Northeast Wall. It is well known by biologists that a cage containing a clan or two of lab rats presents a harmonious community, but when the population gets out of control and the cage gets overcrowded, the rats get strange, go crazy, and eat their young. The first sign of antisocial behavior on Everest came when an American team got territorial and encircled their camp with a fence of rope to keep trespassers out. Then on a foul, windy day in mid-April, while I stood below the North Col at 21,500 feet, watching snow plumes stream over the ice-blue crest 2,000 feet above, I met The Man With An Attitude.

All around me, climbers were setting out and then abandoning their journeys to Camp One on the col, driven back by the gale and signs of impending storm. Wind swirled about in a vortex, occasionally sweeping breathable air away and leaving a momentary vacuum that left one with an awful suffocating feeling. While I zipped up my windsuit to keep spindrift out, I noticed Leo locked in conversation with a climber from another team and then watched them march purposefully toward me.

"Er, this fellow says he's going to cut our tents loose from the North Col and toss them off the mountain," said Leo.

After an introduction I learned the following: The Man With An Attitude was the climbing leader of his expedition; he'd been on Everest a month longer than me and didn't like our intrusion on his ridge; he claimed he'd placed all the fixed ropes himself; if I wanted to use his ropes I had to ask his permission; anyway, it was too late to ask for permission to use his ropes, as he intended to cut them loose so that ingrates like me couldn't use them; and, as Leo said, he planned to slash the ropes lashing our tents to the mountain and let the wind devour them.

It took but a second to identify this character as a dangerous alpine psycho in need of a megadose of Lithium. Leo prescribed different treatment. His heritage was of British barroom brawls and the use of Don Whillans–style fisticuffs to settle climbing disagreements. While Leo shadowboxed in the background, whispering, "Hit him, hit him," I pretended to be a UN negotiator trying to arrange a cease-fire between Serbia and Bosnia.

After a heated discussion in the cold, I got safe passage for us to the North Col by threatening sanctions and reprisals if The Man With An Attitude touched our tents. His threat to destroy our camp was, in his words, "a non-life-threatening protest to our presence." "Well," I said, "I've been on twelve Himalayan expeditions, and that's the first time I've heard that one."

I offer an apologia for The Man With An Attitude: he had been on Everest too long; the mountain was too big for his mind and his body; and he believed the myth of Himalayan solitude—making for a shattered wilderness experience for him when the masses arrived at base camp. His delusions that he'd fixed all the ropes (many teams, including ours, had contributed rope) and that destroying our tents would solve anything, were, however, just plain nuts. As we parted company I wondered how anyone was going to summit with kooks like him around.

BUT SUMMIT PEOPLE DID, in droves.

On May 10, a thick, warm fog rolled up the glacier. For climbers like Russell Brice, a New Zealander who was our expedition leader and who, during four expeditions to the north side, had known only winds that flatten tents and send rocks frisbeeing through the sky, it was a perplexing omen. "This either means the worst storm in history is about to hit, or we're about to get perfect weather." After twenty-four hours the sky was clear.

First to summit, on May 11, were six members of the Japanese/Sherpa team on the Northeast Ridge. This was the first time this immensely long route had been climbed in its entirety, though Russell and Harry Taylor had climbed the route, alpine style, to its junction with the North Ridge in 1988.

After the Japanese success the gauntlet was down. Between May 11 and May 17, about fifty more people summited by the North Ridge. There were first national ascents for Taiwan, Turkey, Latvia, and Rumania. Russians, American, British, Austrian, and Italian climbers succeeded, too. Reinhard

Patsheider, of Italy, set a north-side speed record with a twenty-one-hour oxygenless blitz from ABC to the summit. Britain's Alison Hargreaves made a seemingly effortless oxygenless ascent in "unsupported" style, meaning that although she was always surrounded by other climbers and had radio contact with base camp, she carried her own gear, established her own camps, and had no Sherpa help (as opposed to climbers like me who were vying for bad-style ascents, who happily paid Sherpas to carry their junk, who sucked the guts out of oxygen bottles, and who hauled themselves up fixed ropes). So independent and style-conscious was Alison that she wouldn't even accept a cup of tea from me while on the mountain, lest it be construed as "support." Though hers was the "best" ascent of the season, her publicity machine in Britain got carried away afterward, variously claiming hers as the first female oxygenless ascent, first-ever female ascent, and that it was all done solo. In fact, on her summit day, she was seldom less than fifty feet behind two Italians (who also climbed oxygenless). As for firsts, Junko Tabei of Japan made the first female ascent in 1975, and Lydia Bradey in 1988 was the first woman up without oxygen (though Lydia's claim was hotly disputed at the time, all but misogynists and Luddites credit her ascent now).

Others were gunning for firsts, too. There were contenders for the youngest ascent (age fifteen) and the oldest ascent (age sixty-three), and there was The Man Who Would Bivy Highest.

A member of a commercial expedition, The Man Who Would Bivy Highest hit the spotlight one morning when a team going for the summit found him shivering below the Second Step, at 28,100 feet. He had survived the night dressed only in his climbing suit. Fearing he'd be frostbitten, two Sherpas gave up their summit bids—and the $300 bonus they stood to earn for helping their clients to the top—to assist The Man Who Would Bivy Highest. Radios buzzed as a rescue was mounted, people moved up the ridge to help, and yaks were assembled for his evacuation down the glacier.

When The Man Who Would Bivy Highest passed my tent at 25,600 feet, he was verbally abusing his Sherpa rescuers from behind an oxygen mask. When I saw his gloves dangling from strings on his wrists, I suggested he put them on his dead-fish-colored hands. This prompted him to launch into a tirade about how everyone on the mountain was overreacting to his plight. "I'm in control. I don't need rescuing." He saw no cause to be grateful to anyone for the effort launched on his behalf.

Wary now of alpine psychos, I zipped my tent shut, and from the safety within I suggested to the bivouacker that the world would be a better place if he jumped off the mountain. He stumbled away to impress others with his bonhomie, especially Leo, who, when he handed His Bivouackship a cup of tea at the North Col, had it "thrown back at him" because there wasn't sugar in it.

Miraculously, the bivouacker escaped severe frostbite. In base camp he bragged that he'd set a record for the highest bivy sans oxygen. He believed his accomplishment would create a media storm when he returned to Kathmandu. Perhaps my attitudes are old-fashioned, but sitting out near the summit of Everest doesn't seem so much a record to break as a fuck-up to avoid. Then the theory emerged that The Man Who Would Bivy Highest had intentionally sat the night out to set his record. An American who'd passed Der Bivymeister at 1:00 P.M. at the Second Step said he'd given him a full bottle of oxygen. Although there were still seven hours of daylight left, the bivouacker descended no farther. But unbeknown to Mister Bivouack, in 1994 Mark Whetu and Michael Rheinberger had survived a night without shelter even higher on the ridge. When told this, The Man Who Would Bivy Highest faded into the crowds at base camp and was not missed.

DURING APRIL AND MAY, Tom and I and several score of summit hopefuls reached the wind-ravaged site of Camp Two. For anyone with two feet, this section of the climb up firm, 40-degree snow and scree was easy. But not for Tom, with his spatula-footed, carbon-fiber-ankled, Terminator-like, crampon-adapted, Flexfoot prosthesis. Though he could saunter down a city street with a gait that hinted nothing of a disability, his footing was sketchy on rubble. "I figure I expend a third more energy than an able-bodied person to climb the same distance," he said, explaining his slower pace. He couldn't just kick a foot into snow or edge up on rock, he had to eyeball the append-age his stump was slotted into, place it carefully, and ease onto it. He had no ankle rotation, no calf muscle, no toe to spring off. He also had two trick knees he could invert at will. His leg was also sensitive to cold. He combated this with a battery-powered warming device taped to his stump. After a month, he was running out of artificial feet, having damaged two of his four prosthe-ses on the slog between base camp and ABC. He patched the feet with glue and kept going.

With his strange foot, Tom was easily the most conspicuous, but not the most colorful character on Everest. Aussie climber Jon Muir wore a home-made, Cossack-like, fox-head hat and wielded a mummified chicken claw he'd salvaged from a Tibetan restaurant and planned to leave on the summit. "First chicken-claw ascent. They said it couldn't be done," he'd cackle to confused punters at base camp. Jon, who'd climbed Everest in 1988, was back again to support his wife, Brigitte, in her attempt at an ascent, but he found it hard to take the 1995 mob scene seriously. When a young Turkish candidate suggested he was "willing to die" for Everest, Jon nonplussed him by laughing maniacally and waving his chicken claw around.

Then arrived The Feral Kid, an American youth who appeared at ABC one day, vigorously shook my hand, and began a hard-sell pitch to join our team. He'd "resigned" from his expedition due to irreconcilable differences; now he was a free agent. He rattled out his climbing resume to impress me. It included the ability to whip off one-arm pull-ups, a pointless feat on Everest, where the main use of the bicep is to tie bootlaces. I felt like I was being sold a used car that I didn't want, so I offered this orphan of Everest some advice: "Don't join a team, just solo the mountain." When I offered these words I think I was talking to myself, imagining I was in the next valley, on the solitude of the North Face, where there was not a single person. There, away from the complexity of our film and the hordes, a climber might actually be able to consider himself worthy of the name.

The kid disappeared up the North Ridge with two oxygen bottles scavenged from a Latvian team. I envied his escape from the formality of a structured expedition. He was an animal who'd escaped the zoo, gone wild—a feral climber. I never saw him again, though rumors abounded of a lone youth at the high camp, dossing in abandoned tents, digging in the snow for old food dumps, trying to inveigle himself onto summit teams. Maybe The Feral Kid climbed it, maybe not. He was just another face in the crowd.

More conventional yet no less intriguing was George Mallory, eponymous grandson of the late George Leigh Mallory. After young George summited on May 14, there was little doubt in his mind that his grandfather was the first man up Everest. He based his belief on the fact that in 1924 their teammate, Noel Odell, saw Mallory and Irvine crest the Second Step (in later years Odell seemed unsure of exactly where on the ridge he'd seen them, but in his written dispatches at the time of the disappearance he pinpointed them at the Second Step). Odell sighted them at about 1:00 P.M. The Second Step is 900 vertical feet and a horizontal half-mile before the summit.

"After that, the route is easy. There is nothing to stop you from climbing to the top," young George said enthusiastically of the remaining terrain. Indeed, the weather on June 8, 1924, was reportedly good, though cloudy, and Mallory and Irvine were strong climbers and were using primitive oxygen sets. Although young George had found the Chinese ladder intact, he'd checked out the ladderless variation and felt grandpa could have flashed it, or at least stood on Irvine's shoulders. Anyway, the Chinese Wang Fu-Chou had climbed it in 1960 without the ladder. He'd removed his boots and climbed the rock in his socks, freezing some toes in the process. These were later snipped off.

Though nothing concrete is known about Mallory's and Irvine's last hours, they left some tantalizing clues, such as the ice ax found midway between the First and Second Steps by a 1933 British expedition. Did it signify their high point, the site of a fall, or was it just dumped because it was useless on the rocky ridge? One of their bodies seems to have been found in 1975 by a Chinese porter, Wang Hung-bao, who went for a twenty-minute stroll from his camp at 26,600 feet and returned with the tale of finding "an English dead." Wang's tentmate on the day of the grisly discovery, Zhang Jun Yan, later confirmed Wang's tale. In 1979 Wang revealed his story to Japanese climbing leader Ryoten Hasegawa, but before they could find the corpse, Wang was killed in an avalanche below the North Col. Tom Holzel, an American, had found the whole mystery so compelling that he'd launched an expedition in 1986 to find the bodies and the cameras. Imagine finding a summit photo that proved Hillary wasn't first up Everest! What a scoop! But Holzel found nothing.

Two weeks after I returned from Everest, Holzel revealed to me the long-kept secret of where Wang had found the body, the location of which he'd learned from Chinese climbers. It was eerie to learn that our high camp lay a stone's throw from the possible solution to climbing's most enduring mystery, and our base camp a few yards from Wang's grave.

AS THE SEASON WORE ON, THIEVERY RAISED ITS UGLY HEAD. It began with allegations that precious oxygen bottles stashed at the high camp had been stolen from one expedition by another. Later, two rogue Sherpas were caught red-handed with tents and sleeping bags they'd liberated from a neighboring expedition, an act that left a Sherpa descending from the summit without a sleeping bag to slumber in that night. Tents on the glacier were ransacked by Tibetan yak-men, then tents were uprooted and stolen altogether by yak-men. Locking your tent didn't help; they just ripped out zippers to get inside. Even my ice ax disappeared from beside my tent at 23,000 feet, though I got it back some days later when I met an Eastern European climber toting it down from the summit. But most disturbing to our team was the disappearance of sixty liters of rum, spirited away from base camp.

Was nothing sacred on Everest? Evidently not. Lawsuits were threatened by clients against guides, fax machines spewed out messages to constantly remind us of the real world, and the concrete blockhouse toilets at base camp filled with shit. One could mangle the phrase "If power corrupts, then absolute power corrupts absolutely" to "If mountains corrupt, then Everest corrupts absolutely."

Then the infamous jet-stream winds returned to sandblast the summit on May 18. It occurred to me then that I had not climbed the mountain, that I had missed the good weather, and that I probably would not climb the mountain. I tried to take this in stride, but the threat of failure became a wart on my psyche that I scratched and scratched like a mangy dog. Punters whom I'd helped into their crampons had summited, why not me? I was supposed to be a climber, and these people were—tourists. What was wrong?

The timing was wrong, and getting wrapped up in a film project was wrong, and being trapped in a heavyweight expedition where management decreed when you could climb the mountain and when you could not, was wrong. I'd failed on about half of my eleven Himalayan expeditions, but the failures were always more or less on my terms, an amicable agreement between me and the mountains. Slow learner that I am, I realized at Everest that my self-perceived identity is defined to an unhealthy degree by mountaineering, and I resolved to lighten up, get into the zen of failure, and laugh at the fact that people with minimal mountaineering experience had summited while I was still festering in base camp. But before I could get into any of that feel-good stuff, the weather cleared.

ON MAY 25, TOM, RUSSELL, SHERPAS KARSANG AND LOBSANG, and I hunkered down for the night in the final camp. The summit stood 2,100 feet higher and a horizontal mile in distance southwest of us. At midnight we woke, plugged into Russian-made oxygen masks, and set off into the moonless night.

We followed a trail of frayed ropes anchored to the decrepit rock of the Yellow Band. The bulbous muzzles on our faces made it impossible to see our feet. Cold killed our headlamp batteries. We probed about like blind men. It wasn't easy for Tom, but he forced himself on, pulling on the ropes that snaked up a seemingly endless flow of ramps and cliffs. To speed Tom's progress, the rest of us took his load. The weight was ridiculous. Each of us was weighed down by three oxygen bottles. I also carried a video camera, a radio, a still camera, and a liter of water. My food for the day consisted of 200 calories of GU, an energy paste. At the first glow of sunrise at 4:30 A.M., we stopped at about 27,200 feet to assess our progress.

We unanimously judged Tom's pace to be too slow. We had not even reached the crest of the Northeast Ridge. At this speed he could get to the summit, but not till very late. We'd all be out of oxygen by then, and a nocturnal descent with dead headlamps was an invitation to frostbite, falls, and horror. It was an agonizing moment for Tom, but it was the end of the road for him. He returned to the high camp with Russell while I continued up with Karsang and Lobsang.

The sun was rising when we hit the ridge crest. Makalu, the world's fifth-highest peak, appeared as a massive molar in the east. In the oblique sunlight, Nepal seemed an endless succession of parallel ridges and cloud-filled valleys, of steaming jungles and iced peaks. Tibet's horizon was a sheet of earth-colored velvet, the foreground a swirl of porcelain-white glaciers.

We passed the First Step, then sidled across a limestone shelf festooned with tattered ropes tied to old pitons, some of which I could pull out of the rock with my fingers. Sometimes a tricky free-climbing move had to be made to connect the footpath-width ramps the route followed. At one point I got off route and found myself poised on small, crumbling holds. In my muzzle, mittens, and Frankenstein boots, I had no feel for the rock. I looked between my legs at a huge drop leading to the glaciers, and I saw a pinkish dot about 500 feet down—the body of Michael Rheinberger, an Australian who had summited in 1994. Reaching the top was his life's dream, and his partner, Mark Whetu, a New Zealander, saw him hug the summit and weep with happiness. But Michael had exhausted himself and could only descend a couple of hundred feet before he weakened, forcing them to bivouac in the open. Mark's feet froze, but he continued down the next day; Michael, though, had lost the strength to move, and he remained. Some say he fell down the cliff when he tried to move; others say the wind blew his body there; still others say that a climber had lowered his body off with a rope, so travelers to the summit would not disturb him when they passed.

At the Second Step we encountered the Chinese ladder, flanked left and right by wide fissures that split the wall. Here I wondered if Mallory and Irvine had overcome this obstacle, with their heavy steel oxygen tanks, hobnail boots, and wool tweed jackets. Only the Chinese in 1960 were known for certain to have climbed this cliff. The official Communist-Party book of their ascent says it took three hours to overcome it and that they climbed "with the power of Mao Ze Dong Thought."

Even though I was using bottled oxygen, I'd been gasping desperately for the past hour. Scaling the ladder nearly made me faint. At the top of the step I checked the pressure gauge on my bottle. It registered zero. No wonder I felt so wasted. How long it had been empty I didn't know. I switched onto another bottle, added the spent one to a cluster of abandoned orange torpedoes, and joined the ranks of the world's highest litterbugs.

After an easier quarter-mile of ridge we caught up to Bob, the Frenchman, and three Sherpas. They had set off an hour earlier that morning.

"Hi, Greg," said Bob.

"Hi, Bob," said Greg.

It was then that Bob fell off Mount Everest.

I still don't understand what stopped him from taking the big dive. When I got to him, he was lying on a steeply tilted, coffee-table-size slab of rock, on his back, head pointed down-mountain. Seeing his legs and arms waving about reminded me of the character known as K, in Kafka's book *Metamorphosis*, who turns into a beetle and who, at one point when he tries to walk like a man, falls over and lies on his back wriggling around pathetically. I considered taking a photo—Bob looked really funny—but I thought better of it.

"Help!"

"Don't move an inch!"

Bob was out of reach, and I was damned if I was going to risk reaching over the cliff to offer a hand and getting catapulted over the North Face. I needed a rope but didn't have one. He was sliding off the rock, and his face was turning red as blood flowed to his head; his eyes seemed to plead for fast action. I was about to remove my harness to toss an end of that to him, when I looked at my feet and saw an old hank of rope.

This "seek and ye shall find" discovery didn't give me religion, but it may have if I were in Bob's position. I hacked the rope out of the ice, tied a loop, and cast it to him. He grabbed it. Then Ang Babu arrived, dug out more rope, and tossed it down. When we hauled Bob up, I asked him what caused his fall.

"I was daydreaming," he answered.

THE SUMMIT, WHICH I REACHED AT 9:45 A.M., proved to be a busy spot. For the seven of us up there, there were hands to shake, radio broadcasts to make, and photos to take. Cameras were exchanged in a confusing number of permutations to ensure that everyone had their photo taken with everyone else. The apex of the mountain bristled with a forest of metal poles decorated with fluttering red, yellow, and blue prayer flags. One object up there, a scientific instrument, appropriately resembled a traffic light. I remembered that in 1990 on K2 I had hallucinated the figure of a person while I was alone; on Everest that day, not seeing a person constituted a hallucination.

Bob spun his lariat and then left with the mob. I spent a few minutes on top alone. Quiet at last. Just the flapping of prayer flags and the beat and heave of my heart and lungs. No clouds. A curving horizon. Somewhere out there in the great southern distance the monsoon was rolling toward the Himalaya, pushing aside the jet-stream winds like a cosmic bulldozer to create the freakish spell of calm that surrounded Everest. I pocketed a few small, 199 ancient rocks from a scree patch thirty feet below the top, and then I headed down too.

There were sixty-seven ascents of Everest from Tibet that spring. No climbers or Sherpas died on the Tibetan side, though one young Sherpa fell to his death in Nepal. Record-keepers tell me that mine was the 736th ascent of the mountain. Not exactly an exclusive club, but it felt good to have stood up there.

Editor's note: On May 27, 1998, Tom Whittaker reached the summit of Mount Everest, becoming the first disabled person to complete the ascent.

A climber sucking oxygen at 25,000 feet on Everest's North Ridge.

Lessons in Futility

A Curmudgeon Mouths Off

It was a startlingly clear day on the North Ridge of Mount Everest in the spring of 1995, just the way every climber sees it in his dreams. I was within sight of the summit, closing in on mountaineering's most popularly celebrated feat. Needless to say, it was a moment I'd been anticipating for many weeks, yet never did I expect that my summit bid would dissolve into a theater of the absurd. Sure, I had seen a lot of recklessness on Everest, but nothing quite this blatant: Just 100 feet from the top, I came upon a guided team that included an American client, who, while trudging along beside me, was tripped up by his own feet and started to slide down the cliff of the 10,000-foot North Face.

I was certain he'd fallen to oblivion, but when I peered down after him, I saw that he was alive, lying on his back on a sloping shelf of rock just a few feet below. A shred of fabric on his windsuit had snagged on a tooth of stone. Still, he was groaning in pain, his oxygen mask had been ripped from his face—and the fabric was beginning to give way. It was a hell of a jam to be in at 29,000 feet.

Thankfully, luck prevailed. I found an old rope nearby, and a Sherpa helped me haul him to safety. Soon thereafter he summited—an event he celebrated by twirling a lariat he'd carried with him—but he was still disoriented, and getting him down took all day as he had to be manhandled over rocky steps. A Sherpa finally got him moving on his own by shouting, "If you do not keep going, we will all die." Fortune smiled on us: no afternoon storm ravaged Everest.

The American had none of the climbing skills, self-awareness, or endurance that should be the minimum requirements for trying an 8,000-meter peak. His footwork was that of a raw novice, and he made no attempt to use his ice ax to arrest his fall—a basic survival tactic. Like many others on Everest once he unclipped from the last of the ropes that lined the mountain, he was a time bomb waiting to detonate.

When I returned to the States after my 1995 Everest trip, I brought with me a sense of foreboding. What I'd seen—hordes of novices mobbing the mountain and nearly killing themselves—troubled me deeply. Of approximately 180 climbers from eleven expeditions trying the Tibetan side, nearly half were guided clients from commercial expeditions who would have flunked Climbing 101. Most of these folks operated at the threshold of their endurance even at lower altitudes. They stumbled clumsily, with an unforgiving abyss yawning to either side. (One, it was clear, had never worn crampons before.) They had a sheeplike reliance on guides and Sherpas to carry up all provisions, fix all ropes, establish all camps, and make all decisions for them. Yet the guides were often just as discombobulated by the altitude—they were, after all, merely human. As for the traditional, noncommercial expeditions, aside from a few experienced hands, most also consisted of Himalayan first-timers. Everest, I learned, had somehow become a classroom for the world's highest introductory course in alpinism.

Then came the events of 1996, and this debacle seems to have become the only thing that titillates the general media about climbing. The now-famous *Life* cover photo of twenty-two climbers strung along the South Ridge just before the storm is, I believe, the most disturbing image in climbing history. Yet I fear it has come to be accepted by the general public as the mountaineering norm. In that photo I don't see the glory of summiting Everest; I see a knot of people ready to create a deadly traffic jam should they need to escape a storm.

Sadly, if not yet tragically, the scene on Everest will be much the same when the spring 1997 season kicks off. Commercial operators report that inquiries about guided Everest ascents have risen by almost 20 percent, entirely due to the crush of publicity; yet most were from the utterly unqualified. "We noticed a definite increase in calls," says Manomi Fernando, program coordinator for Mountain Madness, "but the majority were not legitimate." The latest word from Nepal and Tibet indicates that there will be fewer climbers this spring—twenty-four teams, down from thirty in 1996—but the problems of overcrowding will remain. All of the teams in Nepal will be on the

Reality check: a skeleton of an unfortunate climber at 23,500 feet on the North Ridge. Meanwhile, climbers in the background head toward the most prestigious summit on Earth.

same route, the South Col. In Tibet, all but two will climb the North Ridge.

Noncommercial contenders in Nepal will include Japanese, Canadian, Swedish, American, Bolivian, and Malaysian teams, as well as a group from Indonesia guided by Anatoli Boukreev, a survivor of the 1996 disaster [but not of a 1997/98 winter attempt on Annapurna I, on which he was killed by an avalanche]. The latter two teams are large national expeditions, and like the Taiwanese who caused so much trouble on Everest in 1996, those teams are unskilled in high-altitude climbing. The Malaysians, to their credit, did at least train on 23,442-foot Pumori last year, but the Indonesians have not, to anyone's knowledge, undertaken any sort of team trial run.

There will also be five commercial groups on the Nepalese side: three led by British companies, one by New Zealanders, and one by an American. The Kiwi attempt, headed by Guy Cotter (now running the late Rob Hall's former company, Adventure Consultants) has four clients. The American group, led by Todd Burleson of Washington-based Alpine Ascents International, will have just one, a California businessman in his thirties named Charles Corfield. Operating on Burleson's permit, Eric Simonson will also guide a single client, sixty-eight-year-old Leslie Buckland. And like last year, three-time Everest summiter David Breashears will be present, making a documentary about high-altitude physiology in conjunction with guide Ed Viesturs.

All told, it can be conservatively estimated that 170 people will be clogging the South Col route.

Needless to say, the Tibetan side, with its cheaper permit rates, will also be busy. Noncommercial teams from Kazakhstan, Japan, Belgium, Pakistan, Slovenia, and Croatia, among others, have been granted permission, as well as a commercial operation led by New Zealander Russell Bryce. Climbers on the North Ridge will total about 150.

All the guides leading clients in 1997 speak of having been sobered by last year's tragedy. Some point hopefully to a safety advance that will be in wider use this year: fax phones linked to a highly reliable British forecasting service, which provided Breashears and Viesturs several days' notice of approaching storms on their IMAX filmmaking expedition last year. "It gives pretty darn accurate reports of weather and winds, which is crucial," says Viesturs. Most guides also say that it will be easier to enforce critical turnaround times and to deny clients a summit bid if they falter—they can invoke last year's deaths to make their point.

But for this we have little to go on beyond the guides' word. And though I have no beef with those who pay to be escorted up a mountain, nor any problem with the guides who are paid for this service, I do take issue with the grand illusion, championed by the outfitters and swallowed by so many innocents, that mountains above 8,000 meters can be safely guided. As the old saw goes, you pay your money and you take your chances.

In the wake of last year's tragedy, many trip leaders are speaking more candidly about the business. Cotter, for one, says that he will "pave the way, not baby-sit" his clients. Viesturs, who has guided three trips up Everest in the past six years, says he thinks the trip leaders "broke the rules" last year, failing to enforce turnaround times because they wanted their clients to have a shot at the summit. He and Cotter, Viesturs explains, "are going to be very strict with our people." On the surface, this no-nonsense approach sounds prudent, but when speaking in private, many guides all too willingly reveal what lies at its roots. I recall a conversation with one longtime Everest guide who told me of a certain group that planned to hire him. "Do they have any experience?" I asked. "No," he replied, "but that doesn't bother me. If they pay me, I'll take them as far as they can go. This is about business, not climbing." I found this attitude cynical, yet no worse than that of another guide who said of his clients, "Whenever I'm on the mountain with these idiots, I regard that they're trying to kill me."

An unsettling sentiment—but also one that's hard to refute. Many of those around me in 1995 had seen fit to skip training climbs on lesser Himalayan peaks and had motored right onto the big one. Beyond the incredibly lucky lariat-wielding American, there was his elderly French teammate, who had to be pushed from behind and pulled from above by Sherpas simply to get up the mountain. Yet when a Sherpa tried to overtake him on the home stretch to the summit, the Frenchman sternly stopped his escort with a mittened backhand to the chest—he had paid a bundle of cash for this moment and wanted to get there first. This incident seemed to bear out what many "real" climbers feel: that the only skill a commercial operator requires of a client is the ability to write a check for $65,000, the going rate to be guided up Everest.

Equally troublesome, to my mind, were the fellows who made the first Turkish and Romanian ascents of Everest—men who ultimately needed to be rescued, but who nonetheless returned to considerable fanfare in their home countries. Neither of them thanked me or the others who helped them down, and to this day, I'm certain, still don't believe they were ever in trouble.

The Turk, "Nas," was accompanied by a very capable Russian guide; the Romanian, Constanin, was from another commercial group. They had moderate climbing experience and had been guided up other mountains, but none like Everest. Both hoped to make oxygenless ascents, yet they carried oxygen anyway. Struggling in the thin air and weighed down by the heavy equipment, they naturally resorted to using it. And though most sensible parties were summiting around 10:00 A.M., Nas reached the top in midafternoon. Constantin summited at dusk, his oxygen supply depleted.

High winds moved in that night. The alarm was sounded when Nas's guide radioed to say that his charges were exhausted and might not make it through the night. In the morning I climbed toward the two clients with two bottles of oxygen. When I reached Constantin, near the high camp, he refused it, under the misconception that he'd made an oxygenless ascent and accepting it from me would spoil the feat. He was so wasted that not only did I have to repeatedly pick him up out of the snow and clip him to ropes, but I also had to help him take a shit—a grim ordeal at 8,000 meters. Soon after, Nas appeared, staggering down an avalanche-prone slope, clutching only ski poles (an ice ax would better arrest a slip), headed for a cliff. I told him to clip into the ropes, but he refused, muttering something about not needing them. "Who do you think you are, Reinhold Messner?" I shouted, carping at him till he came to his senses and joined the ropes.

Since even Himalayan veterans find clear thinking nearly impossible above 8,000 meters, it's understandable, given their desperate states, that these two don't grasp that they nearly died. Indeed, novices on Everest never seem to remember, or at least choose not to admit, the real and humbling circumstances of their ascents. The Turk later told me that Everest wasn't as hard as he'd expected.

But there was something I saw while helping this pair that struck me, in an odd way, as indicative of the problems on Everest—the wanton disregard for preparation, the blatant me-firstism, the utter lack of responsibility for both the mountain and the sport. On the way down, I noticed that the ice ax the Romanian was using was mine. A few days earlier, it had been stolen from outside my tent.

Death
and Love

Storm clouds wrap their tendrils around K2.

Another Tragedy on K2

On what seemed to be a perfect August day in the Karakoram Range of Pakistan, Alison Hargreaves gazed up at the summit of K2 and must have felt, for a brief moment, a rush of unadulterated luck. After all, there had been six storm-racked weeks in base camp and then a grueling four-day ascent to this 26,000-foot spot at Camp Four, where a party including American Rob Slater was now debating the risks of a final ascent. Yes, everyone was exhausted. Yes, the weather, always full of fang and fury on the world's second-highest mountain, might snap down on them at any time. But the sky was spotless, and the summit was suddenly there like a jagged grail. The decision seemed obvious—the top was twelve hours away.

That evening, Hargreaves indeed summited K2. But as newspapers and radio stations would report a few days later, Hargreaves—considered by many to be the finest woman alpinist of the day—and six others never made it down off the mountain. A storm steamrollered K2 that night with hurricane-force winds and subzero temperatures. And the day that had bugun with so much promise deteriorated into one of mountaineering's most talked-about disasters.

For the thirty-three-year-old Hargreaves, a mother who unlike her male colleagues in the sport was often criticized for leaving her children at home while she risked her life on big mountains, K2 was just one stop on an ambitious, well-publicized project: to be the first woman to climb the world's three highest peaks—Everest, K2, and Kangchenjunga—without supplemental oxygen. The Everest leg, in May 1995, had gone astonishingly smoothly.

The Scottish mountaineer summited with the sun shining brightly the entire time. When she flew home for a few weeks of rest, she was hailed as a national hero.

Meanwhile, Slater, her team's expedition leader and a big-wall climber from the United States had never been above 19,000 feet, but what he lacked in credentials and celebrity he made up for with grit and an almost fanatical approach to big mountains. The thirty-four-year-old had quit his job as a financial broker to train for K2, and before he left for Pakistan, *Climbing* magazine quoted his glib comment: "Summit or die, either way I win." Though he and Hargreaves had never met before arriving at base camp, they seemed to hit it off immediately.

And so on the morning of August 13, a week after splitting with the rest of the team, which had decided to hike back to civilization, Hargreaves and Slater linked up with four climbers from a New Zealand–Canadian team— Bruce Grant, Jeff Lakes, Kim Logan, and Peter Hillary, son of Sir Edmund of Mount Everest fame. They left their tents at Camp Four for the summit via the Abruzzi Ridge.

By midmorning the climbers had ascended the gentle slope called The Shoulder and were clustered together in a steep chute known as The Bottleneck, with five Spanish climbers who had started out from a slightly higher campsite—Javier Escartín, Javier Olivar, Lorenzo Ortíz, Lorenzo Ortas, and José Garces. Considered to be something of a point of no return, The Bottleneck involves an exposed, icy traverse with cliffs above and below. According to Hillary, it was at this juncture that the weather, fair for the previous four days, started to sour.

"Big altostratus clouds were moving in, and a strong wind was blowing snow," Hillary would recall later. "I saw everyone crossing the traverse. Then they disappeared in clouds."

While the rest of the climbers continued in snowy conditions, Hillary and Logan turned back, convinced that a major storm was setting in. Indeed, from a distance one would have seen that K2 had become wrapped in a gauze of clouds. Meanwhile a polar wind was gathering force to the north.

Lakes eventually turned back, too. But as dusk approached, Hargreaves, now climbing with Olivar, pressed on, with Slater not far behind. At 6:45 P.M., more than twelve hours after setting out, Hargreaves and Olivar radioed Camp Four that they'd reached the summit. Oddly, it wasn't snowing on top. "The weather was good, really exceptional," says Ortas, who took the call. "They could have descended easily in the light of the full moon."

That, of course, wasn't the case. According to Ortas, a murderous wind— reportedly blowing at 140 miles per hour—kicked up within the hour. The

A campsite on K2's north ridge, at 25,500 feet.

Spaniards' tents were destroyed, and Ortas and Garces spent the rest of the night huddled in a single sleeping bag. It could only have been worse up higher, where Hargreaves, Olivar, Slater, Grant, Ortíz, and Escartín, all of whom had summited, were working their way down. There were no further radio calls.

One climber who ventured above The Bottleneck, Jeff Lakes, did manage to escape the maelstrom. In a harrowing, thirty-hour descent into the teeth of the storm, he rappelled to Camp Two, where he was dragged into a tent by a New Zealand teammate, only to die from exhaustion and edema during the night.

As with any expedition ending in disaster, the second-guessing began immediately. Had the storm really taken the climbers by surprise? Or were they blinded to the telltale signs of approaching bad weather by the intoxicating prospect of getting to the top? The answer, of course, may never be known.

But according to Garces, whom Hargreaves passed as she made her final approach to the summit, her last hour before the storm must have gone the way she'd imagined it would. The sun was setting, Garces reported, the weather was fair, and Hargreaves was climbing strongly. Her only words to him as she went by were "I'm going up."

The south face of K2.

Death and Faxes

"Alison has become the most famous British climber in history," said Leo Dickinson, the adventure filmmaker and longtime observer of the UK climbing scene. He told me this with a note of sadness in his voice; then he pressed the transmit button on his fax, to send me a sampling of the newspaper headlines that had appeared in Britain in the two weeks since Alison Hargreaves' death, with six other climbers, on August 13, 1995, in a hurricane wind up near the summit of K2.

"Make sure you have a full roll of paper in your fax machine," Leo added. "There's enough press here to wallpaper a house. And be warned, it's pretty sensationalistic stuff."

He wasn't wrong. Among the twenty-or-so front-page and feature stories were tabloid headlines such as "Doomed Treks to Summit of an Icy Grave" and "Hargreaves: A Mother Obsssed." Even the photo captions couldn't resist tasteless puns. One paper ran a snapshot of Alison with the awful line "Hargreaves: Peak Plunge." For the most part, the stories were written by those know-nothing instant experts on mountaineering, journalists who had concocted gems of wisdom such as: "On K2, if anything goes wrong, rescue is virtually impossible. This has led to mountaineers operating on an unwritten code—anyone injured allows the rest of their party to abandon them to their fate." Unwritten as that code may be, I was quite unaware of it.

As I expected, Alison copped *beau coup* flack from the press for being a mother who climbed big mountains, and a mother who got killed in the mountains, leaving two young orphans and a widower. In "K2 Is Not For Mothers," a female columnist wrote in a tone befitting an evangelist: "If Alison . . . had been a drug addict and died from an overdose there would have been few heroic words written about her. Had she killed herself doing something dangerous but frivolous, such as skydiving, there would have been plenty of head-shaking and talk of irresponsibility. But because climbing mountains is part of a noble, romantic tradition, it is viewed as somehow commendable to leave two small children and their father for long periods, while risking her neck on the world's most dangerous peaks. . . . Miss Hargreaves may have been a delightful person . . . but her need to climb mountains and put herself in extreme danger and have children does not denote balance."

"So, Alison," I thought to myself, as yet another cheap story rolled out of the fax machine, "this is how it ends, your life and death under the media microscope, your every action examined and judged by people you've never met." Two months earlier she'd been touted by the press as a hero for climbing Everest. Now the press were smearing her. How quickly fame fades.

Ed Douglas, a climber-writer, explained the flip-flop. "It is the fact that Hargreaves was a mother who was prepared to put her maternal role on hold," Douglas wrote, "that obscures the issue for many people. Even in the nineties, when a woman's right to self-fulfillment is undisputed, there are many who question whether, in leaving her children motherless, she displayed anything remotely approaching heroic qualities." He concluded by reminding readers that in a tragic coincidence, about the same time Alison died, two other well-known British climbers, Paul Nunn and Geoff Tier, were killed in an avalanche on Haramosh II. Both men had children, but neither was criticized for being a climbing father.

Muddled and inaccurate of fact, pathos-soaked and hype-filled in tone, mean-spirited at their worst, the stories were a surreal connection to Alison. Reading about her death did not seem real. But, when I reconciled the content of those press clippings with my vision of what befell those people on K2—caught in a wind so strong that it pinned them down under a crushing hypothermic weight, and then, in all probability, plucked them up and blew them off the mountain—I felt an awful hollowness in the pit of my stomach.

I met Alison Hargreaves on Everest in spring 1995, shared a base camp with her, and dined with her, as did the others of our expedition, day and night, for weeks. I'd feasted on her dynamite high-altitude cheesecakes. I'd watched her get happily rowdy and beer-sprayed at a party one cold Himalayan night. One day I climbed with her to the crest of the North Col, and partway up we paused and leaned like human hang gliders into a blustering pillow of wind. It was her idea; she'd persuaded me to join her in this homage to the elements. It was damn good fun, and she let out a life-affirming joy-squeal into the gale. On days when she penned her thoughts in her journal, while sitting on a rock at base camp, she could look serious. She could also erupt with moments of wry wisdom, crack a smile that let you know she knew the measure of you, and quip, "Life is a ball, isn't it?"

I saw her through a telescope on top of Everest and heard her radio her thoughts down to base camp. When I told her she was my new hero for summiting Everest without oxygen, she jokingly radioed back, "You sarcastic bastard." A day later, Russell Bryce and I met her when she stepped off Everest onto the Rongbuk Glacier. She welcomed the hugs we gave her, as well as a bouquet of plastic flowers. "I'll take these to K2," she said of the flowers, the day she packed her bags and cleared out of camp.

That's as far as I knew her, maybe only skin deep, maybe not very well. Our lives had intersected, she had left an impact on me, that is all, and now I was seeing her reduced to a few column-inches of print in some lowbrow British newspapers, as an obituary or a human-interest piece in *Time* and *People*, or, as the crowds at the August 1995 Outdoor Retailer show in Reno, Nevada, saw, as an online news flash on a computer screen. Millions of people now knew Alison Hargreaves. She was "the girl who died on that mountain, what's it called, K something-or-other?" It was all so surreal.

Admittedly, not all the post-tragedy press about Alison was bad. In fact, the first wave of press expressed shock and sympathy. Full-page obituaries in major British newspapers such as the *Times* lionized her. Some writers even found, with surgical accuracy, the essence of the woman and the climbing scene in which she operated. Describing her appetite for recognition, Stephen Venables wrote that she was "an outstanding British woman climber, unashamed to blow her own trumpet, unembarrassed by her own ambition. Perhaps for that reason she was always something of an outsider, never quite pukka in British climbing circles, where the prevailing ethos remains one of masculine rubbing-shoulders-in-the-pub bravado, veiled by disingenuous understatement."

Kudos to Stephen, and to Jim Perrin, who was poetic about life lost on mountains. To him, her death represented "another hubristic ending, another sturdy, willful, fine life extinguished, another swathe of sadness cut through memory and human association, another dessicated corpse for the Death Zone where life for the devotee of height and adrenaline will always seem more real." Equally touched was travel writer Jan Morris, who wrote "to hear of her death is like a slap in the face from a malevolent fortune, resentful that we had all been given pleasure by a feat of entirely

Alison Hargreaves kicks off her boots at the foot of Everest in the spring of 1995.
She had just made an oxygenless ascent.

harmless, essentially uncompetitive, totally individualist courage."

Fond thoughts all, but the media's crocodilian tears soon dried and gave way to a jaw of snarling teeth. Fleet Street's publications love to trash heroes and establishment figures—witness the treatment of the Royal Family in the British press. I can imagine some chain-smoking editor growling to his minions, "We've had praise, we've had pathos; now it's time to go get some dirt on Alison."

So, off to Skardu, Pakistan, went the journalists, and back came a wave of stories painting Alison as ruthless, obsessed by success, and driven to her death by "summit fever." The unwitting source for some of this slant seemed to be Peter Hillary, who'd been at the high camp the day Alison and the others headed up. I seriously doubt he anticipated the field day the press would have with his words when he spoke his mind and told a reporter, "Alison was a brilliant climber, but she had tremendous commercial pressures on her and she became obsessed. When you spoke to her it was clear that climbing came first and everything else was secondary . . . They had all become blinkered by the summit. . . . They all drove each other on and the others followed."

It may have been that Alison was driven and ambitious; maybe climbing was the most important thing in her life. But isn't every athlete, scientist, or entrepreneur driven and ambitious? Somehow the stories suggested that she suffered from a dirty kind of ambition, from "me-first mountaineering," as one writer put it. It was also implied that because she was the most experienced climber on the hill that day, the men who climbed alongside her were urged on by her, as if she'd cast a spell over them.

Nonclimbers might be fooled by this, but anyone who has been on an 8,000-meter peak knows that no one drives anyone, and that everyone is free to make his or her own decision to go up or down. Journalists, however, must put a spin on their stories, and the Alison-leading-the-pack-to-doom theme became the order of the day in the press. This seemed confirmed by the American climber Scott Fischer, who told me of reporters waiting in Skardu, hounding returning expeditioners as they stepped off jeeps. Reporters were, he said, "fishing for an angle to pin the blame on Alison, for leading less-experienced climbers to their deaths."

When two frostbitten Spaniards returned to Skardu (they had survived the storm and, while descending, found a boot and clothing belonging to Alison and saw a body several thousand feet below the summit that was probably her), one newspaper offered "seven-figure sums in dollars to go up the mountain and retrieve Alison's personal effects, including her diary." This was under the headline "Climber's Husband Attacks 'Scavengers.'" Understandably,

Jim Ballard, married to Alison, denounced the notion of a ghoulish treasure hunt. He also told of hate mail he had received from a busybody who criticized Alison for leaving her children orphans.

The press criticized Ballard, too. In stories such as "Happy Snaps Hid Climbing Tragedy," the quality of his grieving was debated. The story criticized him for urging his children to smile for the cameras while waiting for confirmation of Alison's death, and suggested he was indulging in too much media attention. Quoted were a famous climber, a medical officer, a mountain rescue team leader, a bereavement counselor, and a consulting psychiatrist. Most of them identified Ballard's behavior as being due to—revelation—shock.

Ballard did provide the papers with some strange material, though, especially in a story with the saccharine headline "I Salute My Tiger Alison— Husband's Pride as Children Weep for Climber Lost on Notorious K2." After quoting a Tibetan saying that Alison was fond of—"It is better to have lived one day as a tiger than a thousand years as a sheep"—he said, "I am not sad if she has died. I would have been more sad if she hadn't climbed the mountain." Elsewhere he said, "If she had succeeded she would be at the beginning of her life as a celebrity. She could support the family for life. She would never have to do a climb again."

The last report of Ballard was that he had returned from taking the children to within eyeshot of K2, along with a TV film crew, to make a documentary. (He also whipped up a quick book about Alison and the family's trip to K2.) The trek was a controversial trip, much discussed by the press. Journalists pontificated over whether the pilgrimage was in good taste, yet clamored to accompany the family. In "Homage Is in Bad Taste," I read, "Bad enough—quite bad enough—that Tom and Kate Ballard, aged six and four, should have lost their mother when she fell off a mountain that (some of us think) she had no business being on in the first place, but worse . . . is their misery and grief is now to be served up to us in the guise of entertainment." Ballard will take "the two nippers" on a "preposterous pilgrimage" to K2. "What will [the children] make of looking up a bitter mountain face and being told that mummy's decomposing body is somewhere up there? And all the while having . . . a sodding TV crew pointing cameras at their little faces . . .?"

By the end of the second week, there was little left to report about Alison. Her faxes, letters, and drawings to her children ("Be good to daddy, have a lovely summer, and enjoy your holiday") had been printed, and every photo opportunity (such as pictures of her grief-stricken parents) had been squeezed out of the situation. Then, just when it all seemed over, there was a scoop for *The Independent*. A climber at base camp, Matt Comesky, had   217 interviewed Alison, and the transcript of his tape was published. The interview revealed, the newspaper claimed, "her progression to professionalism and, ultimately, the disillusionment she felt with the 'dishonesty' of modern climbing, fueled by the need to scale popular mountains or combinations of popular mountains in order to attract sponsors."

In fact, the interview was informal and uninformative, but it was given a double-page spread and probably helped sell lots of papers.

Fame, recognition—call it what you will—was certainly what Alison wanted with her well-publicized plan to climb Everest, K2, and Kangchenjunga—the world's three highest peaks—in succession. Even before her ascent of Everest had propelled her to overnight stardom, she was a "professional" climber who took the game seriously, made a little (but not a lot of) money out of climbing, and didn't mind seeing her name splashed about in the press. Sure, her plan to do the Big Three was a career move; yet climbing, she freely admitted, was her best, maybe her only, skill, and she knew being a woman and a mother made her more press-worthy. Unfortunately, the trade she plied was a dangerous one, and motherhood made her an easy target for critics.

If nothing else, the media blitz surrounding Alison's death bolsters my belief that the only time the press gives a hoot about climbing is when someone dies. Which reminds me of a story: I was speaking to a publisher once, about an idea I had to write a book about a climb I'd done in the Himalaya. While I was describing the expedition, the publisher cut to the chase and asked, "Did anyone die?" My answer was no. "Then where is the story?" inquired the publisher. End of book proposal.

The fact that Alison's death has made her a household name is, to me, a sign of the perversity of our times. Her fate has become entertainment, her chosen way to live and die a topic of public debate and moral dissection on the British equivalents of "Oprah." What began in the British media as a genuine expression of grief over the loss of an inspiring, world-class athlete and a well-liked person ended in an orgy of sleazy, nosy, disrespectful, hack journalism.

At grips with the blood red stone.

Unrequited

A Fiction

The rock is red, deep red, and the old man runs his hand over its smooth surface. He is looking for something, trying to remember. He stares up at the cliff that arches above him; then he shifts his glasses on the ridge of his nose. Fractures and bulges of quartz become crisp in his vision, and the shape of the wall settles into the grid of his memory. "This is the place," he whispers, and he settles down on a rock and waits for the memories to take shape.

All day he has been walking along the base of this cliff, touching the stone, breathing the grass-seed-scented air. The tanned young climbers on the rocks have been watching him, worried that his heart will flicker out. "He used to climb around here, a long time ago," he overheard one youngster tell another, and he was flattered to be recognized.

The old man narrows his eyes into slits that stare at the cliff. It is his theory that rocks are like film. They absorb light and time. Concentration recovers these images from the past, in his case, of a youth spent as a climber. When the memories come, they arrive like smoke on a breeze.

He sees himself, his friends. They are young. Strong. Quick-witted. They are easy with each other. The complexities of existence have not yet muddled their lives. The simple act of climbing is enough nourishment for them. In his mind, he watches himself uncoil a rope at the foot of the wall, and he begins climbing. Then his thoughts cede to the present.

Like every route on this cliff, the climb above him has a name: 219

Unrequited. A musclebound young climber whom the old man had encountered on a previous stroll had asked him why he'd named it that, for the climb was one the old man had pioneered. The old man stroked his chin, trying to recall the decades-old tale, but the story remained trapped inside the rock. This bothered him.

The cliffs are part of us, he believed. The routes we adorn them with and the names we give them are invisible signs on a vertical map. The names mark paths we have traveled, sometimes easy, sometimes hard. They are like the titles of paintings, too, reflecting an artist's feelings about a singular moment. Markers, reminders, hieroglyphs of a lost tribe. Each climb and its name contains a tiny personal history to be remembered. That was why he had returned this day, to read the rock, to remember his story.

So the memories become shapes, and the shapes become solid. He sees himself in the rock. He is young again. He is on the wall. His fingers explore the rock like insect antennae, working to solve the anagram surrounding him. Moving up, leaning left, reaching right. In increments. He applies pressure to one flake, counterpressure to another. His shoulders brace like bridge struts. Quivering, he springs like a striking snake and his hand catches a higher hold.

"You did it!" the young woman shouts from below. She feeds the rope out, and he pulls onto a ledge and rigs an anchor. Now it is her turn to climb.

Looking down, he watches her as she rounds a bulge. Her swaying straw colored curls ensnare the sun, and her limbs translate the rock in a language foreign to his. Her style is to dance, his to box and spar. At the final move to grip the ledge, her hand makes an urgent slap. It echoes loudly. The sound brings their eyes together, and they laugh.

She mounts the ledge and they sit, her leg draped over his. The rope connects them to the rock and to each other, and the sun lulls them into a languorous mood.

"I'm wearing your ring," she says with a smirk, stretching out her chalk-dusted pianist fingers to show the gaudy plastic band he'd bought for five cents from a gum machine: their joke on relationships and foreverness.

"Promise you'll meet me? In France after the expedition?" he says. Their climb today—a first ascent he'd been eyeing for months—would be their last outing on this cliff, the place of their first meeting. Tomorrow he would depart on an expedition to climb a distant peak in a distant land, and a climber's wandering life would begin. Part of him wanted to remain with her and with these rocks, but his dreams were of grand adventures. Yet in these weeks before leaving, he found it hard to unclip from her companionship, and from this place of blood-red stone. Perhaps all the friends he

220

The rocks are like film. They absorb light and time.

needed to make, all the rock he needed to climb, were here.

She assures him, "We'll meet in Europe. After all, we're engaged." Another ironic smile and she changes the subject. "Now we have to name this climb. It's our creation. We made it together."

Only the waning sun forces them down. She never made it to France, and he stayed too long away from the place of red quartz. Years pass before they meet again, somewhere in a city. Neither of them has climbed for years. She is in her second marriage. Kids, now grown. Straw hair now gray. But one afternoon in a cafe they talk about those perfect hours as if they'd happened yesterday.

"We made a great threesome," she said before they parted, this time forever.

"Three?"

"You, me, and the stone."

His remembering over, the old man leaves the cliff. He passes the musclebound kid. "About the meaning of that climb, Unrequited," the old man says.

"Yeah?"

"It had to do with love."

About the Author

Greg Child began climbing as a teenager in his native Australia, where he established numerous rock routes before moving to the United States to accomplish similar feats. Among these were two big-wall first ascents—Lost in America and Aurora—on El Capitan in Yosemite. Child has also climbed extensively in the Himalaya, with ascents of many new routes and significant peaks at high altitude, including those of Shivling, Lobsang Spire, Broad Peak, Gasherbrum IV, K2, Trango Tower, and Shipton Spire. A writer and photographer whose work has appeared in adventure magazines around the world, Child won the American Alpine Club's Literary Award in 1987. He is the author of *Thin Air: Encounters in the Himalaya*, *Mixed Emotions*, and *Climbing: The Complete Reference*.

THE MOUNTAINEERS, founded in 1906, is a nonprofit outdoor activity and conservation club, whose mission is "to explore, study, preserve, and enjoy the natural beauty of the outdoors. . . ." Based in Seattle, Washington, the club is now the third-largest such organization in the United States, with 15,000 members and five branches throughout Washington State.

The Mountaineers sponsors both classes and year-round outdoor activities in the Pacific Northwest, which include hiking, mountain climbing, ski-touring, snowshoeing, bicycling, camping, kayaking and canoeing, nature study, sailing, and adventure travel. The club's conservation division supports environmental causes through educational activities, sponsoring legislation, and presenting informational programs. All club activities are led by skilled, experienced volunteers, who are dedicated to promoting safe and responsible enjoyment and preservation of the outdoors.

If you would like to participate in these organized outdoor activities or the club's programs, consider a membership in The Mountaineers. For information and an application, write or call The Mountaineers, Club Headquarters, 300 Third Avenue West, Seattle, Washington 98119; (206) 284-6310.

The Mountaineers Books, an active, nonprofit publishing program of the club, produces guidebooks, instructional texts, historical works, natural history guides, and works on environmental conservation. All books produced by The Mountaineers are aimed at fulfilling the club's mission.

Send or call for our catalog of more than 300 outdoor titles:

**The Mountaineers Books
1001 SW Klickitat Way, Suite 201
Seattle, WA 98134
1-800-553-4453**
e-mail: mbooks@mountaineers.org
website: www.mountaineers.org